The Idea Magazine For Teachers®

PRESCHOOL

1999–2000

YEARBOOK

Jayne M. Gammons, Senior Editor

The Education Center, Inc.
Greensboro, North Carolina

The Mailbox® 1999–2000 Preschool Yearbook

Founding Editor in Chief: Margaret Michel
Senior Editor: Jayne M. Gammons
Executive Director, Magazine Publishing: Katharine P. S. Brower
Editorial Administrative Director: Stephen Levy
Curriculum Director: Karen P. Shelton
Editorial Training: Irving P. Crump
Contributing Editors: Cindy K. Daoust, Michele M. Dare, Ada Goren, Sherri Lynn Kuntz, Michele M. Stoffel Menzel, Karen P. Shelton, Allison E. Ward
Copy Editors: Karen Brewer Grossman, Karen L. Huffman, Tracy Johnson, Laurel Robinson, Debbie Shoffner, Gina Sutphin
Staff Artists: Pam Crane, Nick Greenwood, Rebecca Saunders (SENIOR ARTISTS); Cathy Spangler Bruce, Theresa Lewis Goode, Clevell Harris, Susan Hodnett, Sheila Krill, Rob Mayworth, Kimberly Richard, Greg D. Rieves, Barry Slate, Donna K. Teal
Cover Artist: Lois Axeman
Typesetters: Lynette Maxwell, Mark Rainey
Editorial Assistants: Terrie Head, Melissa B. Montanez, Karen White, Jan E. Witcher
Library: Dorothy C. McKinney (ASSISTANT)

ISBN 1-56234-378-5
ISSN 1088-5536

Printed in the United States of America.

The Education Center, Inc.
P.O. Box 9753
Greensboro, NC 27429-0753

Look for *The Mailbox*® 2000–2001 Preschool Yearbook in the summer of 2001. The Education Center, Inc., is the publisher of *The Mailbox*®, *Teacher's Helper*®, *The Mailbox*® BOOKBAG®, and *Learning*® magazines, as well as other fine products. Look for these wherever quality teacher materials are sold, or call 1-800-714-7991.

Contents

THEMATIC AND CONTRIBUTOR UNITS

DIVE INTO PRESCHOOL!

Invite your little ones to take the plunge into preschool with this "sea-sational" welcome! You'll find getting-ready, open-house, and beginning-of-school ideas that are sure to get everyone right into the swim of things!

ideas contributed by dayle timmons—Special Education-Inclusion, Alimacani Elementary School, Jacksonville, FL

Come Swim in Our School

Reel them in with this invitation to join your school! Duplicate the open newsletter on page 10. Then program the page with the information most appropriate for your beginning-of-the-year activities. For example, provide the details of your open house or orientation. Or write a letter to each child welcoming him to your class. When mailing the information to each family, include a picture of yourself dressed in tropical beach clothing (floral shirt, sandals, sunglasses, and a straw hat) and seated in a lounge chair or playing in a sandbox. As a final touch, include a pinch of sand in the envelope. No doubt you'll create a wave of excitement!

The Water's Fine!

These open house ideas are sure to cause an ocean commotion! To set the mood for a seaworthy start, hang blue and white crepe paper streamers from your ceiling. Also prepare the door decoration described in "Presenting Sea Stars" on page 7. Greet your guests on opening night dressed in the same beachwear you posed in for your photo (see "Come Swim in Our School") and invite them to enter your room filled with the sounds of the ocean (audiotapes available at nature stores). Finally, invite your guests to serve themselves tropical punch and to use a shovel to scoop Goldfish® crackers out of a bucket.

Presenting Sea Stars

The catch of the day (or opening night) will be the excited children who see their names on this door display. To prepare your door, cover it with blue bulletin board paper. Add a scalloped piece of paper to the top of your door frame that can be walked under when entering your room. Mount a title such as "[Your name]'s Sea Stars." Duplicate the starfish pattern (page 9) onto pink, orange, and yellow construction paper to make a class supply. Personalize the starfish; then temporarily affix them to your door. When the children arrive (either on opening night or your first day), invite each child to find his starfish and then to decorate it by gluing on colored sand. When you return the stars to the door, you'll have a display that'll catch everyone's attention.

Bucket Brigade

Prepare these nametags for your little ones to wear on the first days of school. Duplicate a class supply of the bucket on the newsletter (page 10) onto construction paper. Laminate the buckets; then cut them out. Punch a hole on each side of each bucket. Twist the ends of a pipe cleaner half through the holes of each bucket to form a handle. Finally, write a different child's name on each bucket. Hang the buckets on your class coat hooks. When the children come to your room for the first time, help them locate their nametags. To make it easier for each child to find his tag again, have him choose from a selection of ocean-themed stickers to add to his bucket. Then safety-pin the handle of each child's bucket onto his clothing.

Drop It in the Bucket

Hold everything! Why not organize your room with colorful sand buckets! Watch for sand buckets to go on sale at the end of the summer season; then stock up. Use paint pens and stickers to decorate the buckets. Place one on each table or in each center to store supplies such as crayons, scissors, and glue. Or personalize a bucket for each child so he'll have a special place for his things. Hang the buckets on coat hooks or store them in cubbies.

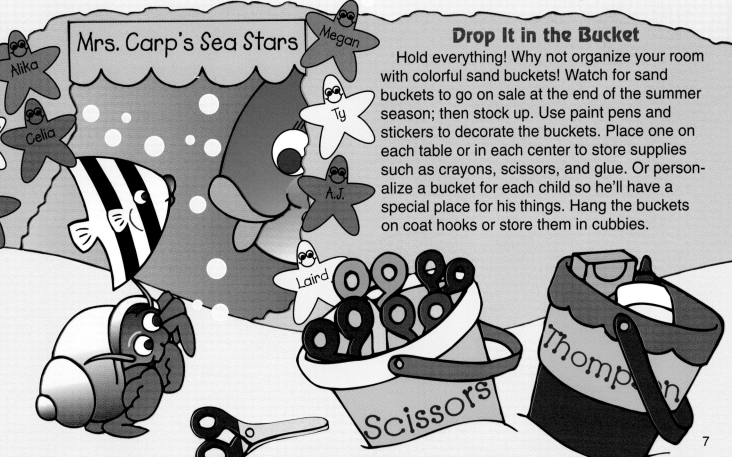

7

What "Shell" We Do?

Looking for a way to help your little ones learn each other's names? Try this idea that they're sure to dig! In advance, duplicate a class supply of the shell pattern (page 11) onto construction paper. Laminate the shells, cut them out, and then write a different child's name on each one. Hide the shells in a tub of sand in your group area. During a group time, sing the following song as you invite each child, in turn, to dig in the sand. When the child has found a shell, insert the name on the shell in the last line of the song. Have that child give the shell to the named child, who then takes a turn digging.

After each child has had a turn digging, put the shells back in the sand. Then, when you need a management tool for taking turns or lining up, dig or have a child dig a shell out again.

Come Dig in the Sand
(sung to the tune of "For He's a Jolly Good Fellow")

Come and dig in the sand, [child's name].
Come and dig in the sand, [child's name].
Come and dig in the sand, [child's name],
To find somebody's shell.
To find somebody's shell,
To find somebody's shell.
Come and dig in the sand, [child's name].
Come and dig in the sand, [child's name].
Come and dig in the sand, [child's name].
You found [second child's name]'s shell!

Hook, Line, and Sinker

Lure your little fishies into traveling as a group with this clever rope. To make this transition tool, collect a class supply of small sand shovels and a length of cotton clothesline rope. At even intervals, tie each shovel's handle onto the rope; then tie a large knot at each end of the rope for the adults to hold. When traveling from place to place, have each child hold on to a shovel while you and your adult helper hold on to the ends of the rope. Here we go!

A Sea Search

You'll want your youngsters to realize that there are other fish in the sea besides their teachers and classmates. Prepare a sea search that will introduce them to additional school faces and will also yield ocean treasures for your classroom. In advance, arrange for people in your school to have sea gifts to give to your group. For example, provide sea creature shapes cut from craft foam for your water table, plastic ocean creatures for your water and sand center, or traditional sand toys such as molds and sieves for an outdoor sand area. Use the transition tool described in "Hook, Line, and Sinker" to travel around your facility. As you make each stop and meet each new person, collect the classroom gifts. "Sea," our school is an exciting place to be!

Sea Snack

It's no fish tale. All the excitement of the beginning of school is likely to make your little ones *really* hungry. Invite them to make these savory snacks to satisfy their appetites. To make one sea snack, a child toasts a piece of bread. He then uses a shell- or starfish-shaped cookie cutter to cut out a shape from the bread. Next he butters the bread, then sprinkles on cinnamon sugar. Simple but savory, and just right for introducing children to your cooking center!

Neptune Kings and Mermaid Queens

Crown your students kings and queens of the sea with this simple project. In advance, cut (or die-cut) a supply of simple ocean-themed shapes from colorful construction paper. Also provide ocean-themed stickers and rubber stamps, if desired. Prepare construction paper strips long enough for headbands. Give each child a strip to decorate as desired; then staple it to fit her head. Now each child is a crowning success at her first pasting project!

A Picture-Perfect Day

Your little ones have really taken the plunge into preschool! Share your pride with parents with this picture-perfect idea. To set up the photo shoot, add beach items—such as a chair, an umbrella, and a beach ball—to your outdoor sand area. In turn, have each child don a beach hat and sunglasses; then take an instant photo of her at the area. Mount the photo on a construction paper copy of the open newsletter (page 10) along with a phrase such as "I really dig preschool!" Send the pictures home the same day. Preschool is a blast!

I really dig preschool!

Open Newsletter and Bucket Pattern

Use with "Come Swim in Our School" on page 6, "Bucket Brigade" on page 7, and "A Picture-Perfect Day" on page 9.

Starfish Pattern
Use with "Presenting Sea Stars" on page 7.

Shell Patterns
Use with "What 'Shell' We Do?"
on page 8.

Classroom by Design

Create a fun and colorful environment for your preschoolers with these simple, yet innovative decorating ideas.

ideas by dayle timmons—Special Education-Inclusion, Alimacani Elementary School, Jacksonville, FL

Curtain Time!

Add warmth and color with these easy-to-make curtains. And the best news is you won't have to sew a stitch! Measure the sides and top of a window. Then obtain a piece of colorful cotton fabric long enough to drape along the top and sides of it. Use pinking shears to cut the ends of the fabric to keep it from unraveling. Next mount a large, self-adhesive hook over each top corner of the window. If the window is very wide, add a hook in the center as well. Hang a plastic bracelet or shower curtain ring on each hook; then drape the fabric through the rings as shown. If desired, fold pleats along the top of the curtain above the window, securing them with staples or hot glue. Once the curtain goes up, take a bow!

Head for the Border

What's so stylish about this fabric-covered bulletin board border? It matches your curtains! Cut a piece of fabric to fit a large piece of lined poster board (available from office supply stores). Iron fusible webbing to the fabric; then iron the fabric to the poster board. Using the lines as a handy guide, cut the poster board into three-inch-wide strips. If desired, laminate the strips to prevent fraying. Make enough border to frame your board. With this idea, your bulletin boards will really have an edge!

They've Been Framed!

Draw attention to your bulletin boards by framing them with fabric. Simply measure the sides and top of each board; then prepare a fabric drape in the same manner used to make the curtains described in "Curtain Time!" Add a few pushpins along the top and sides of the fabric drape to keep the material securely in place.

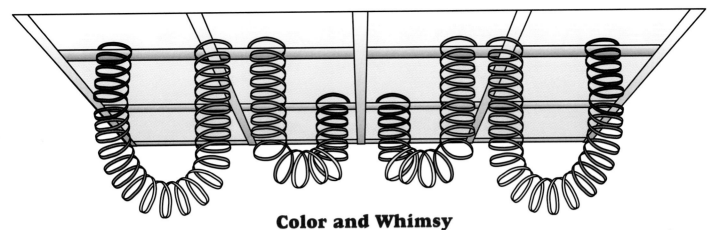

Color and Whimsy

Create rainbows of color on your ceiling with this unique idea! Slip each end of a multicolored, plastic Slinky®-type toy into the tiles of your ceiling so that it hangs down in a loop. (Look for inexpensive versions of this toy at one-price discount stores.) Hang a number of these around your room for a display that causes everyone who enters to do a double take. What a way to top off your classroom decorations!

Made in the Shade

A colorful beach umbrella can brighten any classroom. Purchase an inexpensive beach umbrella. (Watch for sales toward summer's end.) To anchor the umbrella, half-fill a sand pail with plaster of paris. Prop the umbrella in an upright position in the plaster until it dries. Later, fill the rest of the pail with sand and some shells. Finally, place the umbrella on a table in a learning center. Cool idea, dude!

Puppet Window

If you have a three-piece folding puppet theater and not a lot of storage space, this idea is for you! Store the puppet theater in your dramatic play area behind the pretend sink. You will have more storage space and your little ones will have a window they can look out as they wash, wash, wash the dishes!

ABCs and 123s

Wow! This alternative to your traditional alphabet or number line is really eye-catching! Simply use double-sided tape or Sticky-Tac to attach interlocking foam alphabet or number squares to your wall. Or hot-glue the squares to the wall if it is a surface from which the glue can later be removed. If you have an incomplete set of letters or numbers, connect the pieces in random order; then attach them to your bathroom walls as a border.

Crazy About Crayons

Say hello to yellow and yahoo to blue! Get ready for red and set the scene for green! Go crazy over colors with this thematic crayon unit that will have you tickled pink with the learning possibilities!

ideas contributed by Lisa Leonardi, Norfolk, MA

Where Do They Come From?

To introduce your class to this colorful theme, show the group a box of crayons. Invite each child to choose a crayon and to look carefully at it. Ask, "How do you think crayons are made?" Then, using a large crayon, record their answers. Follow up your discussion by showing your group pictures of how crayons are really made, as found in *My First Book of How Things Are Made: Crayons, Jeans, Peanut Butter, Guitars, and More* by George Jones (Cartwheel Books) or *How Is a Crayon Made?* by Oz Charles (available from Scholastic SeeSaw® Book Club, or check your library). Explain that powdered colors called pigment (similar to tempera paint) are mixed with melted wax. Then the wax is poured into crayon molds. Later labels are wrapped around the molded crayons, and then they are put into boxes. Cool!

Creating Crayons

Now that your little ones know how crayons are made, have them watch you make a batch for your classroom. Cut used white candles into chunks (remove the wicks) so that you have enough to half-fill the desired number of foil muffin liners. Put the liners in a muffin pan; then melt the wax in a 240-degree oven for about ten minutes or until the wax is liquefied. Immediately stir one teaspoon of powdered tempera paint into each liner of wax. When the wax has cooled, remove the liners. Now grab some paper and have youngsters put your homemade crayons to the test!

Crayon Discovery Center

You and your youngsters will have to think outside the box of eight basic crayons when visiting this art center. Stock an art area with a variety of types of crayons, such as jumbo, skinny, multicultural, glow-in-the-dark, glitter, scented, changeable, and watercolor crayons. Also provide a variety of materials to color on, such as many colors of construction paper (including black), waxed paper, tissue paper, paper towels, paper bags, aluminum foil, newspaper, and boxes. Invite youngsters to experiment and color to their hearts' content!

Tried-and-True Things to Do

Don't forget all the tried-and-true things your little ones can do with crayons. These techniques might be old favorites to you but new ideas to your preschoolers!

- Tape or rubber-band two or more crayons together so that their tips are even. Have youngsters color stripes galore!
- Tape a crayon to the back of a toy vehicle. To use, a child moves the vehicle along a strip of paper, leaving a crayon trail behind.
- Create a texture rubbing by placing a piece of paper over a textured surface, then rubbing over it with the side of an unwrapped crayon.
- To make a crayon resist, color a picture; then paint over it with watered-down tempera paint or watercolors.
- Transform broken crayon pieces into novelty crayon shapes. First, fill each section of a shaped muffin pan with small pieces of same-colored crayons. Heat the pan in a 250-degree oven for about ten minutes or until the wax melts into a soft, but not watery, substance. When the wax has cooled, re-move the new crayon shapes from the pan.
- Use an iron to melt crayon shavings between waxed paper layers. Cut the joined layers into shapes.

For more ideas, visit the Crayola® Web site: www.crayola.com.

Do Crayons Sink or Float?

Add a splash of color to your water table or discovery center with this experiment. Prepare a chart as shown; then laminate it. Obtain a new box of eight crayons. Gather a group of children around your water table; then ask them to predict whether the crayons will sink or float. In turn, drop each crayon into the water. Use a wipe-off marker to indicate on the chart whether the crayon floats or sinks. Discuss the results. Next, try this experiment comparing the same color of different brands of crayons. (Use the same chart. For example, if you have three brands of red, make three marks to the right of the red crayon.) Wipe off the chart; then leave the marker, chart, and crayons in the center for independent experimentation.

Why do some crayons sink and others float? All crayons are made of wax and pigment. However, some colors and brands of crayons have more pigment than others. This makes them more dense and causes them to sink.

	Floats	Sinks
red		X
orange	X	
yellow		X
green		X
blue		X
purple		X
brown		X
black	X	

15

True Colors

Give youngsters a chance to express themselves with this circle time song. Have the children sit down; then ask each child to select a crayon to hold. Make sure that every child knows the color of his crayon; then sing the following song, changing the color word each time you repeat it. Also vary the movement by including phrases such as *shake your head, move your arms,* and *blink your eyes*. Continue until every child is standing. Then have the children choose new crayons or trade crayons.

Give Crayons a Hand

(sung to the tune of "If You're Happy and You Know It")

If you have a [red] crayon, raise your
    hand.
If you have a [red] crayon, raise your
    hand.
If you have a [red] crayon,
[Stomp your feet] and take a stand.
If you have a [red] crayon, raise your
    hand.

Crayon Families

Open a box of 64 crayons to teach your little ones about color families and to give them a colorful new repertoire of words to use. Empty the box of crayons; then ask your group to help you sort the crayons by color. For example, find all of the different types of blue crayons. Then continue by finding the crayons in the red, yellow, purple, green, orange, and brown families. Using the crayons, make lists of the colors in the families on large sheets of chart paper as shown. Put all the crayons in a container; then place them in an art center for independent sorting practice.

Color Twins

Strengthen visual discrimination skills by adding a second box of 64 crayons to the collection you put in your art center (see "Crayon Families"). After a child at the center sorts the crayons, encourage him to find matching pairs of crayons. Once he thinks he has found a match, have him color with both crayons to compare them.

To foster cooperation skills and creativity, encourage pairs of children to find several color matches. Then direct both children to use the matching crayons to create different masterpieces.

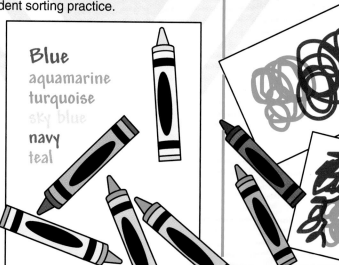

Blue
aquamarine
turquoise
sky blue
navy
teal

Drawing Literature Connections

Order books online. www.themailbox.com

My Crayons Talk

Yakety yak, the crayons in this book talk back. In fact, they sing, brag, and shout too! Read aloud this colorfully fun book by Patricia Hubbard (Bill Martin Books). Then ask your little ones what their crayons might have to say. Direct each child to draw a picture with the crayon of his choice. As he dictates, write on his page what his crayon would say. Bind the pages together between covers to create a class book that will have everybody talking, especially your little ones!

Purple says, "Yum, yum! I'm grape jelly."

The Crayon Box That Talked

Read aloud *The Crayon Box That Talked* by Shane DeRolf (Random House) for a simple lesson on working together. Then give your children a chance to practice cooperation by creating a class mural. Ask each child to select a crayon; then write the child's name on a construction-paper crayon shape that corresponds to the color she selected. Direct the children to use their chosen crayons to draw on the mural; then when everyone has contributed, stand back to admire the collaboration. Display the mural along with the personalized crayons and the following poem:

Together we created
This mural that you see.
By using our own talents,
We made a masterpiece indeed!

My Box of Color

If bananas were blue, would you eat them? Would you swim in an orange ocean? Here's an easy follow-up activity to *My Box of Color* by Lorianne Siomades (Boyds Mills Press) that encourages little ones to be creative. Duplicate a class supply of several simple coloring sheets showing well-known objects such as animals or foods. As you show the group each picture, ask the children what color they would expect that object to be. Then discuss all the different colors that object could be instead. Place the pictures in your art center with a variety of crayons; then sit back and wait to see what happens. If desired, record what your students think about their pictures before displaying them.

If a banana was red, would it taste like an apple?

I made a lollipop banana!

17

Rub-a-dub-dub,
What's in the Sensory Tub?

Icky, sticky, slippery, too,
Bags to see through and bottles of goo,
Squeeze it, shake it, pour it right through,
These sensory ideas give you plenty to do!

These pages are filled to the brim with ideas for sensory tubs, tables, bags, and bottles. "Pour" over them, and you'll get the feel for plenty of fun ways for your little ones to discover learning.

ideas by Nancy Lotzer—Preschool, Hillcrest Academy, Dallas, TX

Sensory Setups

Rub-a-dub-dub, just using your sand or water tub? Provide youngsters with sensory experiences by spilling over into some new and sometimes unusual containers.

all sizes of plastic bottles (with lids)
dishpans
plastic storage boxes
cake pans
plastic jack-o'-lanterns
large appliance boxes
large ceramic planters

all sizes of resealable plastic bags
disposable aluminum roasting pans
small outdoor pools
decorative gift bags
mixing bowls
woven baskets and laundry baskets
large plastic flowerpots or window planters

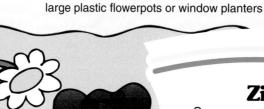

Zippity Zip Bags

Sensory experiences don't have to be messy. Take a peek at these suggestions for filling resealable plastic freezer bags. (After filling, seal the bags with clear packing tape.) Kids love to get their hands on them—especially those children who are tactilely squeamish.

two different colors of tempera paint
a yellow sponge and blue or red water
shaving cream and a drop of food coloring
fingerpaint
jam or jelly

hair gel
hand lotion
gelatin
warm oatmeal
mud

Discoveries by the Dozen

How do you get a bevy of beautiful sensory bottles? Ask parents to save and send in empty, clear plastic bottles of all sizes. Fill each bottle with one liquid, one solid, or mix any liquid with any solid. Prepare contrasting bottles as well. For example, you might put beads in green water (thin) and in a different bottle put beads in green shampoo (thick). Be sure to hot-glue the tops on the bottles after filling.

liquids
colored water
colored soapy water
cooking oil
mineral or baby oil
oil and colored water
shampoo
liquid hand soap
corn syrup

solids
sequins
snippets of yarn or ribbon
colorful plastic paper clips
beads
small thematic erasers
plastic confetti
pieces of craft foam
glitter

Don't forget about the sense of sound when you're filling up your bottles. Fill some bottles with items that make loud sounds to compare with bottles filled with things that hardly make a sound at all.

feathers	small tiles	colored craft sticks
toothpicks	popcorn	beans
rubber fishing worms	dry oatmeal	jingle bells
cake decorations	flour	silk leaves
plastic bugs	sand	pebbles
colorful marker caps	shells	rice or pasta

Words, Wonderful Words

Combine science with language development by helping children describe what they see, hear, and feel as they explore. To further develop literacy, attach labels to bottles and bags or display labels near the sensory area. Have fun with these wonderful words.

Texture Words

smooth	prickly
slick	"tickly"
rough	crumbly
bumpy	wrinkled
oily	thick
silky	thin
slippery	wet
sticky	dry
gooey	soft
gritty	hard
soapy	

Action Words

pour	watch
bury	observe
find	crumble
squeeze	fill
poke	empty
squish	break
smash	dump
scrub	sweep
measure	

Temperature Words

hot	chilly
warm	cold
steamy	icy
cool	frozen

Visual Words

shiny	glittery
dull	full
color words	empty
size words	

Smelling Words

sweet	yucky
good	fruity
bad	stinky

In Our Sensory Table Today:

fingerpaint

slippery

slimy

blue

smooth

squishy

19

Sensational Ideas From A to Z

It just makes sense to incorporate these items into your alphabet sound studies!

A
applesauce in plastic bags
real or pretend apples in water

B
blue beads in blue water
baby doll bathing
large beans with bowls, bottles, spoons, and funnels
balls that sink (golf) and float (Ping-Pong®)
bubble bath in water

C
clothes washing
coins in cornmeal
cereal (such as Cookie-Crisp® or Cocoa Krispies®)
cotton balls

D
dish washing
dry dog food

E
plastic Easter eggs

F
fake flowers to plant in sand or dirt
feathers
flour
fingerpaint in plastic bags

G
green water
plastic grass
green glitter
glue in plastic bags

H
holey items for sand or water such as colanders, funnels, slotted spoons

I
ice: plain, plastic bags filled with water and then frozen, or novelty ice cubes

J
jam, jelly, or Jell-O® in plastic bags
jingle bells

K
ketchup in plastic bags

L
lemon extract in water

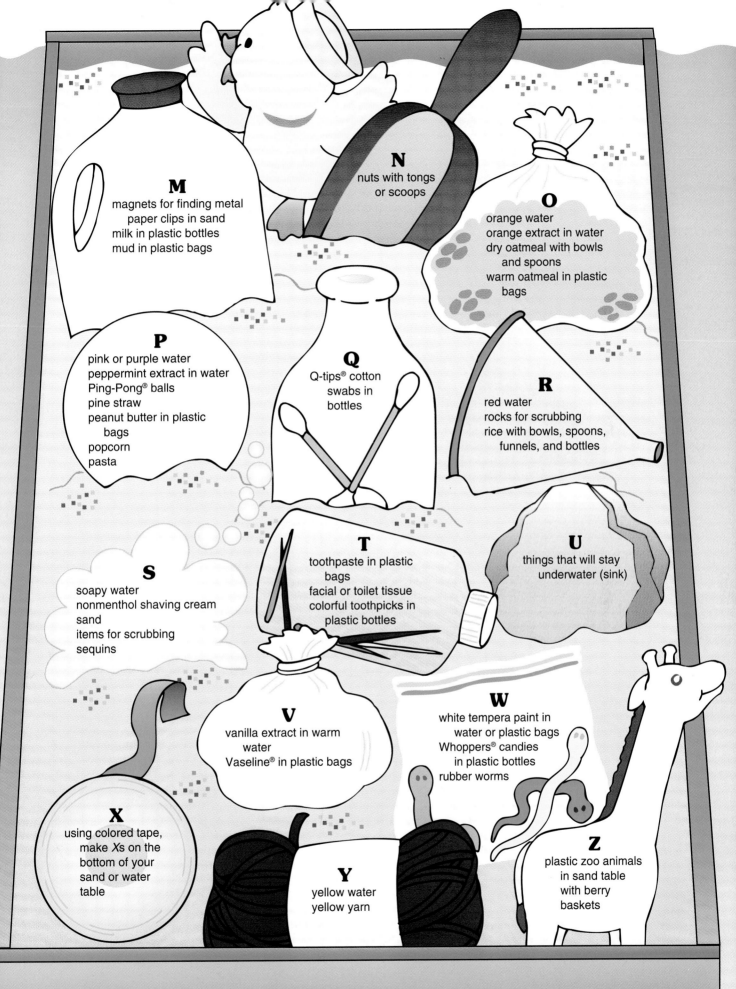

M
magnets for finding metal
paper clips in sand
milk in plastic bottles
mud in plastic bags

N
nuts with tongs
or scoops

O
orange water
orange extract in water
dry oatmeal with bowls
and spoons
warm oatmeal in plastic
bags

P
pink or purple water
peppermint extract in water
Ping-Pong® balls
pine straw
peanut butter in plastic
bags
popcorn
pasta

Q
Q-tips® cotton
swabs in
bottles

R
red water
rocks for scrubbing
rice with bowls, spoons,
funnels, and bottles

S
soapy water
nonmenthol shaving cream
sand
items for scrubbing
sequins

T
toothpaste in plastic
bags
facial or toilet tissue
colorful toothpicks in
plastic bottles

U
things that will stay
underwater (sink)

V
vanilla extract in warm
water
Vaseline® in plastic bags

W
white tempera paint in
water or plastic bags
Whoppers® candies
in plastic bottles
rubber worms

X
using colored tape,
make Xs on the
bottom of your
sand or water
table

Y
yellow water
yellow yarn

Z
plastic zoo animals
in sand table
with berry
baskets

Theme Connections

Keep your sensory tubs, bags, and bottles interesting by using the following items with these favorite themes.

Apples
real and pretend apples
apple baskets
applesauce in plastic bags
apple juice in bottles
apple-scented soap, bubble bath, or shampoo in water table

Autumn
leaves
minipumpkins and bumpy squash
hay
acorns
mashed pumpkin in plastic bags

Birds
feathers
birdseed
decorative birds (from a craft store)

Dental Health
toothpaste in plastic bags
toothpaste and brushes for scrubbing the water table

Dinosaurs
toy dinosaurs in the sand table
rocks, small twigs, leaves

Farm
farm animals in the sand table
chicken feed or cracked corn
hay

Ocean
ocean-themed confetti
aquarium gravel
shells

Pets
cat or dog food, dog biscuits, bowls, scoops
cedar or pine shavings

Plants
artificial flowers for the sand table
watering cans

Rabbits
cotton balls
carrots for washing

Trees
bark mulch
leaves, fresh and dried
cedar or pine shavings

Recycling
biodegradable foam peanuts
margarine tubs, unused burger containers, paper and Styrofoam® cups
shredded newspaper

Transportation
toy vehicles for the sand table
toy boats for the water table

Zoo
zoo animals and berry baskets in the sand table

Pam Crane

Literature Link

The Three Bears
dry oatmeal with three sizes of bowls and spoons
cooked oatmeal in plastic bags

Jamberry
(by Bruce Degen)
jam in plastic bags
fingerpaint with jam in water table

The Little Red Hen
flour, sifters, measuring cups, spoons, bowls

The Rainbow Fish
(by Marcus Pfister)
plastic fish and Mylar® spangles in water table

Little Blue and Little Yellow
(by Leo Lionni)
blue and yellow fingerpaint in a plastic bag

Jack and the Beanstalk
large dried beans and plastic coins in the sand table

The Carrot Seed
(by Ruth Krauss)
baby carrots, small shovels, dirt

Stone Soup
stones, toy vegetables, spoon, small pot in water table

It Looked Like Spilt Milk
(by Charles G. Shaw)
white tempera paint in plastic bags

Order books online. www.themailbox.com

Final Touches
Keep these tips in mind to ensure your sensory activities go smoothly.
- Have children wash their hands before and after playing with sensory materials.
- Change the water in your water tubs daily.
- Frequently clean sensory tubs with bleach and water.
- Monitor the use of small items such as beans and beads.
- Make sure foam packing peanuts are biodegradable.
- Because glitter can be dangerous to little eyes, use glitter only in plastic bags or bottles.
- Be aware of allergies to items such as hay or peanut butter.

WANTED: Parents as Partners

Bet you already know that you need parents as your partners to make each child's preschool experience a success. To help you out, we've rounded up these ideas from teachers who really know the ropes when it comes to communicating and working with parents.

Hello! This week we are having our fall festival!...

Answering Machine Memos

Here's a system that keeps parents up-to-date on current school information, promotes events, and encourages parents to leave messages for teachers—all at everyone's convenience! Each week record a message on your school's answering machine that includes the desired information and requests that parents ask questions or leave messages for specific teachers. Hello! Thank you for calling!

Janice Denney—Preschool
Iola Preschool for Exceptional Children, Iola, KS

How Can I Help?

Many fortunate teachers have been asked by parents, "How can I help?" Use volunteer cards to answer that question and to encourage parents to help in ways that are most convenient for them. When you need a volunteer, identically label two index cards with "Volunteer Card" and the specific request. Clip the cards together; then post them on a parent bulletin board in a highly visible area, such as the class entrance. To volunteer for a task, a parent selects a pair of cards, then pulls them apart. She keeps one card as a reminder. Then she writes her name on the second card and gives it to you for your records.

Cynthia J. Stefanick—Pre-K, Lajes Elementary School, Terceira, Portuguese Azores

Volunteer Card

Trace and cut out 20 bear shapes by Nov. 1.

Ask me where I worked today.

Ask Me Where I Worked Today

Parents are sure to appreciate this idea that helps them ask their children meaningful questions about the school day and reminds them of the learning benefits of play. To implement this tip, draw a simple diagram of your classroom, noting all of your centers. On a separate page, list each of your centers and the benefits of play there. For each child, duplicate the diagram and the list on opposite sides of a colorful sheet of paper. Laminate the sheets.

Each day, use a wipe-off marker to indicate on a child's sheet those centers at which he played. Then have the child take the sheet home to share with a parent. "I worked at sand today and built a castle!"

Betsy Fuhrmann—Pre-K, Dodds Early Start, Springfield, IL

Make Contact

Stick with your effort to make contact with parents with this terrific tip. Cut solid-colored Con-Tact® paper into note-sized geometric shapes. (Or use a die-cutting machine to cut seasonal and thematic shapes out of the paper.) The next time you need to send a reminder home with a child or pass on a word of praise about an accomplishment, use a permanent marker to jot a note onto one of the cutouts. Remove the backing and then press the note onto the child's clothing. These colorful reminders are sure to get parents' attention!

Shoshanna Katz—Two- to Five-Year-Olds, Special Education
Marathon Childhood Center Forest Hills West
Middle Village, NY

Reminder: Pumpkin patch trip tomorrow!

Book orders due on Friday.

It Goes Both Ways

These folders make it easy for information to travel both ways—home and back to school again. Personalize the outside of a two-pocket folder for each child. Invite each child to use markers or stickers to decorate her folder. Encourage parents to check the folders daily for important messages, words of praise, behavior reports, and more. Ensure parents that you'll be checking the folders daily as well for any messages parents may need to send to you.

Barbara Morganweck—Preschool, Handicapped
Downe Township School, Newport, NJ

Thompson

Wishing Well

Need items for your classroom? Make a wish at the wishing well! Mount a wishing well design onto a background; then surround it with self-adhesive notes labeled with your requests. Parents simply take off a note and then send the requested item(s) to school. Prepare this display for an open house or anytime to let parents know of your needs all through the year.

Lucia Roney, Orange Park, FL

Wishing Well

magic markers for art center

snacks for Tuesday, Nov. 9

1 bag of white cotton balls

2 boxes of tissues

1 pair of scissors

package of paper plates

25

A Noteworthy Idea

Even with the best of plans, drop-off times and pickup times can be hectic. Use this communication idea to make sure parents know you value their thoughts and concerns. Write each child's name on his own small spiral notepad. Then store each child's notepad in his cubby. Encourage parents to write messages to you in the notebooks in order to leave you messages. Likewise, when necessary write the parent a message, making sure the child takes his notepad home with him that day.

Lori Secor—Pre-K, Children's Corner Daycare, Albany, NY

Oct. 4

Mrs. Dominguez,
Please send Cassie's permission slip to school by Friday.

Ms. Secor

Cassie

Pam Crane

A Picture Is Worth…

To help parents better understand how their children are learning at school, take some time to create this photo album of your classroom activities and centers. Over a period of time, take pictures of children doing a variety of activities, such as playing in centers, participating in group activities, and taking part in such routines as washing hands or napping. Arrange the pictures in an album along with brief explanations. Invite each child in turn to take the book home; then put it in your reading area for students to look at and discuss. Pictures really are worth a thousand words!

Cindy Lawson—Toddler to Pre-K, Shell Lake, WI

Tomez and Sara develop problem-solving skills at the sand table.

We practice being courteous when we are in line to wash our hands.

Weekly News

Keep 'em Posted

Keep parents posted with a bulletin board provided just for them. Arrange a display area near your school or classroom entrance. Cut one or more pocket folders in half; then staple the halves to your display. Make copies of such items as your weekly newsletter, important forms, or articles to store in the pockets. Encourage parents to check the display often, taking copies of the pages that are of interest to them. To make sure the display remains eye-catching, add pictures of children at the school.

Melissa Batten—Two- and Three-Year-Olds, Sumter, SC

Coffee and Conversation

Parents will quickly reply after getting these student-painted invitations to parent/teacher conferences or group information sessions. For each child, trace a coffee cup shape (similar to the one shown) onto a large, folded piece of construction paper. Cut out the shape leaving the fold intact so that the invitation can be opened. Ask a child to paint the front of the invitation using very strong room-temperature coffee. When the coffee is dry, program the inside of each invitation with a message; then send it home. Now get that coffee brewing, and soon you'll be percolating flavorful conversations!

Nancy Goldberg—Three-Year-Olds
B'nai Israel Schilit Nursery School, Rockville, MD

Dear Mom and Dad,

You are invited for coffee and conversation on Monday, November 9, from 9:30–10:30 A.M. Mrs. Goldberg and Mrs. Speisman will be sharing wonderful stories with you! Plus, you can enjoy the yummy lemon snaps that we made. RSVP to my teachers.

Love,
Nancy

Welcome!
Our children would like for you to find:

 the housekeeping center

☐ the turtle Maria brought to school

☐ our orange and blue paintings

Making a List

You won't have to check twice to see if parents and their children enjoy your open house when you prepare this classroom checklist. Just prior to the event, ask your little ones to list those things or areas in your classroom that *they* would like for their parents to see. Record the items on a checklist; then duplicate a copy for each child's parent. As parents and children arrive, give them a checklist and encourage them to locate the listed items in your room. Take a look—there's lots to see in this special place!

Lucia Roney, Orange Park, FL

"Tour-rific" Open House Idea

Give your little ones the pride of being classroom tour guides with this open house idea. Prepare a coloring sheet similar to the one shown that indicates key areas of interest in your classroom; then duplicate a copy for each child. When each child and her parent arrive at the open house, give them a copy of the sheet and a crayon. Direct the parent to ask his child to show him each listed area, having the child color in the corresponding space after they have spent some time together there. Everyone is sure to have a "tour-rific" time!

Ellen Bruno and Esta Fowler, Rio Rancho Elementary
Rio Rancho, NM

What a Class

Have your older preschoolers make these projects to create the illusion of a classroom full of busy workers for your Open House. For each child, lightly outline a large face shape on a piece of construction paper. Help each child use crayons to add hair, facial features, and skin tone to the outline so it resembles himself. Place the piece of paper on top of another sheet; then cut out the outline shape of the face, cutting through both layers. Glue the cut-out shapes together along the edges, leaving the bottom open. Next, slide the face over a long wrapping paper tube. Secure the tube to a chair; then add paper arms and hands. Label the table at that spot with the child's name. Encourage parents to find their children's portraits when they enter the room.

Eleanore Cirigliano—Preschool, KidsPort Learning Center
Plymouth, MA

Preschoolers Can!

Parents are sure to enjoy looking at this display while waiting for conferences or during an open house. And, as a bonus, it gives a positive message about the many things preschoolers can do. To make the display, take pictures of small groups of children participating in indoor and outdoor activities. Mount each photo to a piece of construction paper; then label the paper "Preschoolers can [action shown]." Arrange the pictures together on a wall or bulletin board. Later, bind the pages together between covers. Title the book "Preschoolers Can!"

Cindy Lawson, Children's EduCare Center, Ft. Wayne, IN

Picture This

When making home visits, keep in mind that many parents may be unable to visit your classroom during school hours. To make the descriptions of your class activities clear, take along photos. In advance of your home visits, take pictures of your classroom activities, making sure to get each child in one or more shots. Have double prints made of the pictures. Organize the first set of pictures in an album. While you are visiting a parent, have her look at pictures that relate to the information you are sharing. Then invite her to choose pictures that include her child to keep from the second set of prints.

Janis Woods—Four-Year-Olds, Ridgeland Elementary
Ridgeland, SC

Appointment Activity Packs

Help parents and children make the most of waiting times at doctor visits with these appointment packs. Prepare several packs by filling large resealable plastic bags with items such as small books, activity sheets, crayons, and informative articles for the parents to read. When a child is picked up from school for an appointment, give him a pack to take along. No more wasted time—waiting times are learning times!

Kim Richman—Preschool, The Learning Zone, Des Moines, IA

10 Reasons You Should Read Aloud to Your Child

Alphabet Cards

A a

Surprise Boxes

Looking for a clever way to send home learning activities to help parents reinforce basic skills? Try clear plastic videocassette boxes! Use dimensional fabric paint and stickers to decorate the outside of a number of empty boxes. Then fill each box with items such as alphabet flash cards, small manipulatives and a card programmed with activity suggestions, or puzzle pieces. Children will enjoy taking the goodies home, and parents will appreciate the learning opportunities provided.

Amy Drake, Fort Wayne, IN

Books on Tape

Looking for a way to involve parents who are unable to come to school? If so, this project is sure to sound like a good idea. Send a letter to parents asking for volunteers to record themselves reading aloud a classroom book. Then send each volunteer a different book, a blank tape labeled with the name of the book, a bell or small instrument (to indicate page turns), and a tape recorder. Also duplicate and send a set of simple directions and suggestions. As the book and tape sets are returned to school, preview them; then place them in your class listening center. Students will be surprised to hear their parents reading a favorite classroom book!

Tracy Tavernese—Pre-K, Holy Child School, Old Westbury, NY

The Little Red Hen

The Little Red Hen

SPOTS, the Fire-Safety Dog

Make these adorable dalmatian puppets and booklets just in time for Fire Prevention Week.

puppet and book idea contributed by
Tonya Warren—Preschool, Kid Connection, Inc., Liberal, KS

Dalmatian Pup Puppet

Do your youngsters know that dalmatians are the unofficial mascot—or good luck charm—of firefighters? Once they find out, they're sure to want a dalmatian pal of their own! To make a puppet, trace two of the dog patterns and two of the ear patterns (page 31) onto white felt. Cut out the patterns. Glue the dog patterns together, leaving the bottom open; then glue the ears onto the back of the puppet. Use dimensional fabric paint to add facial features to the dog. Finally, use Q-tips® cotton swabs to paint black dimensional-paint spots on the puppet. To make a hat for the puppet to wear, trace the hat pattern onto red tagboard; then cut it out. Label the hat with a child's initials or with Spots's name.

Where Is Spots?

Give Spots a chance to show off his fire-safety savvy with this interactive booklet. To make one, duplicate the booklet (pages 32–33) onto white construction paper or tagboard. Cut out the cover, the pages, and the boxes on each page along the bold lines. Bind the pages in sequence along the left side. Have each child color his booklet. Then demonstrate how to manipulate a Spots puppet behind the cutout boxes as you read each page. "Woof, woof!" That means "hot reading!"

Storytime With Spots

Have your own Spots puppet read this story about a real firehouse dog to your little ones. *Firehouse Dog* by Amy and Richard Hutchings (Cartwheel Books) follows Hooper the dog and his fire-fighting friends through a day on the job. After the story, teach youngsters this song about what a fire dog sees and invite their puppets to bark along!

At the Fire Station
(sung to the tune of "Down at the Station")

At the fire station early in the morning (during the daytime/late in the evening),
Spots the fire dog is watching, don't you know?
He sees the firefighters [riding in the fire truck].
"Clang! Clang!" sounds the bell. Off they go!

Each time you sing the song, substitute one of the following phrases for the underlined words:

…sliding down the fire pole.
…building their muscles.
…putting on equipment.
…eating in the kitchen.
…resting in the bedroom.

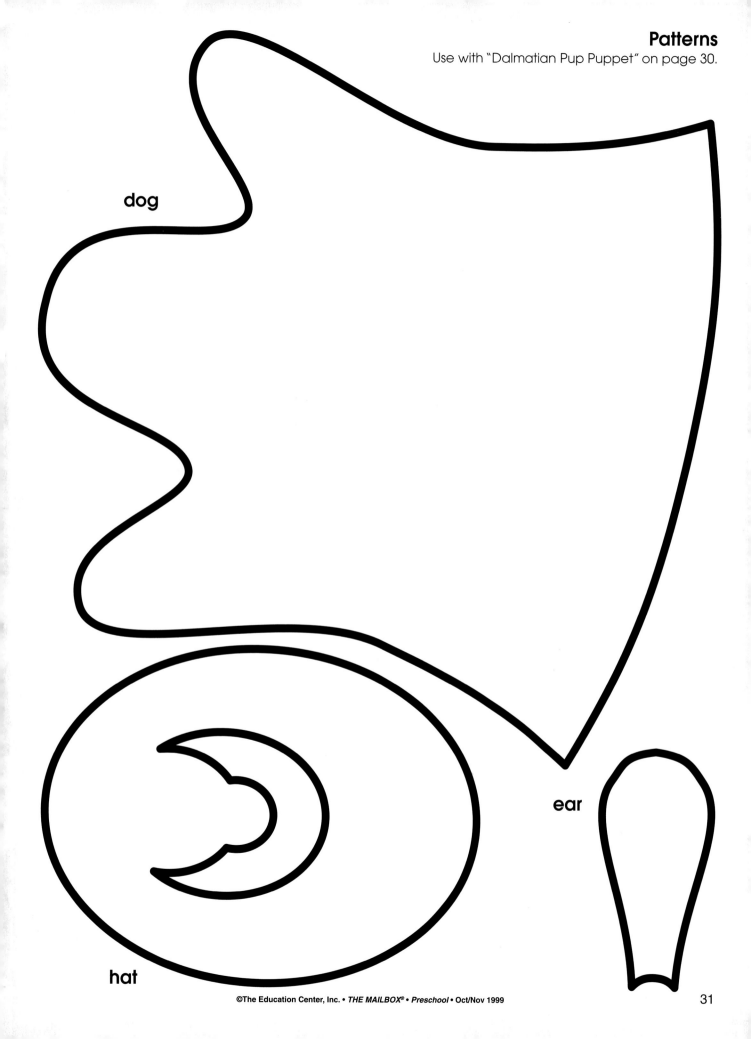

dog

hat

ear

Booklet

Use with "Where Is Spots?" on page 30.

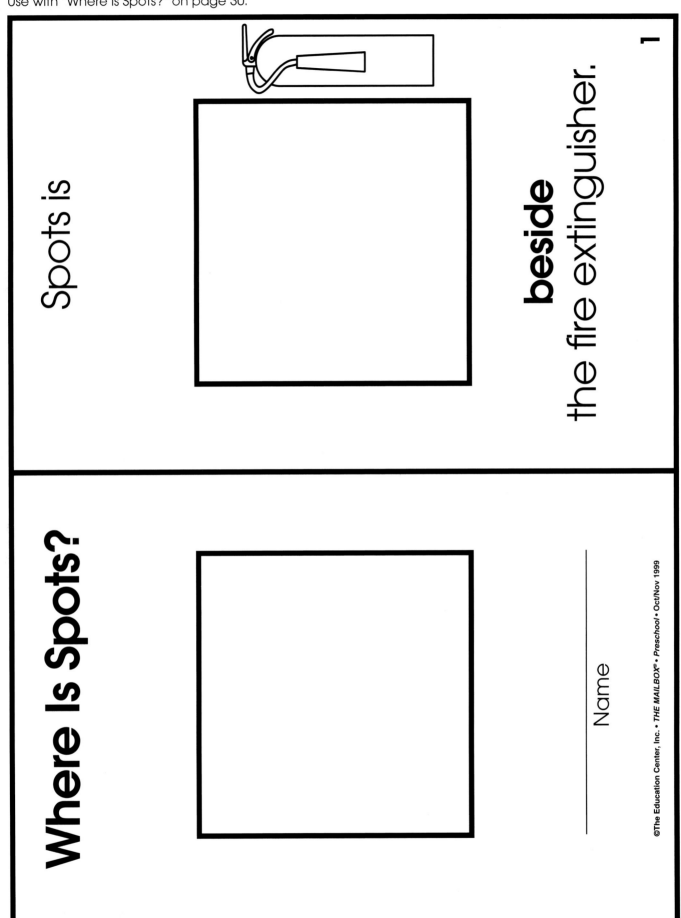

Spots is

beside
the fire extinguisher.

1

Where Is Spots?

Name _____

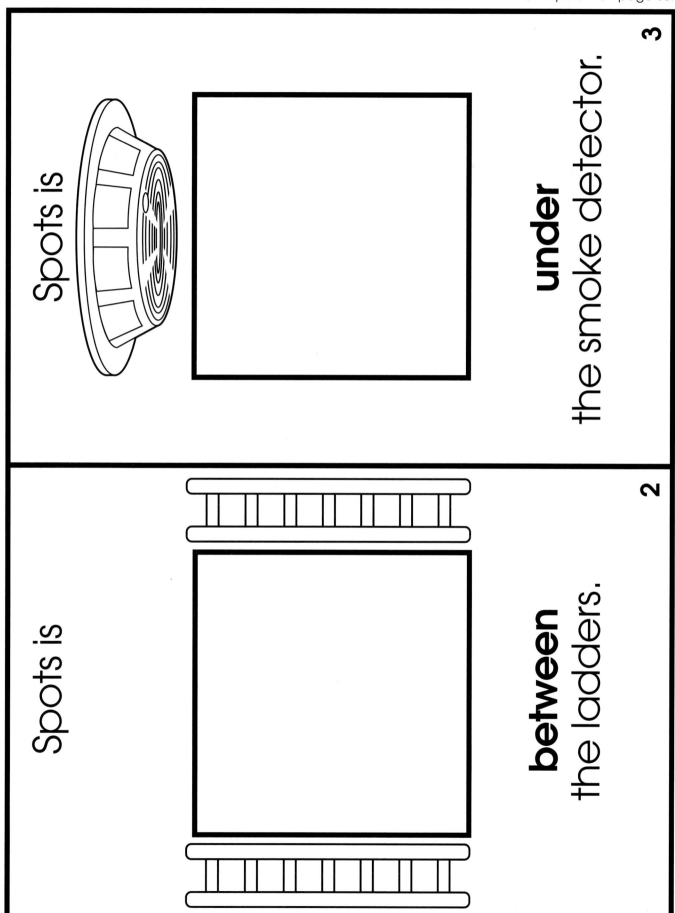

3

Spots is

under
the smoke detector.

2

Spots is

between
the ladders.

Gobblin' Good Party Ideas

Well "wattle" you know? It's time for a class party! Use these ideas to plan your celebration and you're sure to have a gobblin' good time!

ideas by Susan Bunyan, Linn Elementary, Dodge City, KS

Pilgrim Hat Table Toppers

Help your little ones make these place cards for themselves and any guests attending your party. To make one, trace the bottom of a six-ounce Styrofoam® cup onto black construction paper. From the black paper, cut out the circle along with a four-inch circle, a strip of paper (as shown) sized to fit around the cup, and a small rectangle. From yellow paper, cut out a larger rectangle and a strip that measures about 1" x 3". Glue the small black circle to the bottom of the cup. Next glue the strip around the cup and the larger circle to the top of the cup. Personalize the yellow strip; then glue it to the hat along with the black and yellow rectangles. Arrange these place cards on your tables for a seating arrangement that's simply tops!

Talking Turkey

Have students make these turkey puppets to invite children in other classes or to invite their parents to join your party. To make one, glue a five-inch brown circle onto a wide craft stick. Fold a two-inch orange square in half. Use a brad to attach the square and a wattle cutout to the circle as shown. Glue on white paper reinforcers for eyes. Cut out the desired number of feathers from colorful construction paper. Fringe their edges; then glue them to the back of the circle. Complete the invitation by programming the wattle and turkey with a message like the one shown. Encourage students to use their puppets to extend verbal invitations to your party.

Poultry Party Hats

This festive headgear is sure to get everyone in the mood to party! To make one headband, glue together a 4" x 18" and a 4" x 6" strip of tan construction paper. To the front of the band, glue a five-inch brown circle. Add black paper eyes, a red wattle, and a folded orange square for a beak. Bend several 2" x 18" strips of colorful construction paper in half; then glue the ends to the back of the band for feathers as shown. Finally, fringe the rounded part of two brown half circles; then glue them on the side of the band for wings. Encourage youngsters to put on their hats and strut with pride!

Turkey, Anyone?

What's a Thanksgiving celebration without a turkey? You'll have a class full of turkeys when you invite everyone to wear their party hats and join you in singing this song.

I'm a Little Turkey

(sung to the tune of "I'm a Little Teapot")

I'm a little turkey
Fluffy and brown.

My wings flip-flop
When I turn around.

I have a lot of feathers
On my back,

And a big orange beak
That goes "click clack"!

Candy Corn Countdown

Treat your partygoers with this tasty game. To play you'll need a bag of candy corn and a large poster-board model of a candy corn. Have the players stand in a circle. Stand in the center of the circle, holding the cutout. Choose a child to start. Point to the white part of the candy corn and ask that child to name the color. Point to the orange part of the candy corn and ask the next child to name the color. Point to the yellow part of the candy corn and ask the next child to name the color. Give this child a real candy corn; then direct him to sit down where he was standing. Continue in this manner until only one child is standing. Declare that child the winner and ask him to help you with the next round of play by holding the candy corn as you point or by distributing the candy.

Gobble, gobble!

Gobble, gobble!

Gobble, gobble!

A Turkey's Dinner

Liven up your party with this guessing game that will have the group gobbling and flapping their wings. Have the class stand in a circle. Teach them the following poem. Then, each time you recite the poem, ask a different child to name either a food or an object that is not a food. If the child names a food, the turkeys in the group should gobble. If the child does not name a food, the turkeys should flap their wings.

"Gobble, gobble!" said the turkey
As he rubbed his fluffy tummy.
My Thanksgiving dinner
Is going to taste yummy.

So he got out his fork,
And he got out his plate.
Now, can you tell me
What that little turkey ate?

white
orange
yellow

Take to the Air!

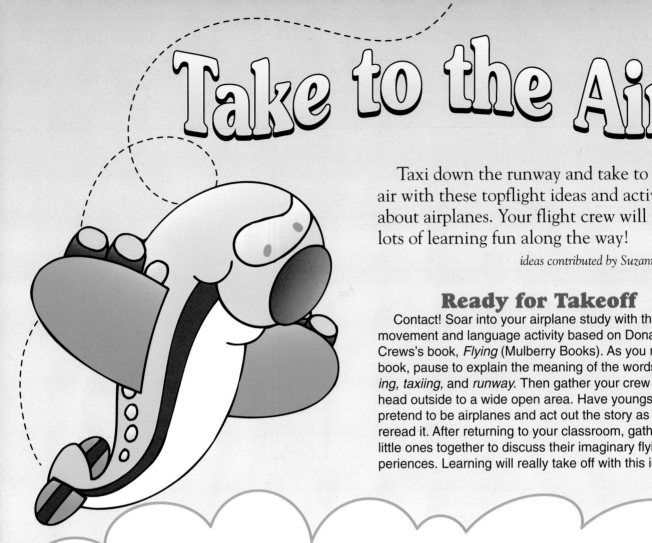

Taxi down the runway and take to the air with these topflight ideas and activities about airplanes. Your flight crew will log in lots of learning fun along the way!

ideas contributed by Suzanne Moore

Ready for Takeoff

Contact! Soar into your airplane study with this movement and language activity based on Donald Crews's book, *Flying* (Mulberry Books). As you read the book, pause to explain the meaning of the words *boarding, taxiing,* and *runway.* Then gather your crew and head outside to a wide open area. Have youngsters pretend to be airplanes and act out the story as you reread it. After returning to your classroom, gather your little ones together to discuss their imaginary flying experiences. Learning will really take off with this idea!

Parts Are Parts

Your youngsters will be singing the parts of a plane with this catchy tune. Before breaking into song, show students several pictures of airplanes. (*Let's Fly From A to Z* by Doug Magee, published by Cobblehill Books, is an especially helpful photo-illustrated book.) If pictures are not available, locate a toy plane. Explain that the fuselage is the main part of an airplane where the pilot, passengers, and luggage are located. The cockpit, galley, and seats are inside the fuselage. Then point out other parts of the plane such as the wings, tail, and wheels. Ready to sing?

Those Planes! Those Planes!
(sung to the tune of "Dem Bones, Dem Bones")

Those planes, those planes, those airplanes!
Those planes, those planes, those airplanes!
Those planes, those planes, those airplanes!
These are the parts of a plane.

The body of a plane is the *fuselage.*
The body of a plane is the *fuselage.*
The body of a plane is the *fuselage.*
That is part of a plane.

The [wheels] are connected to the fuselage.
The [wheels] are connected to the fuselage.
The [wheels] are connected to the fuselage.
[Wheels] are part of a plane.

Repeat the verse, replacing "wheels" with "wings" and "tail."

The [cockpit] is in the fuselage.
The [cockpit] is in the fuselage.
The [cockpit] is in the fuselage.
The [cockpit] is part of a plane.

Repeat the verse, replacing "cockpit" with "galley" and "seats."

Those planes, those planes, those airplanes!
Those planes, those planes, those airplanes!
Those planes, those planes, those airplanes!
We've learned the parts of a plane!

Up, Up, and Away!

How do airplanes fly? The answer is all around us—air! Use this simple activity to demonstrate how air helps move an airplane. Give each child a 3" x 11" strip of copier paper. Direct her to hold the strip at one end; then challenge her to lift the other end *without touching it.* After youngsters have experimented on their own, have each child hold the strip close to her bottom lip and blow *hard* across the top of the paper. The other end of the strip will move up! How did that happen? Explain that the air moving across the top of the paper made the air under the paper push the strip up. Airplanes fly in much the same way. As an airplane rolls along the runway, it moves faster and faster. The air moves across the top of the wings so fast that the air under the wings pushes the whole plane up, up,…and away!

Pam Crane

Cleared for Landing

Invite your little ones to act out this airplane poem during your circle time. To prepare, label each of five lengths of white bulletin board paper with dotted lines down its center and a different numeral from 1 to 5. Have students sit in a circle around the numbered runways and review each number with them. Next invite five children to pretend to fly like airplanes around the circle. As you recite the poem below, have each child, in turn, land on a runway.

Five little airplanes flying in the sky,
Come in for a landing from way up high.

The first little airplane shining in the sun,
Is the first to land on runway number 1.

The second little airplane carrying its crew,
Lands very slowly on runway number 2.

The third little airplane, such a sight to see,
Lands quietly on runway number 3.

The fourth little airplane can't wait anymore,
And lands very quickly on runway number 4.

The fifth little airplane is the last to arrive,
And finally lands on runway number 5!

LeeAnn Collins—Director, Sunshine Preschool, Lansing, MI

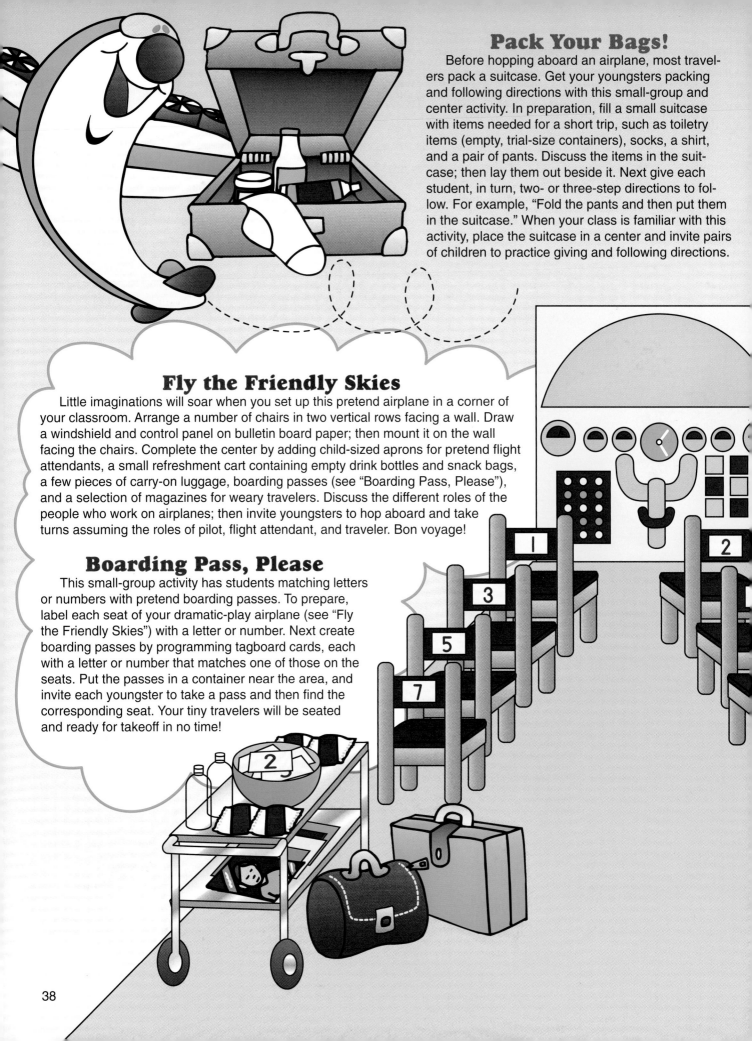

Pack Your Bags!

Before hopping aboard an airplane, most travelers pack a suitcase. Get your youngsters packing and following directions with this small-group and center activity. In preparation, fill a small suitcase with items needed for a short trip, such as toiletry items (empty, trial-size containers), socks, a shirt, and a pair of pants. Discuss the items in the suitcase; then lay them out beside it. Next give each student, in turn, two- or three-step directions to follow. For example, "Fold the pants and then put them in the suitcase." When your class is familiar with this activity, place the suitcase in a center and invite pairs of children to practice giving and following directions.

Fly the Friendly Skies

Little imaginations will soar when you set up this pretend airplane in a corner of your classroom. Arrange a number of chairs in two vertical rows facing a wall. Draw a windshield and control panel on bulletin board paper; then mount it on the wall facing the chairs. Complete the center by adding child-sized aprons for pretend flight attendants, a small refreshment cart containing empty drink bottles and snack bags, a few pieces of carry-on luggage, boarding passes (see "Boarding Pass, Please"), and a selection of magazines for weary travelers. Discuss the different roles of the people who work on airplanes; then invite youngsters to hop aboard and take turns assuming the roles of pilot, flight attendant, and traveler. Bon voyage!

Boarding Pass, Please

This small-group activity has students matching letters or numbers with pretend boarding passes. To prepare, label each seat of your dramatic-play airplane (see "Fly the Friendly Skies") with a letter or number. Next create boarding passes by programming tagboard cards, each with a letter or number that matches one of those on the seats. Put the passes in a container near the area, and invite each youngster to take a pass and then find the corresponding seat. Your tiny travelers will be seated and ready for takeoff in no time!

Test Flight

Use this center idea to help develop eye-hand coordination and gross-motor skills. In preparation, cut out several large cloud shapes from white bulletin board paper; then arrange them on the floor of an open area. Next follow the directions (at the right) to create several paper airplanes. Place the planes in a container and then set it a short distance from the clouds. Demonstrate how to *gently* throw the planes; then challenge each youngster to toss a plane and have it land on a cloud.

How to Make a Paper Airplane:

Step 1: Fold paper in half as shown.

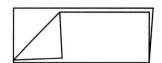

Step 2: Fold corner as shown.

Step 3: Fold same corner again as shown.

Step 4: Fold same corner once again as shown.

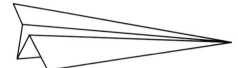

Step 5: Repeat Steps 2–4 on the unfolded side.

Beautiful Biplanes

Little propellers will be spinning with this craft idea! To make one biplane, duplicate and cut out a construction paper copy of the patterns on page 41. Trace the propeller pattern onto tagboard and then cut on the resulting outline. Punch a hole through the middle of the propeller; then use a brad to attach it to the middle of a three-inch masking tape strip. Tape the strip across one open end of a toilet paper tube. Paint the tube. When the paint is dry, cut a slit in the top of the back of the plane; then slip the tailpiece into the slit. Next glue the wing cutouts to the plane. As a final touch, add stickers or foil stars to the plane. Hang the planes around your room. Look, there's something special in the air!

On the Move!

Use the planes from "Beautiful Biplanes" to practice positional relations skills and identification of body parts. Invite each child to fly her airplane above her head, behind her back, under her chin, over her shoulder, in front of her body, beside her body, beneath her legs, and more. Or have students try these acrobatic airplane moves as shown: nosedive, loop, and roll.

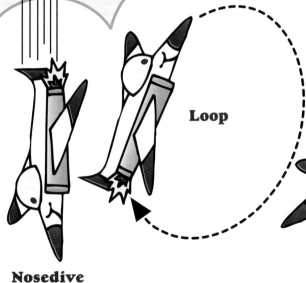

Nosedive

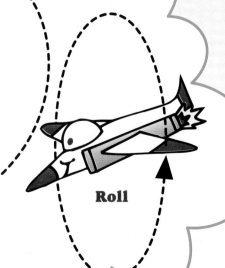

Loop

Roll

Flannelboard Flight

Language skills will take off with this poem and flannelboard activity! In preparation, cut out pieces of felt similar to the ones at the right. As you recite the poem, assemble the pieces as shown to create an airplane. When students are familiar with the poem, place the felt pieces in a center for students to use independently.

First an oval,

Then a door.

Add two wings.
But, wait! There's more!

Add a tail and windows, too.
Here's an airplane just for you!

On Cloud Nine!

This display has your entire class flying high! Cut out a large airplane shape from bulletin board paper. Draw a window on the plane for each child in your class; then mount a different child's self-portrait in each window. If desired, add your own self-portrait to the front window of the plane. Mount the plane on a light blue background along with some student finger-painted clouds and a catchy title.

Miss Ewing's Class Has Really Taken Off!

Appetizing Airplanes

Follow the recipe below to create a snack that makes a direct flight to little tummies!

Ingredients for one airplane snack:
$1/2$ banana, peeled
1 pretzel stick
2 $1/2$ Keebler® Town House® crackers
peanut butter

Spread peanut butter on the middle and ends of the banana. Place the pretzel stick and crackers in the peanut butter as shown; then eat!

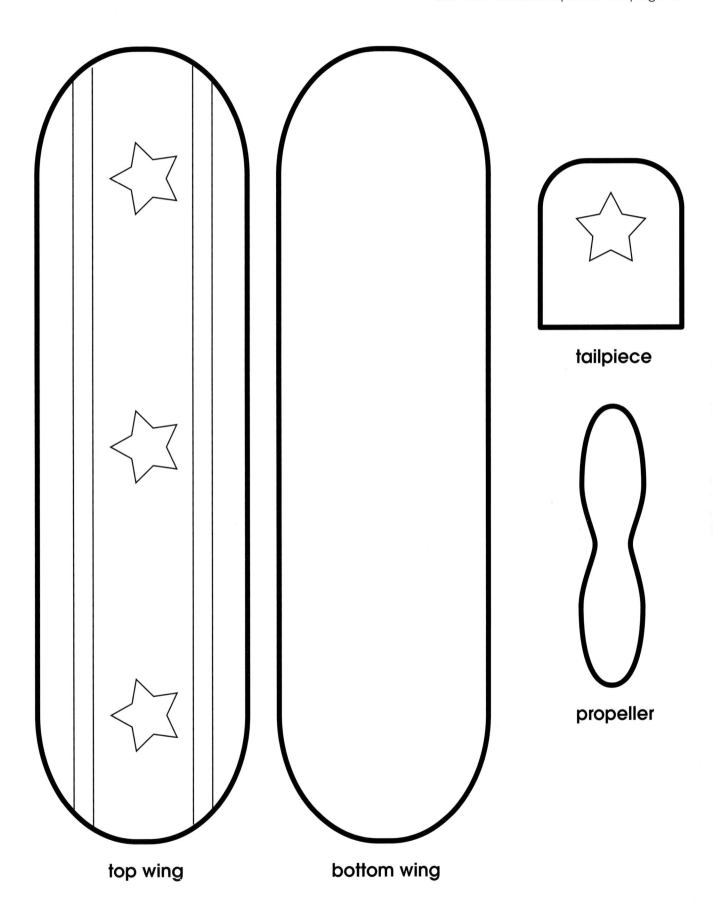

tailpiece

propeller

top wing

bottom wing

Hanukkah Patterns

Use with "My Hanukkah Counting Book" on page 43.

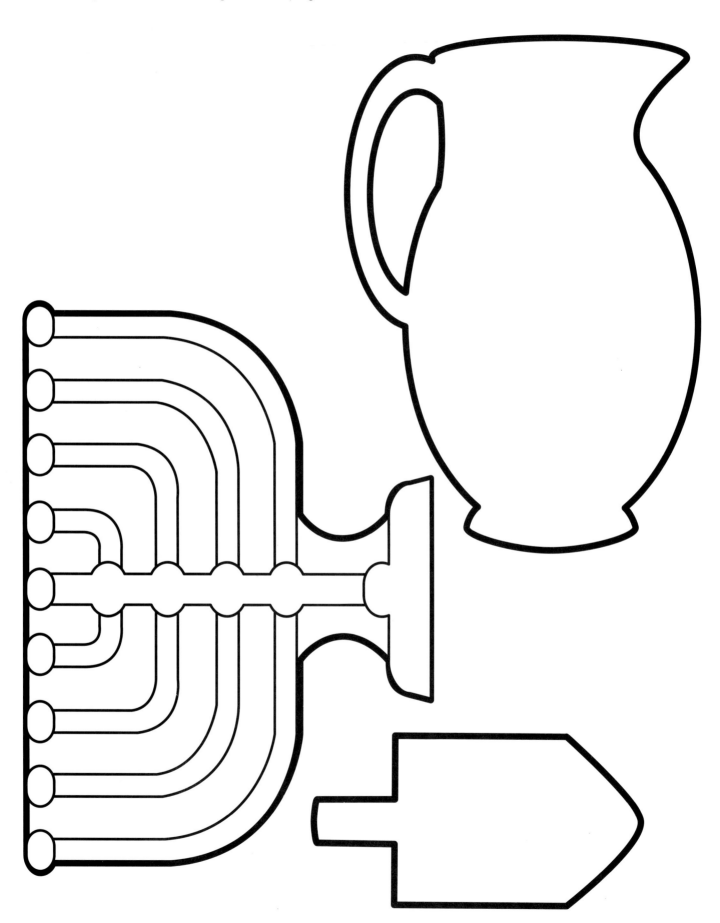

My Hanukkah Counting Book

Remember the eight days of Hanukkah with the eight pages of this unique counting book. To prepare, program a cover and eight pages as shown. Then duplicate a cover and a set of pages for each child. Read through the directions below and prepare the necessary materials. Then have each child follow the directions to complete her counting book.

Nancy Goldberg—Three-Year-Olds, B'nai Israel Schilit Nursery School, Rockville, MD

My Hanukkah Counting Book

Illustrated by Kim

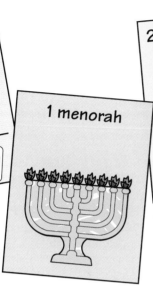

1 menorah

2 stars of David

3 presents

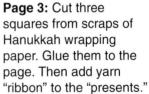

4 gelt coins

Cover: Write your name. Decorate the cover with Hanukkah stickers.

Page 1: Use a gold or silver crayon to color a copy of the menorah pattern (page 42). Cut it out and glue it to the page. Glue on tissue paper flames.

Page 2: Make two stars of David from four blue construction paper triangles. Glue them to the page. Add glitter.

Page 3: Cut three squares from scraps of Hanukkah wrapping paper. Glue them to the page. Then add yarn "ribbon" to the "presents."

Page 4: Carefully unwrap two pieces of chocolate gelt. Glue the wrappers to the page. Then eat the gelt!

5 oil drops

6 latkes

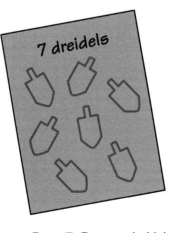

7 dreidels

8 candles

Page 5: Trace a pitcher (pattern on page 42) onto construction paper. Cut it out and glue it to the page. Then use a brown marker to draw five drops of oil.

Page 6: Glue a precut construction paper frying pan to the page. Press a circle-shaped sponge into brown tempera paint. Then print six round latkes in the pan.

Page 7: Press a dreidel-shaped sponge (pattern on page 42) or cookie cutter into blue tempera paint. Then print seven dreidels on the page.

Page 8: Cut eight candles from construction paper. Glue them to the page. Then add a glitter flame to each one.

An Exceptionally Shapely Tree

Trying to decide how to decorate your classroom tree this holiday season? Decorate it with gorgeous child-crafted ornaments in a variety of shapes. Children will think and talk about the characteristics of each shape as the ornaments are being made, but the typical holiday hubbub will revive the subject of the ornament shapes time and again.

Assist each student as needed in making each of these six ornaments and label them with his name and the date. Then send the sets of ornaments home in spiffed-up boxes to extend conversations about shapes well beyond your classroom.

by Lucia Kemp Henry

Not As Frosty, Just As Fun

Associate circles with snowballs and every child will be anxious to make his own. To make a snowball ornament, cut a circle from a sheet of Styrofoam® by pressing an empty can into it to create the circular cutout. Poke a slender knitting needle through the shape near its edge, and then insert a cord or ribbon for hanging the ornament. Spread glue on one side of the snowball cutout; then cover the glue with torn pieces of cotton ball. For sparkle, drip glittery dimensional paint over the cotton. Or drizzle glue onto the cotton; then sprinkle it with clear glitter. If desired, repeat the decorating process on the other side, after the cotton-covered side has dried. At last, there's a snowball that will last from year to year!

The Three-Sided Wonders

Surely evergreen trees are the favorite triangles of the holiday season. Create a triangle tracer (from a 4" x 5" rectangle) for this project and use a glue stick to adhere green patterned wrapping paper to two or three large sheets of construction paper. Cut the construction paper into 4" x 5" pieces. To begin making a triangular tree ornament, help a child count the sides of the tracer, trace the shape onto one of the pieces, and cut along the tracing lines. Glue part of a craft stick to the construction-paper side of the triangle for a tree trunk. Punch a hole near the top of the tree, and use ribbon to make a hanger. Have the child put tiny glue dots all over the gift-wrap side of the tree, cover each dot with a sequin, and then finish the tree by topping it with a self-adhesive foil star. Isn't it amazing how quickly you can light up a tree? A triangular tree, that is!

One Side, Two Sides, Three Sides, Four!

As your students are making these one-of-a-kind ornaments, encourage them to use lots of descriptive language. To make an ornament, start by using red and yellow crayons to draw stripes or plaids on white construction paper. Brush this artwork with a thin, green tempera paint wash to create a crayon-resist design. When the paper is dry, use pinking shears or other fancy paper-edging scissors to cut a four-inch square from the artwork. Use a gold glitter pen to add sparkle to the square; then glue the square to a slightly larger square cut from felt. When the glue is dry, hole-punch the square and insert a pipe-cleaner hanger. Now that the ornament's ready for hanging, better count the sides one last time. 1, 2, 3, 4!

Delightful Gifts of the Season

Children see fascinating rectangular gift boxes everywhere they go this time of year. Help each child add a special rectangular gift to the classroom tree. Gather a supply of miniature gift boxes, soap boxes, and matchboxes. Cover each box with tissue paper and make a small bow for each box from wire-edged $5/8$" ribbon. Hot-glue a thin cord hanger to each bow for hanging the ornament. Precut a supply of assorted small rectangular shapes from colored construction paper. To make an ornament, have each child select and glue rectangles to the wrapped box of his choice. Then have him glue a bow to his package. What a lovely rectangle!

Razzle-Dazzle Cookie Look-Alikes

Here's a sparkling cookielike ornament that makes a festive diamond ornament. Prepare and roll out a batch of baking dough. Cut out a diamond-shaped ornament using a cookie cutter, poke a hole near one end with a drinking straw, and then place the shape on a foil-lined baking pan. Using permanent marker, label the foil near the ornament to indicate whose it is. When each child has made a cutout, bake the ornaments and let them cool. Help each child locate his ornament and twist a pipe-cleaner half into a hanger for the ornament. Have each child frost his ornament with thick, white tempera paint and sprinkle the wet paint with tiny colored beads for imitation candy sprinkles. They look rather yummy. Do we have time to make some real cookies— diamond-shaped, of course?

Baking Dough
2 cups flour
1 cup salt
water
Mix the dry ingredients; then add enough water to create a workable dough. Invite children to cut the dough with cookie cutters. Bake the dough at 300°F for 1 to $1 1/2$ hours (depending on the thickness).

All Five Points Twinkling Bright

Bring the beauty of a starry winter's night to your classroom tree with this twinkling ornament. Start with five-inch squares of white tagboard and blue tissue paper. Brush water-thinned glue onto a square of tagboard; then place a tissue-paper square on it. Brush another coat of the thinned glue on the tissue paper and allow it to dry. Use a commercial or homemade star-shaped stamp to print a yellow star in the middle of the square. Immediately sprinkle the star design with gold glitter. When the stars are dry, cut around each imprint, leaving a blue margin. Punch a hole in each star and attach a glittery ribbon or cord for hanging. How many points does your star have?

Delivering the Ornaments to Another Fine Tree

When it's time to remove the ornaments from your classroom tree, send them on their way to stimulate conversations about shapes in your students' homes. To deliver them with special flair, you'll need small cardboard pizza boxes, spray-painted white and decorated by the children. Cut a sheet of construction paper to fit the bottom of each box. Place each ornament in a child's set on the paper and trace around it; then line the bottom of the box with the paper that shows the place for each ornament. Have the child tuck his ornaments in their places inside the box and take them home to decorate his tree—this year and next.

Santa's Little Helpers

Uh-oh! Santa's hardworking elves need some extra help this year. Preschoolers to the rescue!

by Ada Goren

Attention! Elves Needed!

Before students arrive on the first day of your elves unit, use red and green chalk to write on your chalkboard a message similar to the one shown. When youngsters notice the message, read it aloud to your class. No doubt you'll receive an enthusiastic response to Santa's request! Ask youngsters what they know about Santa's elves. Then teach children this song to sum up the duties of an elf.

(sung to the tune of "The Mulberry Bush")

Oh, what do Santa's little elves do,
Little elves do, little elves do?
Oh, what do Santa's little elves do?
[They help make lots of toys.]

Continue with additional verses, substituting these phrases for the underlined words:

They help wrap up the gifts.
They help feed the reindeer.
They help load Santa's sleigh.
They help check Santa's list.

Hello, boys and girls!

My elves are VERY busy this year. I think we need some extra help. Please tell your teacher if you would like to be honorary elves. She will show you what to do. Merry Christmas!

Love,
Santa Claus

Can you help us?

Elf Duty #1: Making Toys

Everyone knows that toy making is an elf's primary responsibility. So invite your honorary elves to get busy right away preparing bags of Sparkling Peppermint Play Dough to give to some good little boys and girls (See "Thanks, Honorary Elves" on page 48). In advance, prepare a batch of play dough following the recipe on this page. As each little elf reports for duty at the toy factory (art center), give her a portion of dough on a square of waxed paper. Have her squeeze two drops of red or green food coloring onto her dough and then knead it in. Next sprinkle a generous amount of iridescent glitter onto her waxed paper and have her roll her play dough through it to pick it up. Then have her knead the glitter into the dough. Label a zippered plastic sandwich bag as shown; then have the elf drop her play dough into the bag and zip it closed. Set the finished gifts aside for wrapping.

Sparkling Peppermint Play Dough
(makes 12 portions)

2 cups water
2 cups flour
1 cup salt
4 teaspoons cream of tartar
4 tablespoons oil
4 tablespoons peppermint extract

made by A.J. the elf

Combine all ingredients in a heavy saucepan. Cook over medium heat, stirring constantly with a wooden spoon, until mixture thickens and pulls away from the sides of the pan. Form dough into a ball, place on waxed paper, and allow to cool.

Elf Duty #2: Wrapping Gifts

Give your little elves a fine-motor workout as they participate in another elf essential: wrapping gifts. Set up a painting station where your youngsters can create these festive gift bags. To make one bag, lay a white paper lunch bag flat on the table, with the bottom folded under. Dip a candy-cane-shaped sponge into your choice of red or green tempera paint; then print a candy cane onto the bag. Use a small paintbrush dipped in white tempera paint to add stripes to the candy cane. (Don't worry about the colors blending.) Next dip a small circle-shaped sponge into your choice of red or green paint and print a few peppermint discs around the candy cane. Use the paintbrush to add white swirls. Set the bags aside to dry.

When the paint is dry, have a child place her bag of Sparkling Peppermint Play Dough (page 46) inside the gift bag. Fold the top of the bag down to the back side. Then have the child use a hole puncher to punch two holes a slight distance apart through all the layers of the folded section. Help her thread a candy cane through the holes as shown. And that's a wrap!

Elf Duty #3: Feeding the Reindeer

Caring for Santa's reindeer is a big responsibility. Help your honorary elves practice in case they are called upon to perform this task. Make a copy of page 49 on brown construction paper; then cut the boxes apart and label each stall with a different reindeer's name—Dasher, Dancer, Prancer, Vixen, Comet, Cupid, Donner, and Blitzen. Use the pattern on page 8 to make eight feed buckets from white or gray construction paper. Label each of the buckets with a different reindeer's name. (If desired, make an extra reindeer, glue a tiny red pom-pom to its nose, and make an extra feed bucket so you can include Rudolph.) Laminate all the pieces for durability.

To use this center, a child matches each feed bucket to the corresponding reindeer. As a variation, write a numeral next to each reindeer's name. Then duplicate a large supply of blank buckets. Have a child count out the corresponding number of feed buckets to give to each reindeer.

Break Time for Elves

Busy elves need a break? Stop for this energy-boosting snack. It'll fuel up your elves for more hard work!

High-Energy Elf Snack
(serves one)

1 tablespoon creamy peanut butter
1 tablespoon honey
dash of cinnamon
pretzel sticks

In a three-ounce paper cup, combine peanut butter, honey, and cinnamon. Stir with a craft stick until well blended. Dip pretzel sticks into peanut butter dip and enjoy.

Elf Duty #4: Loading Santa's Sleigh

Just before Christmas Eve, elves are busy loading all the toys and goodies into Santa's sleigh. This job requires organization, teamwork, and lots of heavy lifting! Your honorary elves can practice this duty in your dramatic-play area. In advance, use a utility knife to cut two sleigh runners from large sheets of cardboard or poster board. Use heavy-duty tape to attach the runners to the sides of a wagon, and—ta da!—Santa's sleigh is ready. Provide boxes in all shapes and sizes, empty Christmas stockings, and a few Santa hats. Add some wrapping paper, scissors, and tape, so the elves can do some last-minute wrapping. Then invite your youngsters to take it from there—they'll know just what to do!

Elf Duty #5: Checking Santa's List

Who helps Santa keep all those deliveries straight? The elves, of course! So a good elf must be able to recognize children's names. Help your honorary elves practice recognizing the names of their classmates with this pocket-chart activity. Print each child's name on a sentence strip. Then glue a photo of each child to an index card. Randomly place the names and photos in two columns in a pocket chart. Invite your youngsters to match the names and faces. As an extension, make a photo class list by lining up children's photos on a sheet of copy paper and then photocopying the page. Write in each child's name next to his photo. Leave this list near the pocket chart, and challenge little ones to put the names and photos in the same order as your list.

Thanks, Honorary Elves!

They've made toys, wrapped gifts, and practiced all the other important elfin duties. To show them that Santa appreciates their effort, make each of them a special certificate. For each child, duplicate the award on page 50 onto red or green construction paper. Personalize each award; then roll it up and tie a length of curling ribbon around it. To make this awards ceremony extra special, ask an adult helper to dress up as Santa and visit your classroom. Have Santa hand out the certificates, and then further surprise your youngsters by presenting them with the wrapped gifts that they themselves made (See "Elf Duty #1: Making Toys" on page 46)! You told them that they were making those toys for some good little boys and girls, and it was true!

Bucket Pattern
Use with "Elf Duty #3: Feeding the Reindeer" on page 47.

Award
Use with "Thanks, Honorary Elves!" on page 48.

_____
(child's name)

consider yourself

One Helpful Elf!

Thanks for all your hard work!

Santa Claus
_____
(signature)

GET READY FOR RED!

Roses are red; apples are, too. This unit on red is "red-y" for you!

ideas contributed by Suzanne Moore

SEEING RED

Use this guessing game to introduce youngsters to this red-hot unit! In advance, collect a number of red items (such as plastic foods from your house center, a jar of strawberry jam, an apple, a stop sign from your blocks center, a button, a jar of cherries, etc.) and put them into a large red gift bag. During a group time, gather your class around the bag; then sing the following song. Just before you sing the last line, have a child pull an item from the bag; then substitute the name of the item for the underlined word. Continue until each item has been removed from the bag. Then have students examine the items for their similarities and differences. When your little ones have concluded that all of the objects are red, use a red marker to list the items on chart paper. Challenge the group to name additional red things to add to the list. If desired, also encourage the children to bring in more red items to add to the bag.

(sung to the tune of "The Muffin Man")

Oh, do you know what's in the bag,
The big red bag, the big red bag?
Oh, do you know what's in the bag?
A(n) [apple]'s in the bag!

Art Center

RED HEART ART

Got all your marbles? Good! Have youngsters use them to create these racy red hearts to decorate your classroom. To make one, cut a white construction paper heart to fit in a heart-shaped pan or box. Place the paper in the pan; then pour a spoonful of red paint onto it. Next place a marble or two in the pan. Gently tilt the pan repeatedly to roll the marble through the paint. Carefully remove the paper and set it aside to dry. To embellish his heart, encourage a child to glue on his choice of sequins, glitter, or other red craft items. A work of "heart"!

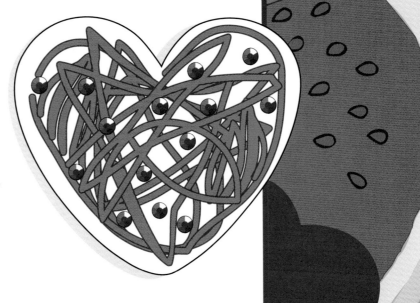

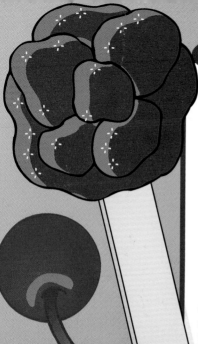

Red Roses, Red Roses

Roses are red…and so is this rose-scented play dough! Follow the recipe to make a batch of dough for your budding sculptors. Put the play dough in a center along with green craft sticks. Then encourage your little ones to make roses to put on the craft stick stems.

Rosy Red Play Dough

3 cups flour
$^{3}/_{4}$ cup salt
3 tablespoons cream of tartar
$^{1}/_{8}$ cup powdered red tempera paint

$^{1}/_{8}$ cup red glitter
2 cups water
2 tablespoons cooking oil
10 drops rose-scented potpourri oil

Mix the dry ingredients together in a large, heavy pot. Stir in the water, oil, and potpourri scent until the mixture is smooth. Continue to stir the mixture over medium heat until it forms a ball. Put the dough onto a floured board, and knead it until it is cool. Store the dough in an airtight container.

Dramatic-Play Area

Mary Wore a Red Dress

Stock your dress-up area with red clothing, shoes, and jewelry. Then invite youngsters to visit the area to create some red-hot costumes. As you admire a child's attire, revise the traditional song to include the child's name and each item of red clothing she is wearing. "Sarah's wearing a red hat, red hat, red hat. Sarah's wearing a red hat all day long!"

Water Table

Caught Red-Handed!

Have your little ones reach into your water table to pull out floating red objects. To prepare the center, tint the water with red food coloring. Or for really red water, drop a Tub tints® fizzing water coloring tablet into your water table. (For purchasing information, visit www.tubtints.com.) From red craft foam, cut the shapes of red objects such as apples and hearts; then add the shapes to the water.

To vary the center, remove the objects and provide youngsters with plastic heart-shaped containers for scooping and pouring the water.

Cooking Center

RECIPE FOR RED

What color could be more delicious than red? To make a simple red treat, have students spread strawberry jam on bread that has been toasted and quartered or cut into a heart shape. This lip-smacking red treat will inspire your little ones to sing!

(sung to the tune of "If You're Happy and You Know It")

Oh, I love the color red, R-E-D! (R-E-D!)
Oh, I love the color red, R-E-D! (R-E-D!)
Oh, I love the color red,
Like the jam spread on my bread!
Oh, I love the color red, R-E-D! (R-E-D!)

ROSES ARE RED

Roses are red, and tasty, too! Well, maybe not all roses are tasty, but these roses made at your cooking center sure have flavor. In advance, cut red Fruit by the Foot® into six-inch-long strips. To make one rose, roll a fruit strip around the tip of a pretzel stick. As you roll, press the bottom edge of the strip to the pretzel. If desired, press a small piece of green fruit roll onto the pretzel for a leaf. Finally, stop to smell the roses. Then eat!

Becky Saunders

Reading Center

"RED" ANY GOOD BOOKS LATELY?

Have a lamp in your reading center? If so, put a red lightbulb in it; then stock the center with these titles to ensure that your children are well-read. In addition, encourage the readers to point out the red items in each book by using a red pointer (red straw, unsharpened red pencil, or red craft stick).

Red Is Best
Written by Kathy Stinson
Illustrated by Robin Baird Lewis
Published by Firefly Books

Who Said Red?
Written by Mary Serfozo
Illustrated by Keiko Narahashi
Published by Aladdin Paperbacks

Little Red Plane
Big Red Fire Truck
Written & Illustrated by Ken Wilson-Max
Published by Cartwheel Books

Clifford® the Big Red Dog®
Written & Illustrated by Norman Bridwell
Published by Scholastic Inc.

Is It Red? Is It Yellow? Is It Blue?An Adventure in Color
By Tana Hoban
Published by William Morrow & Co.

Mary Wore Her Red Dress and Henry Wore His Green Sneakers
Adapted & Illustrated by Merle Peek
Published by Clarion Books

Big Red Barn
Written by Margaret Wise Brown
Illustrated by Felicia Bond
Published by Harpercollins Juvenile Books

Dr. Seuss on the Loose!

Got a classroom with the winter doldrums? Call the doctor—Dr. Seuss, that is! There's no better medicine than his rollicking rhymes to get your little ones laughing and learning!

ideas contributed by Lisa Leonardi

Enter the World of Seuss

Oh, my! On the door—what's that? It's a giant red-striped hat! Welcome your students to a Dr. Seuss unit with a larger-than-life version of the signature hat worn by Seuss's most popular character, the Cat in the Hat. To assemble this door decoration, first cover your classroom door with white bulletin board paper. Then cut two L-shaped pieces of the same paper (about six inches longer than the height of the door) and attach them on either side of the door, as shown. Trim the outer edges of the resulting hat shape, so that it is slightly wider at the top. Add a thin strip of white paper at the bottom on each side of the door, to form the hat brim. Paint wide red stripes across the hat. Finish by adding the title shown above or beside your doorway.

Dr. Seuss is on the loose in Miss Paigel's room!

Introducing Dr. Seuss

Chances are, most of your little ones have some books by this beloved author at home. So why not ask them to bring them in? Send home a copy of the parent note on page 59 with each child. Gather Dr. Seuss books from your library as well, so you'll have plenty to go around. (Be sure to check out the books you'll need for the activities on pages 55–59 or order them from our Web site: www.themailbox.com.)

When you have a good Seuss selection, invite youngsters to be seated on the floor, take turns looking at the books, and discuss as a group what they see. Have youngsters check out the covers and the illustrations. Point out that while all these books were written by the same person—Dr. Seuss—he did not illustrate all of them. Help youngsters find some Seuss-illustrated books and contrast them with a few not illustrated by him. Next, randomly read a page or two from various stories. Can your little ones tell anything about Dr. Seuss's writing? Point out his rhyming text and his love for made-up words. Explain that a lot of Dr. Seuss's stories are very silly. Then get busy reading and learning with the following preschool-appropriate Seuss books!

Read, Read, Read!

Each year on March 2, the National Education Association sponsors a reading campaign that encourages parents and children to celebrate the joy of reading and the birthday of Dr. Seuss. For more information about Read Across America, visit www.nea.org/readacross.

The Cat in the Hat

What's the "purr-fect" Dr. Seuss story to start with? *The Cat in the Hat,* of course! After sharing this classic story, invite little ones to do some more rhyming with this famous feline. To prepare, make a replica of the cat's striped hat and the red box from the story. Roll a 14-inch square of white poster board into a cylinder that's slightly wider at one end; then staple it in place. Adhere strips of red tape around the cylinder. Then cut tabs (as shown) in the narrow end. Next, cut the center from a sturdy white paper plate. Staple the cylinder's tabs onto the top side of the plate and then tape over the staples. Punch a hole on each side of the resulting hat rim; then knot a length of red yarn to each hole. Next, cover a flip-top laundry detergent box with red paper. Inside the box, place simple drawings of items from the story, such as a ball, a book, a ship, a fish, a cake, and more.

Invite youngsters to play a rhyming version of "Fun-in-a-Box." Have a child wear the poster board hat, tying the yarn under his chin to hold it on. Direct him to pull a picture from the red box and then name a word that rhymes with the word pictured. When he correctly names a word, recite this rhyme before having another child play.

Yes, [wall] rhymes with [ball].
I am quite sure of that!
Thanks for the rhyme,
My dear Cat in the Hat!

Green Eggs and Ham

After sharing this Seuss classic, you'll no doubt want to serve your youngsters some green-tinted scrambled eggs and slices of ham. Then give little ones a turn to do the serving with this idea for your dramatic-play area. To make green eggs, cut some abstract shapes from white craft foam; then hot-glue a green foam circle to the center of each shape. Cut a ham shape from green craft foam, too, and add black marker lines to make it resemble the ham in the story. Place the foam eggs and ham in your dramatic-play center, along with a serving tray. Encourage little ones to role-play Sam-I-am, offering the tray to their classmates and posing the question: "Do you like green eggs and ham?" What will the response be? Just wait and see!

Mr. Brown Can Moo! Can You?

Mr. Brown is quite the impressionist—he can sound like just about *anything!* Ask your little ones to try their hands—and voices—at making sounds with this response rhyme. First have the class recite the first verse of the rhyme to a student volunteer. Then help the volunteer respond with the second verse, inserting her choice of an object or animal and its sound. Then have the class echo the sound.

Class: Oh, the wonderful things
[Child's name] can do!
If you show us, [child's name],
We'll try it, too!

Child: I can sound like a [pig].
I can go [oink, oink].
That's what I can do.
Can you try it, too?

Pam Crane

Marvin K. Mooney Will You Please Go Now!

Where *was* Marvin K. Mooney and *why* was he asked to leave? We'll never know, but youngsters will enjoy the many imaginative ways Dr. Seuss describes for Marvin to travel. Use this story to jump-start a transition time between activities. When it's time for your class to travel from one place to another, choose one of the methods in the story. Demonstrate for little ones how to dramatize this way of moving; then get going! You can go on skates or on a cow—your youngsters will go if you show them how!

I Am Not Going to Get Up Today!

Almost everyone can relate to the sleepyhead character in this story who has no intention of getting out of bed. Spark some dramatic play by dressing up in a robe and slippers to read this Seuss story. Bring along a comfy pillow and blanket, too! After sharing the book, invite little ones to take turns putting on the robe and slippers and getting into the pretend bed. Ask the sleepyhead's classmates to brainstorm ways to get him out of bed. Encourage him to respond like the character in the story: I am not going to get up today! After giving every child a turn, place the robe and slippers in your library center for some snuggly Seuss reading.

For another Dr. Seuss book on a related topic, share *Great Day for Up.* Your lazy little ones will hear Seuss's call to rise and shine—but be prepared for the surprise ending!

I Can Read With My Eyes Shut!

The Cat in the Hat is back and he's reading everything in sight! Since your preschoolers no doubt love reading, too, have them tell all about it in this class book. Invite each child to pose with a book of his choice in a particular place or position. Mount the developed picture on a sheet of construction paper, and then write the child's dictation below his picture to describe how or what he can read. If desired, arrange the pages so the text of your book rhymes, Seuss-style!

Anna can read dressed in blue,

Brad can read about a zoo.

The Foot Book

Youngsters will be "toe-tally" amused when you take off your shoes and socks and share *The Foot Book.* After reading the story, have your little ones use their own bare feet to show off what they know about opposites. Call out a phrase from the story, such as "slow feet," and encourage little ones to shout out the opposite, "quick feet." Then have them use their own feet to demonstrate these two phrases. Continue with other phrases, such as:

left foot/right foot
low foot/high foot
feet up/feet down
feet under/feet over
loud feet/quiet feet
feet forward/feet backward

The Shape of Me and Other Stuff

Dr. Seuss makes use of silhouettes to illustrate this book about the shapes of objects and animals, real and imagined. Follow up this story with a center that will challenge your youngsters to match the shapes of many things. To prepare, use a die-cutting machine to punch out pairs of shapes from black construction paper. Mount one die-cut shape from each pair onto a colorful square of construction paper, and then label the square with the name of the animal or object. Laminate the resulting cards and the loose shapes. To use this center, a child matches each loose die-cut shape to its mate on a card.

apple

Our
Many
Colored
Days

by
Miss Leonardi's Class

On red days,
we do exciting
things, like ...

...going to the circus!
Carly

...getting a haircut!
Teddy

...going on an
airplane trip!
Ruthie

My Many Colored Days

This Seuss book has a different look and feel than most of his other works, but it's sure to be a favorite with your preschoolers. They'll love the bright, colorful pages and very simple rhyming text. After reading it, make this class book that links colors to your students' moods. To begin, cut a person shape (similar to the one at the beginning of the book) from each color mentioned in the story. Program each page as shown below. Then invite a few youngsters to complete the sentence on each page. Bind the pages together and add a cover with the title "Our Many Colored Days." Send the finished book home with each youngster, in turn, so he may share it with his family.

On Red Days, we do exciting things like...
On Blue Days, we do fun things like...
On Brown Days, we do slow things like...
On Yellow Days, we do busy things like...
On Gray Days, we just like to watch...
On Orange Days, we do silly things like...
On Green Days, we do quiet things like...
On Purple Days, we are sad like when...
On Pink Days, we do happy things like...
On Black Days, we do loud things like...

What's Your Favorite Seuss Story?

Your preschoolers are bound to have opinions on which Seuss book is tops! Invite them to pass along their preferences with a sticky-note system. Place a pad of sticky notes and some pencils in your library center, along with all the Seuss books you've shared. Encourage each child to write her name on a sticky note and affix the note to the inside cover of a favorite Dr. Seuss story. As youngsters revisit the books, they can identify friends' names and get some reading recommendations, all at the same time!

More of the Good Doctor

Dr. Seuss's wonderful imagination makes his stories unforgettable, and his creative use of language makes them useful for reinforcing phonemic awareness skills, such as hearing alliteration and rhyme. So—whether you share these stories for the fun of it or to teach language to your little learners—here are some more Seuss selections just right for preschool.

Hop on Pop
Fox in Socks
One Fish, Two Fish, Red Fish, Blue Fish
There's a Wocket in My Pocket!

All the books in this unit are published by Random House, Inc., with the exception of *My Many Colored Days,* which is published by Alfred A. Knopf, Inc.

Order books online.
www.themailbox.com

Parent Note

Use with "Introducing Dr. Seuss" on page 54.

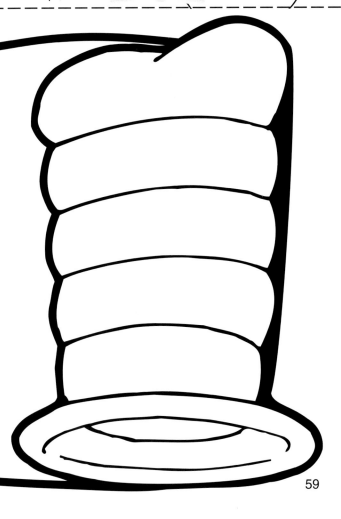

A "Study of Seuss"—
What's that you say?
We're reading Dr. Seuss's books,
And we're starting today!

Do you have some Seuss books?
Send them in—don't delay!
Yes, we're reading his books.
Send them in right away!

May we borrow your books?
Can we look at them, please?
Any Seuss books you have
Would fill us with glee!

Please print your name in
Every book that you send.
We'll send the books back
When we've come to the end.

Thanks!

Monkeying Around With Movement

Your little ones are sure to go bananas over these ideas that will keep 'em moving!

Monkey See, Monkey Do

Monkeys love to mimic one another, so lead your class in this activity that improves listening and large-muscle skills. Chant the following rhyme while demonstrating the action named. Repeat the chant, substituting a different action each time, such as hop, slide, or run. Or invite children to take turns being the lead monkey.

Monkey see, monkey do.
I can [jump].
How about you?

Michele Menzel—Special Education, Appleton Area School District, Appleton, WI

Monkey Limbo

Monkeys must be limber to swing through the trees, so get out a length of rope and get your youngsters in shape with Monkey Limbo. Hold one end of the rope and ask an adult volunteer to hold the opposite end so that the rope is stretched between you. Have your little ones pretend that the rope is a jungle vine; then invite them to move like monkeys as they limbo under it. Continue to lower the rope with each round. Next invite your little ones to jump over the rope. (Make sure that your little ones move slowly through these rounds and that the rope does not get high enough that the children could possibly trip over it.) Now you're swingin'!

From Tree to Tree

Do your little ones have as much energy as monkeys do? Have them practice moving from tree to tree with this gross-motor activity. Lay a course of plastic hoops on the floor of an open area so that the rims of the hoops touch. Explain that each hoop is a tree; then demonstrate how to move like a monkey and hop into each hoop. Encourage each child to hop through all the hoops once. Then rearrange the hoops to create a different course. To increase youngsters' spatial awareness, invite several children to each stand in a different hoop. Then have them hop from hoop to hoop at the same time. From tree to tree, I'm a monkey, you see!

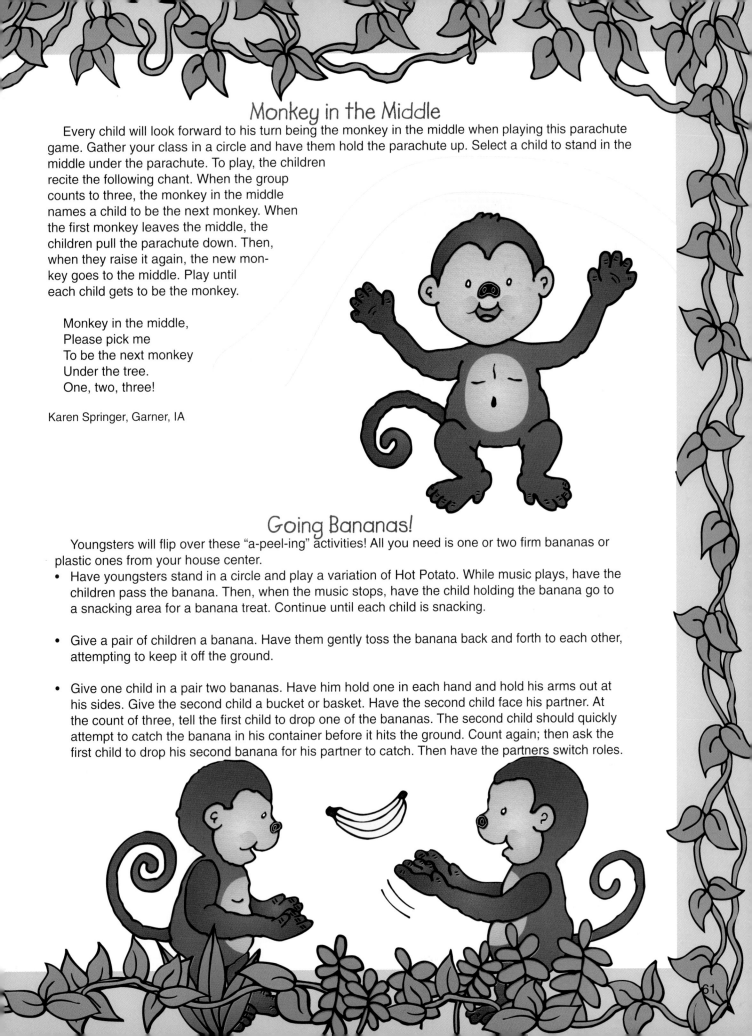

Monkey in the Middle

Every child will look forward to his turn being the monkey in the middle when playing this parachute game. Gather your class in a circle and have them hold the parachute up. Select a child to stand in the middle under the parachute. To play, the children recite the following chant. When the group counts to three, the monkey in the middle names a child to be the next monkey. When the first monkey leaves the middle, the children pull the parachute down. Then, when they raise it again, the new monkey goes to the middle. Play until each child gets to be the monkey.

Monkey in the middle,
Please pick me
To be the next monkey
Under the tree.
One, two, three!

Karen Springer, Garner, IA

Going Bananas!

Youngsters will flip over these "a-peel-ing" activities! All you need is one or two firm bananas or plastic ones from your house center.

- Have youngsters stand in a circle and play a variation of Hot Potato. While music plays, have the children pass the banana. Then, when the music stops, have the child holding the banana go to a snacking area for a banana treat. Continue until each child is snacking.

- Give a pair of children a banana. Have them gently toss the banana back and forth to each other, attempting to keep it off the ground.

- Give one child in a pair two bananas. Have him hold one in each hand and hold his arms out at his sides. Give the second child a bucket or basket. Have the second child face his partner. At the count of three, tell the first child to drop one of the bananas. The second child should quickly attempt to catch the banana in his container before it hits the ground. Count again; then ask the first child to drop his second banana for his partner to catch. Then have the partners switch roles.

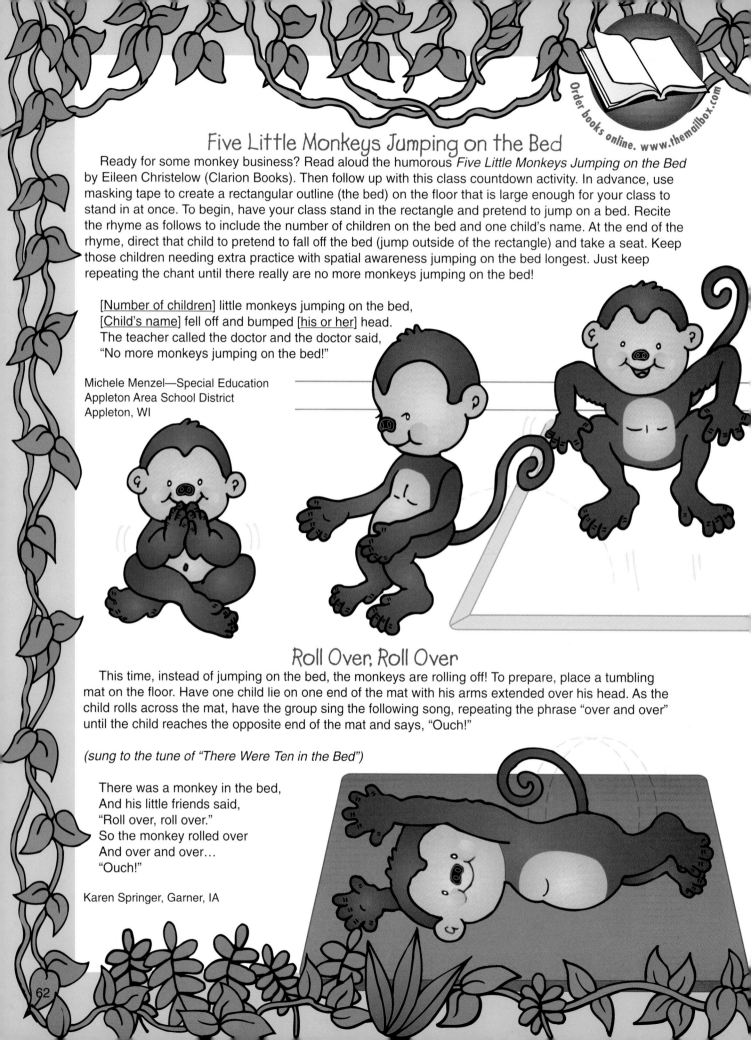

Five Little Monkeys Jumping on the Bed

Ready for some monkey business? Read aloud the humorous *Five Little Monkeys Jumping on the Bed* by Eileen Christelow (Clarion Books). Then follow up with this class countdown activity. In advance, use masking tape to create a rectangular outline (the bed) on the floor that is large enough for your class to stand in at once. To begin, have your class stand in the rectangle and pretend to jump on a bed. Recite the rhyme as follows to include the number of children on the bed and one child's name. At the end of the rhyme, direct that child to pretend to fall off the bed (jump outside of the rectangle) and take a seat. Keep those children needing extra practice with spatial awareness jumping on the bed longest. Just keep repeating the chant until there really are no more monkeys jumping on the bed!

[Number of children] little monkeys jumping on the bed,
[Child's name] fell off and bumped [his or her] head.
The teacher called the doctor and the doctor said,
"No more monkeys jumping on the bed!"

Michele Menzel—Special Education
Appleton Area School District
Appleton, WI

Roll Over, Roll Over

This time, instead of jumping on the bed, the monkeys are rolling off! To prepare, place a tumbling mat on the floor. Have one child lie on one end of the mat with his arms extended over his head. As the child rolls across the mat, have the group sing the following song, repeating the phrase "over and over" until the child reaches the opposite end of the mat and says, "Ouch!"

(sung to the tune of "There Were Ten in the Bed")

There was a monkey in the bed,
And his little friends said,
"Roll over, roll over."
So the monkey rolled over
And over and over…
"Ouch!"

Karen Springer, Garner, IA

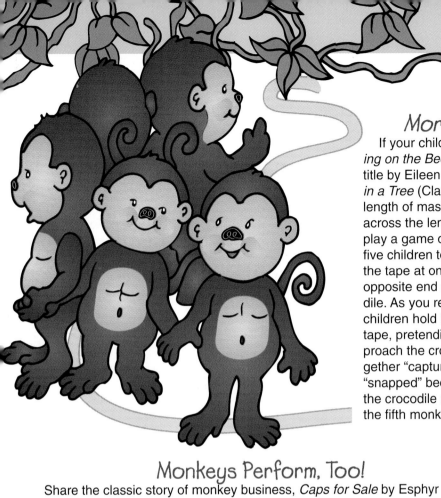

More Five Little Monkeys

If your children enjoyed *Five Little Monkeys Jumping on the Bed*, then they'll also enjoy hearing another title by Eileen Christelow, *Five Little Monkeys Sitting in a Tree* (Clarion Books). Following the story, tape a length of masking tape in a wavy fashion on the floor across the length of your room or down a hallway. To play a game of cooperation and coordination, invite five children to hold hands and stand side-by-side on the tape at one end. Direct a sixth child to stand at the opposite end of the tape and pretend to be the crocodile. As you recite the rhyme from the book, have the children hold hands as they carefully move along the tape, pretending it is a tree branch. When they approach the crocodile, have him snap his arms together "capturing" one child. Have the child who was "snapped" become the crocodile, while the child being the crocodile moves to the end of the line to become the fifth monkey.

Monkeys Perform, Too!

Share the classic story of monkey business, *Caps for Sale* by Esphyr Slobodkina (HarperTrophy), with your class. Then teach them this song that summarizes the simple tale. Be sure to get everyone in the act as they sing!

(sung to the tune of "The Farmer in the Dell")

The peddler sells his caps.	*Stand very straight; walk slowly.*
The peddler sells his caps.	
Hi-ho, the derry-o, the peddler sells his caps.	
The peddler falls asleep....	*Sit down slowly; sit straight.*
The monkeys take his caps....	*Pick up pretend caps.*
The peddler then gets mad....	*Stomp feet.*
They throw down his caps....	*Throw down pretend caps.*
The peddler sells his caps....	*Stand very straight; walk slowly.*

Sharon Winter—Four-Year-Olds, Our Lady of Hope/St. Luke Pre-K, Baltimore, MD

Balancing Act

For another movement-related follow-up to *Caps for Sale,* place a box of hats and caps in a center. Challenge a child to put a number of hats on his head and then walk slowly around with them. Or have a partner help the child place the hats on his head before he walks around. As a variation, have a child select a numeral card to determine how many caps to balance on his head.

Marcia Buchanan—Pre-K, Special People in Northeast, Inc., Philadelphia, PA

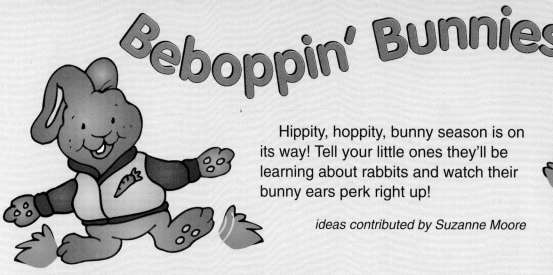

Beboppin' Bunnies

Hippity, hoppity, bunny season is on its way! Tell your little ones they'll be learning about rabbits and watch their bunny ears perk right up!

ideas contributed by Suzanne Moore

"Every-bunny" Get "Hoppy"!

To get off to a hip-hoppin' start, pair up the children so everyone has a bunny buddy. Then teach them the bunny jive. You just do the bump, give a jump, and then thumpity-thump-thump a foot on the ground. Repeat the rhyme over and over until everyone has the hang of the bunny jive. Faster, faster, the bunnies are on the way!

Hip-hoppin' hooray!
Do the bunny jive this way:
With a bump and a jump and a thumpity, thump, thump.
  (Partners bump hips.
  Jump up with hands in front like bunny paws.
  Extend leg and thump foot on the ground three times.)

The bunnies are on the way!
Let's have bunny fun today!

Bunny Basics

"Hare's" a fun way to introduce your litter to some basic bunny facts. From construction paper, cut a class supply of several simple vegetable shapes, such as cabbage, carrots, and radishes. Record each of the following facts on a different shape; then hide the shapes around the room or around a playground area. Direct your class to hop like rabbits in a garden to find the vegetables; then have them put their finds into one basket. When all of your bunnies have bounced back to your group area, read and discuss the facts on the shapes. Next have your class help you sort the shapes into garden rows. Put the shapes back in the basket and then put the basket in a center so that little rabbits can sort the veggies over and over again.

Rabbits sleep during the day. At night they look for food.

Rabbits have long front teeth that never stop growing.

Rabbits have long ears that turn in many directions. They are great listeners!

Some rabbits live together underground. Their houses are called warrens.

A rabbit warns other rabbits of danger by thumping the ground with his back feet. The other rabbits stay very still!

A bunny's eyes are on the sides of his head so that he can see everywhere around him.

Rabbits are herbivores. They eat mostly plants.

A boy rabbit is called a buck. A girl rabbit is called a doe. A baby rabbit is called a kitten.

Rabbits have long back legs for running fast or hopping.

Bunny Salad Bar

Nibble, nibble. Munch, munch, crunch. Rabbits love to eat plants, and so do people. Set up a bunny salad bar so that your little ones discover that bunnies and kids have similar tastes. If desired, just set out dip and several different types of cut-up vegetables for sampling. Encourage students to write their names on sticky notes to put on the table indicating their favorites of the available vegetables. Or set up a real salad bar. While students munch on the garden goodies and drink some V8® Splash fruit drink, share these stories about bunnies who do *not* like the traditional rabbit favorites.

Cabbage Moon
Albert won't eat cabbage. Then he finds out why the moon changes its shape.
Written by Tim Chadwick
Illustrated by Piers Harper
Published by Orchard Books

Rabbit Food
No veggies for John! Maybe Uncle Bunny would be a good role model. Or would he?
Written & Illustrated by
 Susanna Gretz
Published by Candlewick Press

Show Me the Bunny!

Students will bound over to this art center to make a hare. At the center, show a small group of children pictures of different kinds of bunnies. Discuss the different colors and markings of the bunnies. To make a paper bunny, help a child spread his fingers apart; then trace the child's hand (excluding the thumb) and his foot onto his choice of white, brown, or black construction paper. Direct the child to cut out the shapes or tear them. Then have him glue the pieces together. Have the child use additional scraps of paper to add eyes and spots to the bunny if desired. Then have him add the finishing touch—a cotton ball tail!

Julie Shields—Four-Year-Olds
Brookeland Elementary, Brookeland, TX

I'm All Ears

All ears serve as great sound catchers, but not many are better than a rabbit's ears! Try this easy experiment that proves that bigger is better—for catching sounds, that is! Put some music in a tape or CD player. Turn the music on with the volume completely down. Tell your little ones to make bunny ears with their hands on their heads when they can hear the music. Turn up the volume until all of the children have bunny ears. Then turn the volume back down.

Next show your children how to improve their own listening skills by placing their hands behind their ears, palms facing forward, and pushing their ears slightly forward. Play the music at a medium volume. Have youngsters compare the sound by repeatedly making their ears like bunny ears as described and then listening in normal fashion.

clink clink

whoosh whoosh

Now Hear This!

Set up a listening center where every child can put on bunny ears and practice her listening skills. To prepare, make a simple headband with bunny ears. Fill a number of film containers with different materials, so that pairs of containers have matching sounds. When visiting the center, a child puts on the bunny ears and finds the containers that make matching sounds.

A Rabbit Habit

Encourage your little ones to make good listening skills a habit with a listening stick. To make one, paint a tongue depressor white. When the paint is dry, use markers to draw a face on the depressor. Cut ears from craft foam. Using a Q-tips® cotton swab, apply blusher to what will be the insides of the ears and to the cheeks of the face. Glue the ears to the back of the tongue depressor. During a group time, have the child whose turn it is to speak hold the rabbit as a reminder to the rest of the group to do their best bunny listening.

If desired, help each child make a bunny. Write a message similar to the one shown on each child's stick before sending it home.

Nick is all ears!

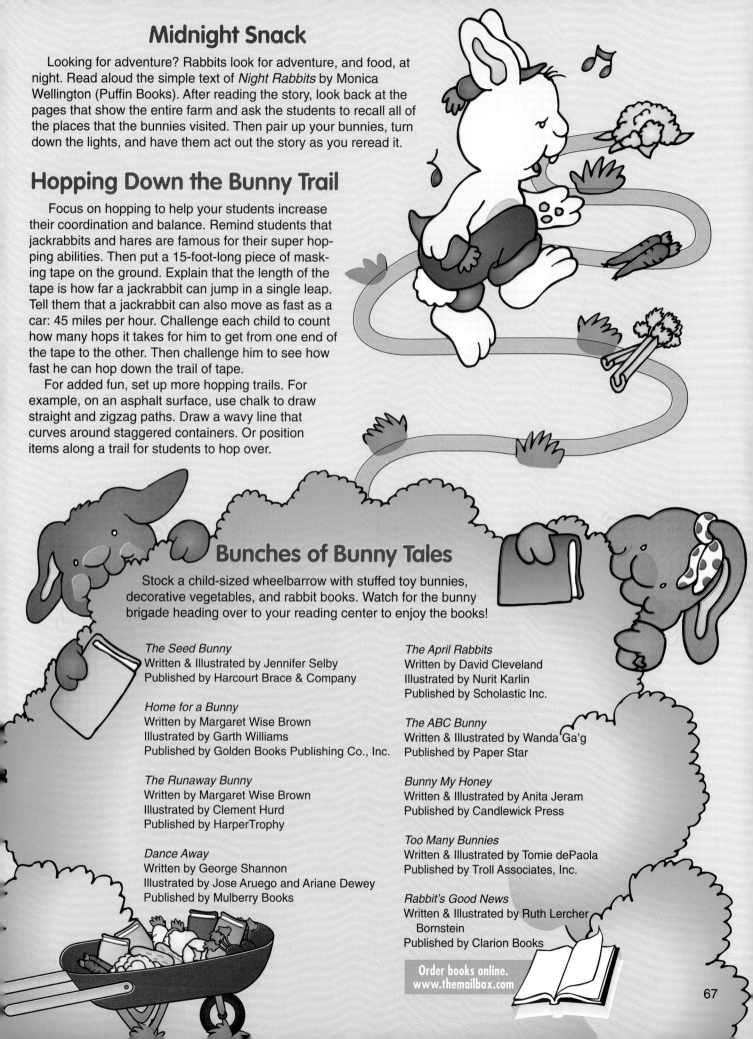

Midnight Snack

Looking for adventure? Rabbits look for adventure, and food, at night. Read aloud the simple text of *Night Rabbits* by Monica Wellington (Puffin Books). After reading the story, look back at the pages that show the entire farm and ask the students to recall all of the places that the bunnies visited. Then pair up your bunnies, turn down the lights, and have them act out the story as you reread it.

Hopping Down the Bunny Trail

Focus on hopping to help your students increase their coordination and balance. Remind students that jackrabbits and hares are famous for their super hopping abilities. Then put a 15-foot-long piece of masking tape on the ground. Explain that the length of the tape is how far a jackrabbit can jump in a single leap. Tell them that a jackrabbit can also move as fast as a car: 45 miles per hour. Challenge each child to count how many hops it takes for him to get from one end of the tape to the other. Then challenge him to see how fast he can hop down the trail of tape.

For added fun, set up more hopping trails. For example, on an asphalt surface, use chalk to draw straight and zigzag paths. Draw a wavy line that curves around staggered containers. Or position items along a trail for students to hop over.

Bunches of Bunny Tales

Stock a child-sized wheelbarrow with stuffed toy bunnies, decorative vegetables, and rabbit books. Watch for the bunny brigade heading over to your reading center to enjoy the books!

The Seed Bunny
Written & Illustrated by Jennifer Selby
Published by Harcourt Brace & Company

Home for a Bunny
Written by Margaret Wise Brown
Illustrated by Garth Williams
Published by Golden Books Publishing Co., Inc.

The Runaway Bunny
Written by Margaret Wise Brown
Illustrated by Clement Hurd
Published by HarperTrophy

Dance Away
Written by George Shannon
Illustrated by Jose Aruego and Ariane Dewey
Published by Mulberry Books

The April Rabbits
Written by David Cleveland
Illustrated by Nurit Karlin
Published by Scholastic Inc.

The ABC Bunny
Written & Illustrated by Wanda Ga'g
Published by Paper Star

Bunny My Honey
Written & Illustrated by Anita Jeram
Published by Candlewick Press

Too Many Bunnies
Written & Illustrated by Tomie dePaola
Published by Troll Associates, Inc.

Rabbit's Good News
Written & Illustrated by Ruth Lercher
  Bornstein
Published by Clarion Books

Order books online.
www.themailbox.com

67

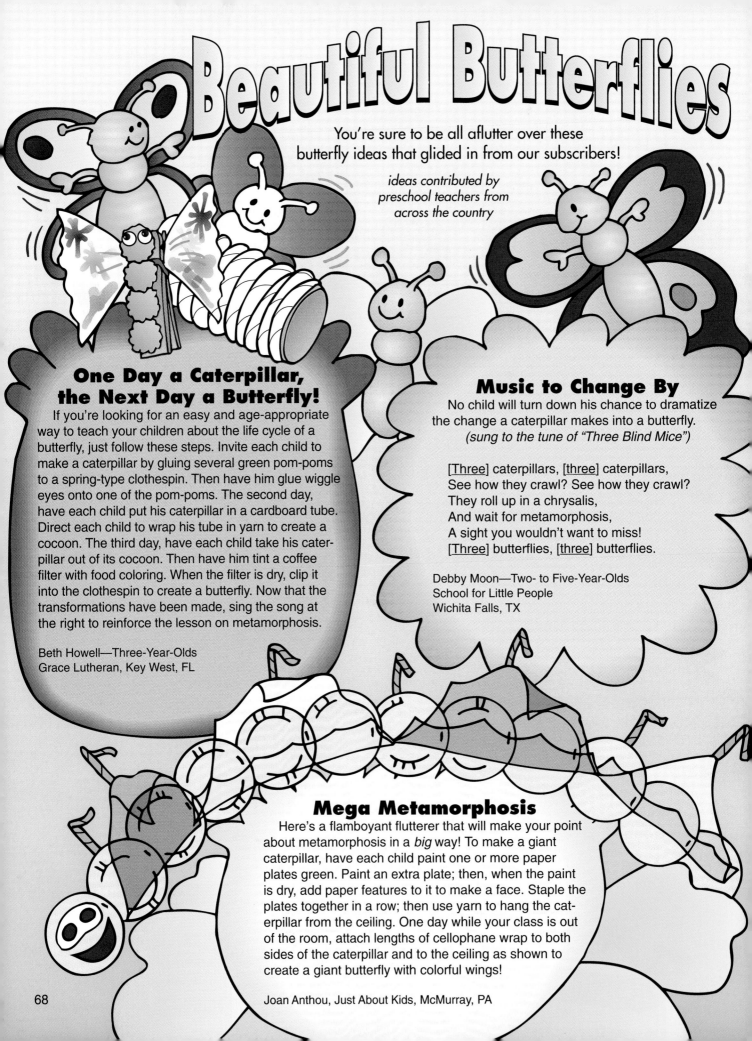

Beautiful Butterflies

You're sure to be all aflutter over these butterfly ideas that glided in from our subscribers!

ideas contributed by preschool teachers from across the country

One Day a Caterpillar, the Next Day a Butterfly!

If you're looking for an easy and age-appropriate way to teach your children about the life cycle of a butterfly, just follow these steps. Invite each child to make a caterpillar by gluing several green pom-poms to a spring-type clothespin. Then have him glue wiggle eyes onto one of the pom-poms. The second day, have each child put his caterpillar in a cardboard tube. Direct each child to wrap his tube in yarn to create a cocoon. The third day, have each child take his caterpillar out of its cocoon. Then have him tint a coffee filter with food coloring. When the filter is dry, clip it into the clothespin to create a butterfly. Now that the transformations have been made, sing the song at the right to reinforce the lesson on metamorphosis.

Beth Howell—Three-Year-Olds
Grace Lutheran, Key West, FL

Music to Change By

No child will turn down his chance to dramatize the change a caterpillar makes into a butterfly. *(sung to the tune of "Three Blind Mice")*

[Three] caterpillars, [three] caterpillars,
See how they crawl? See how they crawl?
They roll up in a chrysalis,
And wait for metamorphosis,
A sight you wouldn't want to miss!
[Three] butterflies, [three] butterflies.

Debby Moon—Two- to Five-Year-Olds
School for Little People
Wichita Falls, TX

Mega Metamorphosis

Here's a flamboyant flutterer that will make your point about metamorphosis in a *big* way! To make a giant caterpillar, have each child paint one or more paper plates green. Paint an extra plate; then, when the paint is dry, add paper features to it to make a face. Staple the plates together in a row; then use yarn to hang the caterpillar from the ceiling. One day while your class is out of the room, attach lengths of cellophane wrap to both sides of the caterpillar and to the ceiling as shown to create a giant butterfly with colorful wings!

Joan Anthou, Just About Kids, McMurray, PA

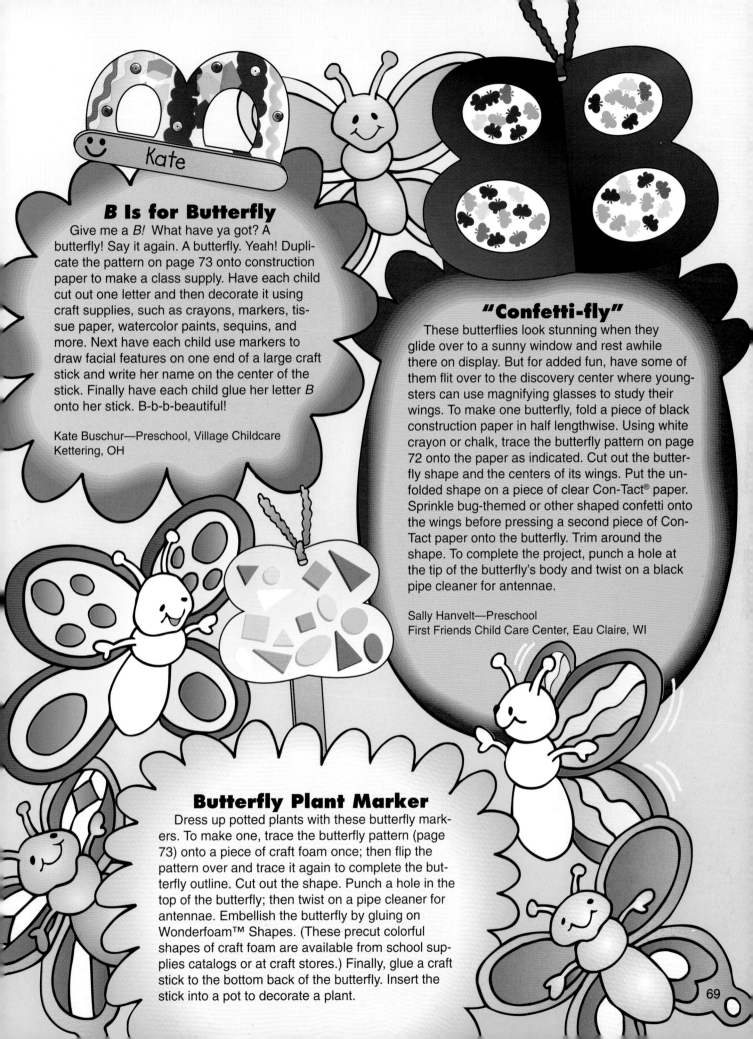

B Is for Butterfly

Give me a *B!* What have ya got? A butterfly! Say it again. A butterfly. Yeah! Duplicate the pattern on page 73 onto construction paper to make a class supply. Have each child cut out one letter and then decorate it using craft supplies, such as crayons, markers, tissue paper, watercolor paints, sequins, and more. Next have each child use markers to draw facial features on one end of a large craft stick and write her name on the center of the stick. Finally have each child glue her letter *B* onto her stick. B-b-b-beautiful!

Kate Buschur—Preschool, Village Childcare
Kettering, OH

"Confetti-fly"

These butterflies look stunning when they glide over to a sunny window and rest awhile there on display. But for added fun, have some of them flit over to the discovery center where youngsters can use magnifying glasses to study their wings. To make one butterfly, fold a piece of black construction paper in half lengthwise. Using white crayon or chalk, trace the butterfly pattern on page 72 onto the paper as indicated. Cut out the butterfly shape and the centers of its wings. Put the unfolded shape on a piece of clear Con-Tact® paper. Sprinkle bug-themed or other shaped confetti onto the wings before pressing a second piece of Con-Tact paper onto the butterfly. Trim around the shape. To complete the project, punch a hole at the tip of the butterfly's body and twist on a black pipe cleaner for antennae.

Sally Hanvelt—Preschool
First Friends Child Care Center, Eau Claire, WI

Butterfly Plant Marker

Dress up potted plants with these butterfly markers. To make one, trace the butterfly pattern (page 73) onto a piece of craft foam once; then flip the pattern over and trace it again to complete the butterfly outline. Cut out the shape. Punch a hole in the top of the butterfly; then twist on a pipe cleaner for antennae. Embellish the butterfly by gluing on Wonderfoam™ Shapes. (These precut colorful shapes of craft foam are available from school supplies catalogs or at craft stores.) Finally, glue a craft stick to the bottom back of the butterfly. Insert the stick into a pot to decorate a plant.

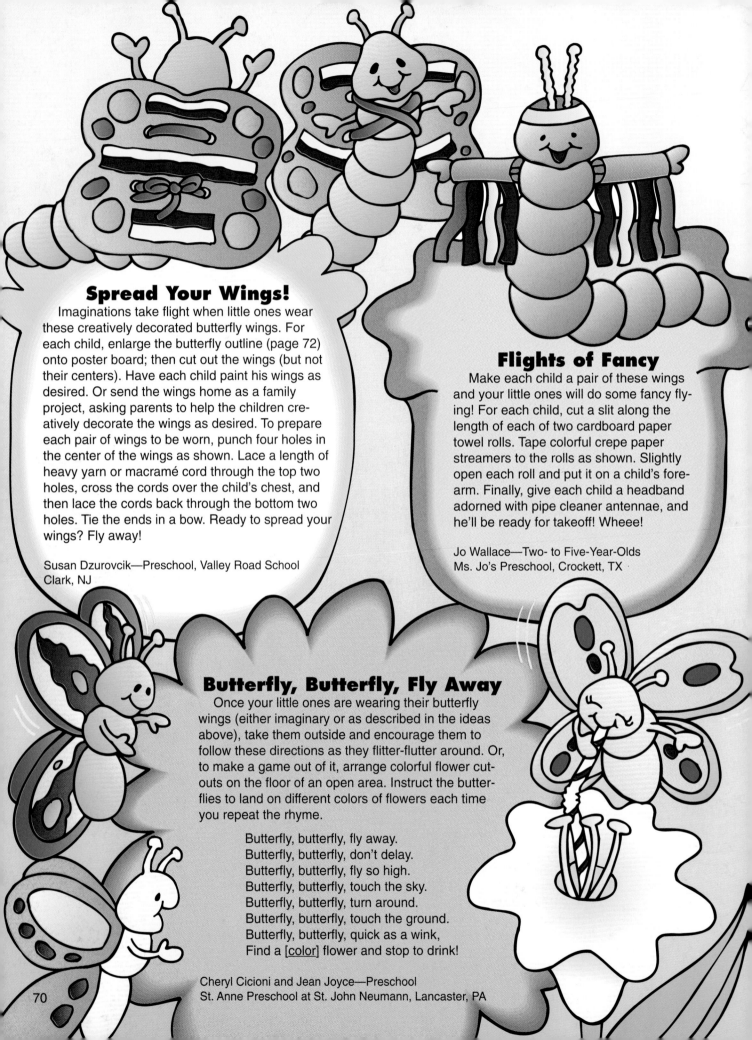

Spread Your Wings!

Imaginations take flight when little ones wear these creatively decorated butterfly wings. For each child, enlarge the butterfly outline (page 72) onto poster board; then cut out the wings (but not their centers). Have each child paint his wings as desired. Or send the wings home as a family project, asking parents to help the children creatively decorate the wings as desired. To prepare each pair of wings to be worn, punch four holes in the center of the wings as shown. Lace a length of heavy yarn or macramé cord through the top two holes, cross the cords over the child's chest, and then lace the cords back through the bottom two holes. Tie the ends in a bow. Ready to spread your wings? Fly away!

Susan Dzurovcik—Preschool, Valley Road School
Clark, NJ

Flights of Fancy

Make each child a pair of these wings and your little ones will do some fancy flying! For each child, cut a slit along the length of each of two cardboard paper towel rolls. Tape colorful crepe paper streamers to the rolls as shown. Slightly open each roll and put it on a child's forearm. Finally, give each child a headband adorned with pipe cleaner antennae, and he'll be ready for takeoff! Wheee!

Jo Wallace—Two- to Five-Year-Olds
Ms. Jo's Preschool, Crockett, TX

Butterfly, Butterfly, Fly Away

Once your little ones are wearing their butterfly wings (either imaginary or as described in the ideas above), take them outside and encourage them to follow these directions as they flitter-flutter around. Or, to make a game out of it, arrange colorful flower cutouts on the floor of an open area. Instruct the butterflies to land on different colors of flowers each time you repeat the rhyme.

Butterfly, butterfly, fly away.
Butterfly, butterfly, don't delay.
Butterfly, butterfly, fly so high.
Butterfly, butterfly, touch the sky.
Butterfly, butterfly, turn around.
Butterfly, butterfly, touch the ground.
Butterfly, butterfly, quick as a wink,
Find a [color] flower and stop to drink!

Cheryl Cicioni and Jean Joyce—Preschool
St. Anne Preschool at St. John Neumann, Lancaster, PA

Bit o' Butterfly

No butterfly study is complete without a butterfly-themed snack. To make one of these treats, slice a piece of toast in half diagonally. Spread jelly on both pieces of toast; then arrange colored candy pieces on top. Or spread flavored cream cheese on the toast; then top it with colorful round cereal pieces. Arrange the toast pieces and an oval-shaped cookie on a plate as shown. Finish the treat by adding licorice antennae and two candy or cereal pieces (for eyes) to the cookie.

Loryl Fisher—Preschool
Happy Hands Methodist Preschool
Lemont, IL

Flutter By

To make one of these fantastic finger puppets, fold a 4" x 6" piece of card stock in half. Draw a butterfly wing on the fold; then cut it out, making sure to cut through both layers of paper but not through the fold. Cut two slits, about $3/4$" apart, perpendicular to the fold. Unfold the wings and then invite a child to decorate them with various craft supplies. When the butterfly is decorated, invite the child to slip one or two fingers through the slits. Use a marker to add a smiley face to the child's finger. Watch that butterfly fly away!

Molly Nagel
Cheshire, CT

Take a Dip, Take a Sip

What do butterflies do when they get thirsty? They sip nectar through their long, tube-shaped tongues! In this activity, your little ones can pretend to be butterflies as they dip straws into "nectar-filled flowers" and sip away. To make a class supply, duplicate the flower pattern (page 73) onto colorful construction paper; then cut out the flowers and their centers. Have each child use crayons to decorate his flower; then tape the underside of the flower onto the sides of a nine-ounce cup as shown. Carefully fill the cup with fruit punch. Invite each child to pretend to be a butterfly as he uses his tongue (straw) to take a sip.

Debra Holbrook—Four-Year-Olds, SBEC, Olive Branch, MS

71

Pattern

Use with "'Confetti-fly'" on page 69 and "Spread Your Wings!" on page 70.

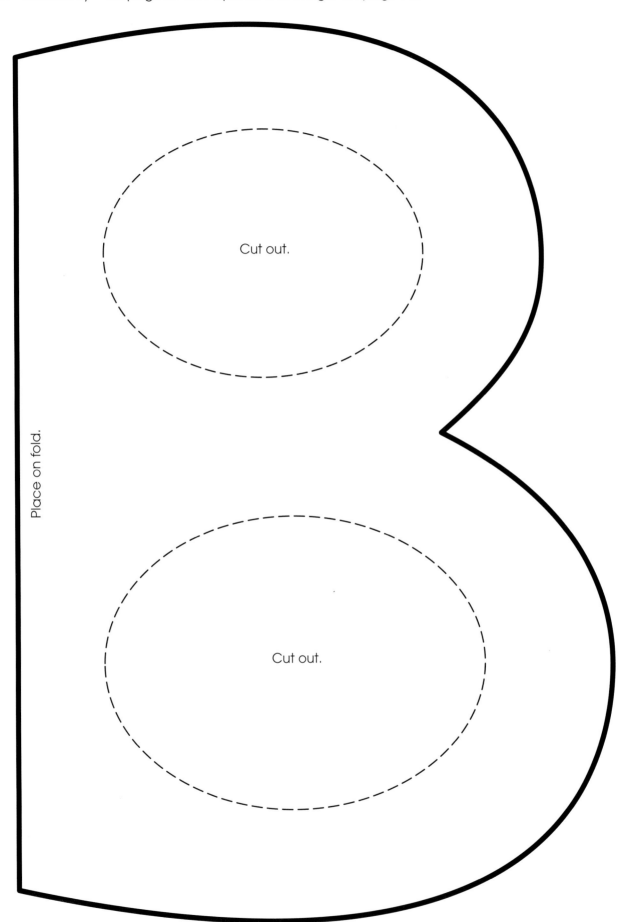

Place on fold.

Cut out.

Cut out.

Patterns
Use with "*B* Is for Butterfly"
and "Butterfly Plant
Marker" on page 69.

Use with "Take a Dip,
Take a Sip" on page 71.

Let's Mess Around!

A Preschool Chemistry Unit

Preschoolers doing chemistry? Why not? Explain to your little ones that scientists don't know all the answers, so they experiment—or "mess around"—to test things and see what will happen. So, for now, forget about finding a "right" answer or even explaining *why* things happen as they do. Just dress your youngsters in lab coats (men's short-sleeve dress shirts) and stock your classroom with some common tools and substances. Then let the experiments begin. Come on—let's mess around!

ideas contributed by Nancy M. Lotzer

A Chemist's Vocabulary

There will be lots of opportunities throughout this unit to introduce youngsters to scientific terms. Go ahead! If your little ones can say "Tyrannosaurus rex," they'll love these words, too!

mixture
solution
dissolve
react/reaction
liquid
solid
chemist/chemicals/chemistry
experiment
coloring agent

Billions of Bubbles

Each child will need:
personalized clear plastic cup   drinking straw
bubble wand (pipe cleaner twisted into wand)

The class will need:
small box of laundry soap   teaspoon
bottle of white dishwashing liquid $1/4$ cup measuring cup
bottle of blue dishwashing liquid   water source
bottle of children's bubble bath

Which type of soap makes the best bubbles? Let's find out! Have each child measure $1/4$ cup water into her cup. Then have her choose a type of soap to test. Write each child's choice on a chart for later reference. Help each child add a teaspoon of the chosen soap to her cup and then have her stir it with her straw. Set the cup aside until everyone has made a bubble solution. Then have everyone take their cups and wands outdoors and blow some bubbles! Once you return to the classroom, have each child dictate her results and write them next to her soap choice on the chart. What's the class consensus? Which soap made the best bubbles?

Our Bubble-Making Choices

Lee–bubble bath
    It made good bubbles.
    There were lots of little ones.

Anya–laundry soap
    It made lots of soap.
    The bubbles were little.

Kari–blue dish soap
    BIG bubbles! They floated
    way up.

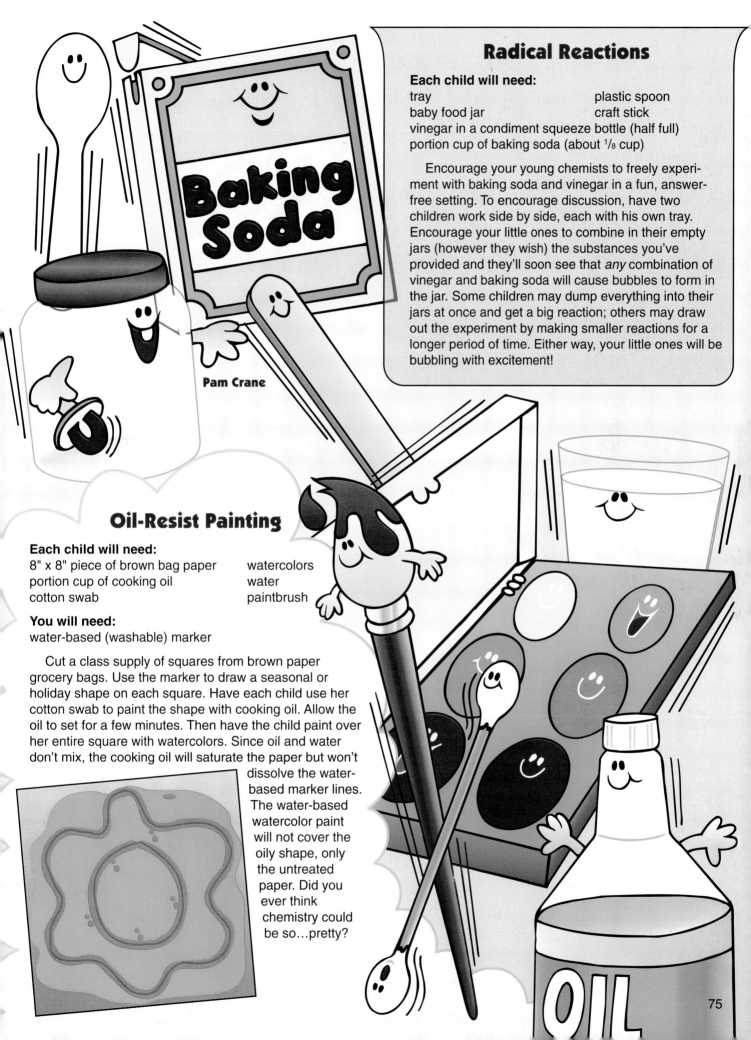

Radical Reactions

Each child will need:

tray

baby food jar

vinegar in a condiment squeeze bottle (half full)

portion cup of baking soda (about ⅛ cup)

plastic spoon

craft stick

Encourage your young chemists to freely experiment with baking soda and vinegar in a fun, answer-free setting. To encourage discussion, have two children work side by side, each with his own tray. Encourage your little ones to combine in their empty jars (however they wish) the substances you've provided and they'll soon see that *any* combination of vinegar and baking soda will cause bubbles to form in the jar. Some children may dump everything into their jars at once and get a big reaction; others may draw out the experiment by making smaller reactions for a longer period of time. Either way, your little ones will be bubbling with excitement!

Pam Crane

Oil-Resist Painting

Each child will need:

8" x 8" piece of brown bag paper

portion cup of cooking oil

cotton swab

watercolors

water

paintbrush

You will need:

water-based (washable) marker

Cut a class supply of squares from brown paper grocery bags. Use the marker to draw a seasonal or holiday shape on each square. Have each child use her cotton swab to paint the shape with cooking oil. Allow the oil to set for a few minutes. Then have the child paint over her entire square with watercolors. Since oil and water don't mix, the cooking oil will saturate the paper but won't dissolve the water-based marker lines. The water-based watercolor paint will not cover the oily shape, only the untreated paper. Did you ever think chemistry could be so…pretty?

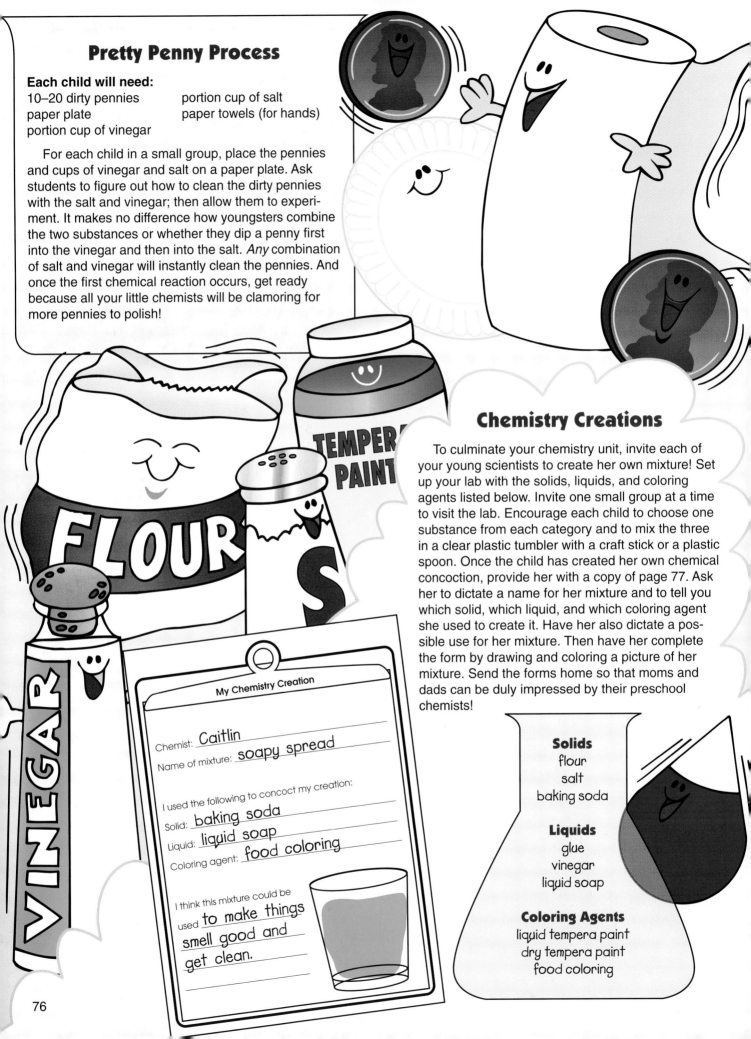

Pretty Penny Process

Each child will need:
10–20 dirty pennies
paper plate
portion cup of vinegar
portion cup of salt
paper towels (for hands)

For each child in a small group, place the pennies and cups of vinegar and salt on a paper plate. Ask students to figure out how to clean the dirty pennies with the salt and vinegar; then allow them to experiment. It makes no difference how youngsters combine the two substances or whether they dip a penny first into the vinegar and then into the salt. *Any* combination of salt and vinegar will instantly clean the pennies. And once the first chemical reaction occurs, get ready because all your little chemists will be clamoring for more pennies to polish!

Chemistry Creations

To culminate your chemistry unit, invite each of your young scientists to create her own mixture! Set up your lab with the solids, liquids, and coloring agents listed below. Invite one small group at a time to visit the lab. Encourage each child to choose one substance from each category and to mix the three in a clear plastic tumbler with a craft stick or a plastic spoon. Once the child has created her own chemical concoction, provide her with a copy of page 77. Ask her to dictate a name for her mixture and to tell you which solid, which liquid, and which coloring agent she used to create it. Have her also dictate a possible use for her mixture. Then have her complete the form by drawing and coloring a picture of her mixture. Send the forms home so that moms and dads can be duly impressed by their preschool chemists!

My Chemistry Creation

Chemist: Caitlin
Name of mixture: soapy spread

I used the following to concoct my creation:
Solid: baking soda
Liquid: liquid soap
Coloring agent: food coloring

I think this mixture could be used to make things smell good and get clean.

Solids
flour
salt
baking soda

Liquids
glue
vinegar
liquid soap

Coloring Agents
liquid tempera paint
dry tempera paint
food coloring

Use with "Chemistry Creations" on page 76.

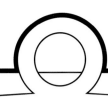

My Chemistry Creation

Chemist: ____

Name of mixture: ____________________________________

I used the following to concoct my creation:

Solid: ____

Liquid: ____

Coloring agent: _____________________________________

I think this mixture could be

used ______________________

____

____

____

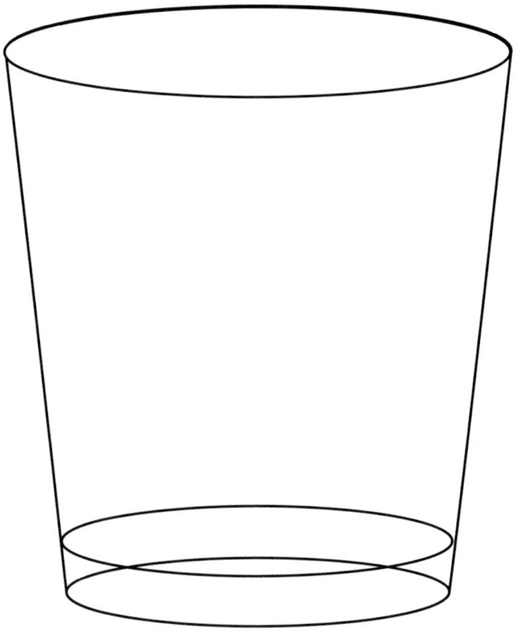

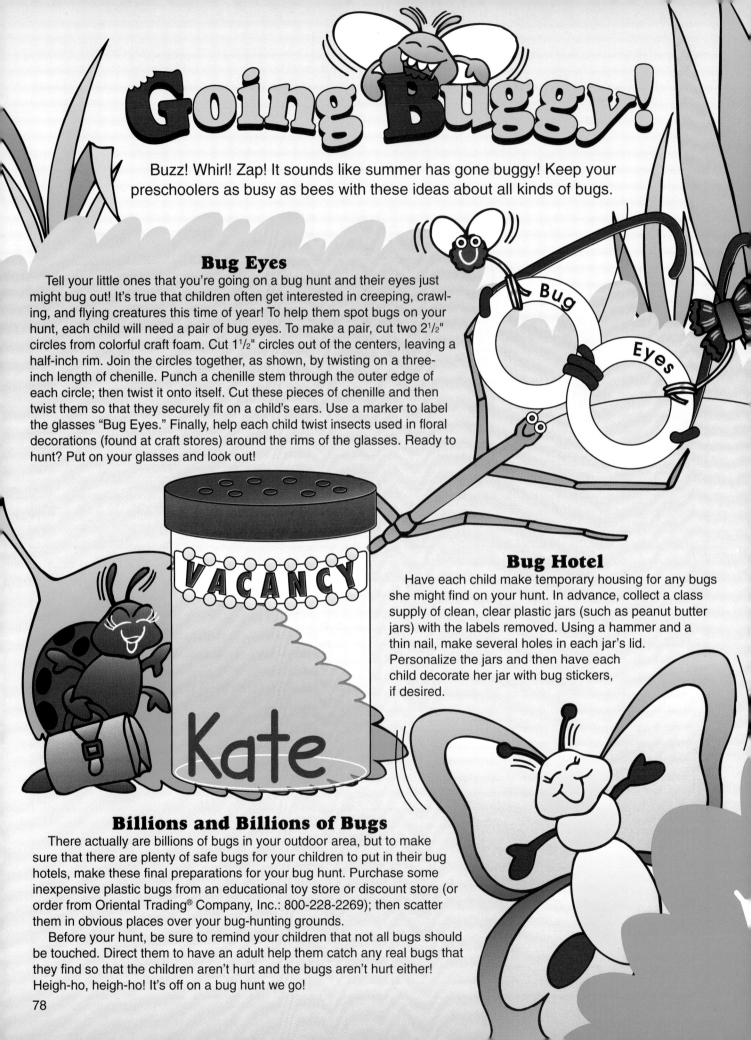

Going Buggy!

Buzz! Whirl! Zap! It sounds like summer has gone buggy! Keep your preschoolers as busy as bees with these ideas about all kinds of bugs.

Bug Eyes

Tell your little ones that you're going on a bug hunt and their eyes just might bug out! It's true that children often get interested in creeping, crawling, and flying creatures this time of year! To help them spot bugs on your hunt, each child will need a pair of bug eyes. To make a pair, cut two 2½" circles from colorful craft foam. Cut 1½" circles out of the centers, leaving a half-inch rim. Join the circles together, as shown, by twisting on a three-inch length of chenille. Punch a chenille stem through the outer edge of each circle; then twist it onto itself. Cut these pieces of chenille and then twist them so that they securely fit on a child's ears. Use a marker to label the glasses "Bug Eyes." Finally, help each child twist insects used in floral decorations (found at craft stores) around the rims of the glasses. Ready to hunt? Put on your glasses and look out!

Bug Hotel

Have each child make temporary housing for any bugs she might find on your hunt. In advance, collect a class supply of clean, clear plastic jars (such as peanut butter jars) with the labels removed. Using a hammer and a thin nail, make several holes in each jar's lid. Personalize the jars and then have each child decorate her jar with bug stickers, if desired.

Billions and Billions of Bugs

There actually are billions of bugs in your outdoor area, but to make sure that there are plenty of safe bugs for your children to put in their bug hotels, make these final preparations for your bug hunt. Purchase some inexpensive plastic bugs from an educational toy store or discount store (or order from Oriental Trading® Company, Inc.: 800-228-2269); then scatter them in obvious places over your bug-hunting grounds.

Before your hunt, be sure to remind your children that not all bugs should be touched. Direct them to have an adult help them catch any real bugs that they find so that the children aren't hurt and the bugs aren't hurt either! Heigh-ho, heigh-ho! It's off on a bug hunt we go!

Heigh-ho, Heigh-ho! It's Off on a Bug Hunt We Go!

Start off your hunt by singing this repetitive song to the tune of "Heigh-ho, Heigh-ho!"

Heigh-ho, heigh-ho,
It's off on a hunt we go.
Look here and there
Bugs are everywhere!
Heigh-ho, heigh-ho, heigh-ho.
(Repeat.)

What's the Buzz on Bugs?

Give your young entomologists a chance to share what they already know about bugs. First, ask children to name as many kinds of bugs as they can. Record the names on a piece of white poster board that has been cut to resemble a jar. Also record any thoughts or questions they have about bugs.

Now really go buggy by sharing any of the following preschool-appropriate nonfiction books and stories about bugs. Be sure to add to your jar any new information you catch!

grasshopper   cricket
mosquito   ladybug
ant   bee
wasp

Why do bugs have so many legs?

Why do some bugs sting?

Bugs! Bugs! Bugs!
(This colorful book is perfect for reading aloud to your preschoolers.)
Written & Illustrated by Bob Barner
Published by Chronicle Books

Bugs
Written by Nancy Winslow Parker and
    Joan Richards Wright
Illustrated by Nancy Winslow Parker
Published by William Morrow and
    Company, Inc.

What Is an Insect?
Bugs, Bugs, Bugs!
Where Do Insects Live?
What Do Insects Do?
Spider Names
(This nonfiction emergent readers series is available from Scholastic Inc. For ordering information, call 1-800-724-6527.)

Books by Eric Carle
The Honeybee and the Robber
The Very Busy Spider
The Very Clumsy Click Beetle
    (Philomel Books)
The Grouchy Ladybug
    (HarperCollins Children's Books)
The Very Quiet Cricket
The Very Lonely Firefly
    (The Putnam Publishing Group)

And just for fun...
Alpha Bugs: A Pop-up Alphabet
Bed Bugs: A Pop-up Bedtime Book
Feely Bugs: To Touch and Feel
Giggle Bugs: A Lift-and-Laugh Book
Written & Illustrated by David A. Carter
Published by Little Simon

Bugs on the Web

To find really cool bug stuff your kids will love, visit Insect Lore's Web site: www.insectlore.com. Or call to request a catalog (1-800-LIVE-BUG).

Order books online.
www.themailbox.com

Singing in the Key of "Bee"

Your circle time will be crawling with excitement when you sing and move with these buggy songs!

Buzzzz!
(sung to the tune of "Jingle Bells")

Buzzing through the air,
From a beehive every day,
Over the fields we go,
Buzzing all the way.
Trying not to sting,
Making honey sweet,
Oh, what fun it is to buzz,
From a beehive every day.

Oh! Buzz, buzz, buzz,
Buzz, buzz, buzz,
Buzzing all the way.
Oh, what fun it is to buzz,
From a beehive every day.
(Repeat chorus.)
Buzzzz!

Cindy Guerriero—Preschool
Riverhead Country Day School
Riverhead, NY

Buggy Movements

As your youngsters learn about new bugs, have them help you add new verses to the following two songs!

Do You See Bugs?
(sung to the tune of "The Muffin Man")

Do you see a grasshopper, a grasshopper, a grasshopper?
Do you see a grasshopper? It leaps around like this.
(Squat down and hop.)

Do you see a butterfly, a butterfly, a butterfly?
Do you see a butterfly? It flits around like this.
(Flap arms and dart around.)

Do you see a brown spider, a brown spider, a brown spider?
Do you see a brown spider? It creeps around like this.
(Bend at waist and touch floor with hands.)

Do you see a bumblebee, a bumblebee, a bumblebee?
Do you see a bumblebee? It flies around like this.
(Make buzzing sound while pretending to fly.)

Christa J. Koch—Pre-K, Wesley Circle of Friends
Bethlehem, PA

I Wish I Were...
*(sung to the tune of
"The Oscar Mayer® Weiner Song")*

Oh, I wish I were a butterfly, a butterfly.
That is what I'd truly like to be.
'Cause if I were a butterfly, a butterfly,
I would flutter by so merrily.

Oh, I wish I were a bumblebee, a bumblebee...
I would carry pollen merrily.

Oh, I wish I were a cricket, a cricket...
I would sit and chirp so merrily.

Oh, I wish I were a firefly, a firefly...
I would blink my light so merrily.

Oh, I wish I were a beetle, a beetle...
I would chew on plants so merrily.

adapted from an idea by Cheryl Bowman—Two-Year-Olds
Mercy Child Development Center, Des Moines, IA

Flashing Fireflies

Your little ones will light up at the chance to practice counting with these fireflies. If desired, share with your class *Ten Flashing Fireflies* by Philemon Sturges (North-South Books Inc.). Then prepare for this small-group activity by duplicating the firefly pattern (page 84) onto brown construction paper several times. Collect the same number of flashlights (with easy on/off switches) as you have fireflies. Trace the bulb end of each flashlight onto the end of a different firefly. Cut out each firefly and the corresponding circle in its tip; then tape each flashlight to the corresponding firefly as shown. Seat several children in a dark area of your room; then give each child a firefly. Each time you show or say a different numeral, encourage the children to flash their firefly lights that number of times. What a bright idea!

Chrissy Yuhouse, Latrobe, PA

Moths Love the Light!

Some of your children may have noticed that at night, moths and other bugs fly around bright lights. Moths search for food at night, but sometimes the lights distract them. If the light is turned off, the moths are likely to fly away. Invite your children to pretend to be moths in this movement activity that will have them fluttering for more. Give each child two pieces of white tissue paper, two white crepe paper streamers, or two lengths of white toilet tissue. Invite each child to hold one piece in each hand as he dances around the room to some lively music. Turn the lights off and direct the children to stop and land (squat down). Restart the moth make-believe when the lights are turned back on. Continue until everyone is all fluttered out.

Chrissy Yuhouse

Gross-Motor Garden

Youngsters will make a beeline for this outdoor activity that has them buzzing in and out of flowers just like busy bees sucking nectar and gathering pollen. In advance, cut several large flower shapes from cardboard. Cut out the flowers' centers to create holes large enough for a child to crawl through. Ask the children to paint the flowers. Then, when the paint is dry, take the flowers outside for use in this floral obstacle course. Give each flower to a different child. Direct those children to stand in different areas of the playground and to hold the flowers upright and touching the ground. Encourage the remaining children to buzz around the playground and to crawl in and out of the flowers. If desired, designate a piece of playground equipment as the hive where tired bees can rest after they've delivered the pollen they collected on their legs.

81

Create-a-Bug

There are already millions of species of bugs, but why not invite youngsters to scurry over to your art center to make some more? To prepare the area so that each child can make his own one-of-a-kind bug, cut large circles and ovals from various colors of construction paper. (Save the scraps for decorating the bugs.) Cut a supply of thin rectangles from black construction paper to serve as legs and antennae. Cut a pair of oval wings from laminating film or cellophane wrap for each child. Finally, stock the area with scissors, markers, glue, and various art supplies, such as paper scraps, sequins, and more.

If desired, explain that some kinds of bugs—insects—have three body parts and six legs. Then invite each child to glue together his choice of circles and ovals to construct his bug or insect. If desired, staple a pair of wings on his bug. Then encourage him to glue on legs and antennae and to decorate the bug as desired. Hang these creative creatures from your ceiling and everyone will know your class has gone buggy!

Buzzing to the Beat

The buzzword for this freestyle art and music activity is fun! In advance, duplicate the bug patterns (page 84) onto various colors of construction paper a number of times. Cut the bugs out; then glue or tape each one onto a crayon as shown. Hide the crayons in a tub of plastic grass. Then put the box, large sheets of drawing paper, and an audio recording of instrumental music in a music center. When visiting the center, a child carefully digs around in the grass until he finds one or more bug crayons. As the music plays, he pretends that the bug(s) is flying over his paper, leaving a freestyle design as it moves. Sometimes the bugs move slowly to the music; sometimes they move quickly. Either way they create beautiful bug art!

Seeing Spots

Spots here, spots there. Youngsters will count spots everywhere with this counting activity. Getting ready is easy. Just spread an inexpensive round, red plastic tablecloth on the floor. Then gather at least ten black plastic plates (or laminated construction paper circles) and a large die. Seat your class around the spotless red ladybug. Have the group chant the following rhyme. Roll the die and then ask students to put the correct number of spots on the ladybug's back.

Ladybug, ladybug, where are your spots?
You look funny without any dots!
How many spots will you get? 1, 2, 3,…

Walkingstick Snack

Create these twig treats that are fashioned after a most amazing bug—the walkingstick. If possible, find a picture of this bug that looks like a twig. Then make some walkingstick snacks. To make one, just spread peanut butter on a pretzel rod. Put three pairs of pretzel stick legs on the pretzel rod; then add two pieces of black licorice antennae. Eat quick before they walk away!

Chrissy Yuhouse
Latrobe, PA

Bee Tea

Think you swallowed a bug? If it was the walkingstick bug snack described above, then it was probably delicious! Now wash those buggy snacks down with some Bee Tea. To make a cup of tea, a child fills a five-ounce cup with cold water. He then stirs in an amount of powdered sweetened tea (check the amount on the package directions) and a spoonful of honey. Wrap a decorative bee around a straw for each child. Honey, this tea is delicious!

Go Buggy!

If your students really go buggy over bugs, make this card game that can be played similarly to Go Fish or Concentration. To prepare a game of Go Buggy!, copy the game cards (page 85) onto construction paper four times. If desired, color and laminate the cards. Cut the cards out. To play, identify the bugs with your class. Pass four cards to each player in a small group of students; then place the deck of cards facedown on the floor. Have each player, in turn, ask the child to his right for a specific card that matches a card he is holding. If the child has that card, he gives it to the first player who then places the match on the floor. If the child does not have the card, he tells the first player to "go buggy." The first player takes the top card off the deck and keeps that card in his hand unless it matches one of his cards. Continue play in this manner until all the matches have been made.

To play a game of Bug Memory (Concentration), have a pair of children spread two sets of the cards facedown on the floor and then play the game like Concentration until they have matched all of the pairs of cards.

Pam Crane

Bug Patterns

Use with "Flashing Fireflies" on page 81.

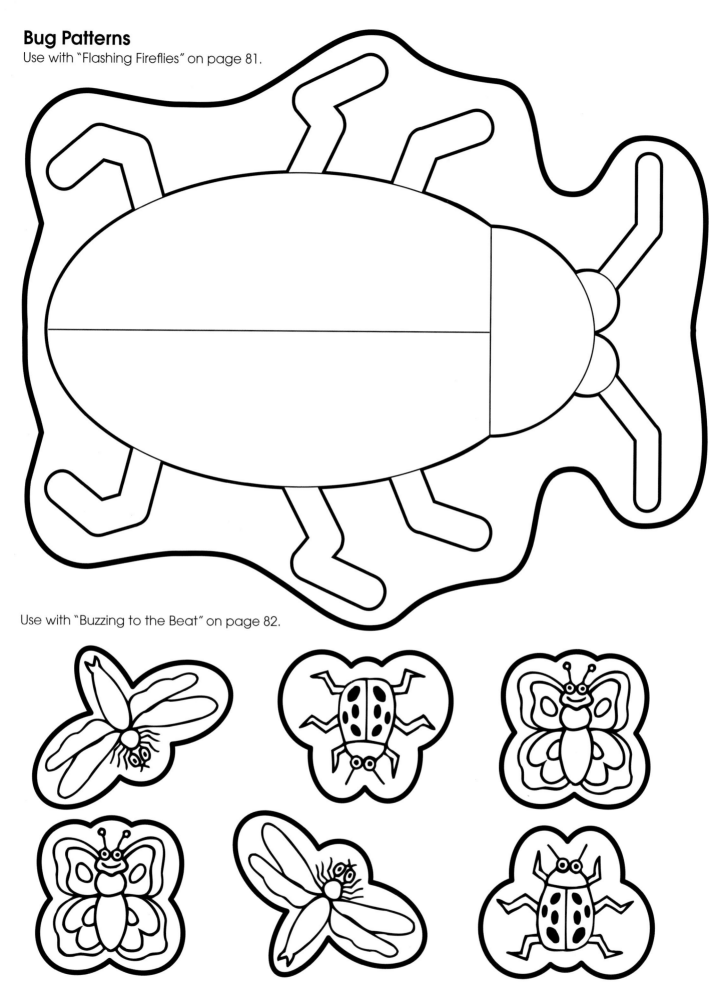

Use with "Buzzing to the Beat" on page 82.

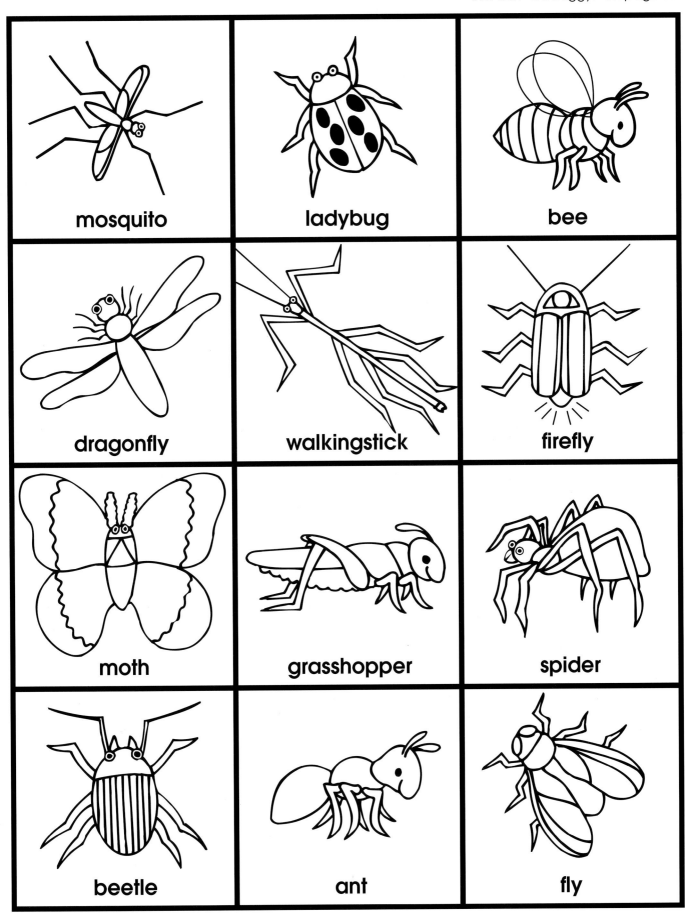

mosquito

ladybug

bee

dragonfly

walkingstick

firefly

moth

grasshopper

spider

beetle

ant

fly

"Pet-tastic" Patterns

Unleash your cat and dog lovers on this set of pet-inspired pattern projects. Once your youngsters have trained with these spotted puppy dog and striped cat activities, they'll be nothing less than pattern pros!

by Lucia Kemp Henry

Pet Lotto

Help your little ones begin to recognize patterns with this lotto activity that will have the players pairing pups and cats by their patterns and colors. To make one lotto activity, duplicate two copies of page 88 onto tan construction paper and two copies onto gray paper. Cut one sheet of each color along the lines to create cards. Cut the remaining sheets only along the edge of the set of cards to make the lotto boards. To use, invite pairs of students to lay the boards and cards on a table. Have the students take turns placing each lotto card on its matching space on one of the two boards. Once the students understand how to play, encourage them to repeat the activity on their own.

Spot and Stripe Patterns

Here's a "grr-eat" way to stretch your preschoolers' skills in identifying spotted and striped patterns. You'll also extend their understanding of how patterns repeat. To prepare, reproduce the dog and cat cards (page 89) onto white construction paper at least three times. Color each dog with a simple pattern of spots such as big and small or brown and black. Similarly, color the cats with stripes to create patterns, such as wide and thin stripes or red and yellow stripes.

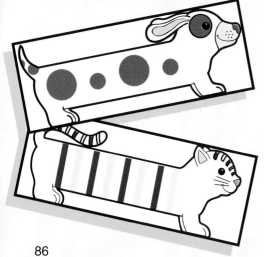

During a group time, explain that patterns are lines and shapes that repeat. Then have your students identify the spots or stripes on each animal. Also help them identify the pattern on that animal. When your group time is over, place the cards in a math or art center for use with "Colorful Pet Patterns" on page 87.

Colorful Pet Patterns

Extend the use of the pet reproducibles on page 89 with this patterning art project. To prepare, duplicate the cards to create at least a class supply. Cut out the dog and cat cards; then put them in a center along with crayons and the examples created for "Spot and Stripe Patterns" on page 86. Encourage each child to color a pattern on a pet either by copying one of your examples or creating his own. Be sure to invite children to identify the patterns on their pets during a group time. Hey, does that cat have green and blue stripes?

Pairing Up Pets

More matching and patterning is in store for your preschoolers with these pet pairs. Make a dog and a cat tracer from the patterns on the lotto cards. Trace pairs of dog and cat shapes from different colors of scrapbook paper (from craft stores) with stripes and polka dots, and then cut them out. Ask a small group of children to help you find the matching pairs of pets. Then have them identify the visual patterns on the cutouts. Next, help them arrange some of the cutouts in a line to create a pattern. For example, you could create a dog and cat pattern, a striped cat and spotted cat pattern, a blue pet and yellow pet pattern, and more. Keep it simple and patterning is sure to be "pet-tacular" fun!

Pet Style

Who's the "teacher's pet"? Each and every student who wears one of these simple-to-make headbands! Help each child paint a pattern of spots or stripes on a strip of tagboard. When the paint is dry, cut out paper ears to attach to the strip. Then staple the ends of the strip together to fit the child's head. Isn't wearing a pattern just the cat's meow?

Patterns

Use with "Pet Lotto" on page 86 and "Pairing Up Pets" on page 87.

Red, White, and Blue Gala

by Michele Stoffel Menzel

Star-Spangled Learning Centers

Celebrations don't have to stop after the Fourth of July! Continue the fun of the holiday by setting up these star-spangled centers using red, white, and blue materials and leftover holiday supplies.

Catch the Spirit!

Get set for your celebration by duplicating a class supply of the note on page 95 onto red, white, or blue construction paper. Invite students to add patriotic punch to the notes by decorating them with foil star stickers, patriotic stickers, or glitter. Then, just prior to the Fourth of July, send home each child's note to announce your learning center celebration; request that parents donate their leftover holiday supplies; and suggest that students wear red, white, and blue clothing on the days you have your patriotic centers in place.

Patriotic Pizzazz

When the leftover party items you've requested arrive, turn your room into a celebration station by starting with the decor. Have your children help you decorate the room by hanging streamers from the doorway, mounting metallic star-shaped garland at children's eye level, placing holiday-themed tablecloths on the tables, or mounting small flags at each center. Even invite children to paint stars on classroom windows using paint to which a small amount of soap has been added. Look around…a festive flair is in the air!

Star-Spangled Style

If you sent home the note on page 95 announcing your events, then you will have already suggested that the children wear red, white, or blue clothing during the days you have your patriotic centers in place. To make sure that each child has a patriotic item to wear, have her paint a bandana or a kerchief. To prepare, cut a class supply of white fabric squares the size of handkerchiefs. To decorate her square, a child spreads red, blue, or silver glitter fabric paint onto a star-shaped sponge, then presses the sponge onto the square. She continues using different sponges and colors of paint. Once the paint dries, help each child tie on her fabric to form a bandana or a kerchief. How's that for star-spangled style?

Listening Center
Wanted: Star Seekers!

Youngsters' size- and color-recognition skills are sure to shine when they participate in this movement activity. Teach children the song below; then record them singing it several times—each time substituting different color words (*red, white,* or *blue*) and size words (*big* or *small*). Place the tape in your listening center. Then create a path of laminated red, white, and blue construction paper stars in varying sizes. As children visit this center, invite them to play the tape while they jump along the path and pick up stars.

(*sung to the tune of "Pick a Bale of Cotton"*)
Gonna jump down, turn around,
Pick a **big, red** star;
Jump down, turn around,
Pick a star today.

Oh, stars!
Pick a **big, red** star.
Oh, stars!
Pick a star today!

Fine-Motor Center
"Spark-tacular" Sculptures

If you have little ones who tune in to learning through touch, then try this colorful dough activity. Use your favorite recipe to prepare a batch each of uncolored dough, red dough, and blue dough to which silver glitter has been added. When a child visits the center, give her a small ball of each color of dough. Invite her to knead the dough together so that the colors begin to mix; then encourage her to mold her dough into a colorful sculpture. If desired, add star-shaped cookie cutters to the center for more "spark-tacular" fun!

Outdoor Center
Hip, Hip, Hooray! It's a Sidewalk Parade!

Everyone loves a parade! So take a small group outside to a blacktop on the playground or to a sidewalk. Also take a supply of sidewalk chalk in patriotic colors, an audiotape of marching music, and a tape player. Using the chalk, outline a parade path; then have children work together to decorate the path with stars, flags, and fireworks. Invite children to form a line at the beginning of the route and then have them march to the music. Direct the children to take turns leading each other along the route. Hip, hip, hooray!

Dramatic-Play Center
Happy Birthday, America!

Your little ones might not fully understand that the Fourth of July is America's birthday, but they are sure to know that every birthday calls for a party! Here's a great center idea that makes use of the party supplies that parents donated, such as holiday-themed paper plates, tablecloths, napkins, cups, plastic utensils, party favors, and confetti. Place all of these items in your dramatic-play area; then let children prepare for birthday celebrations over and over! As they do, they'll have the opportunity to practice sorting, matching, counting, and one-to-one correspondence. The chance to practice these skills is a real reason to celebrate!

Sensory Table
Sparkling Stars and Things

This idea is so simple, yet it provides tons of patriotic fun! Simply add patriotic-themed party confetti to your sand and water tables along with sieves and slotted spoons. Invite little ones to stir, scoop, and sift. As children find the confetti, encourage them to sort, count, and pattern the pieces into red, white, and blue plastic bowls. What a great day for patriotic play!

Art Center
Oh My Stars!

Invite youngsters to add to the red, white, and blue decor by making these star-spangled banners. For each child, use masking tape to create star shapes on a piece of fingerpainting paper. Have each child paint his entire sheet with any combination of red and blue paint. Then, when the paint dries, assist each child as he carefully removes the tape. Oh my, I spy stars!

Science Center
Fireworks Display

This see-and-touch discovery center invites little ones to watch changes in the shape, color, and texture of frozen paints *and* to create paintings that explode with color! Prepare for this discovery by layering each section of a Styrofoam® egg carton with red, white, and blue BioColor® (available from Discount School Supply, 1-800-627-2829). Firmly close the lid; then insert a separate craft stick through the lid and into each section of the carton. When the paint is frozen, take the carton out of the freezer and let it sit for just a few minutes. Put some of the individual sticks of paint in the center for children to use and observe; then put the carton back in the freezer.

Encourage children to use the frozen paints to draw on white construction paper. Then, as the paint melts, have each child paint a design beside her original drawing. When the paint melts completely, encourage her to fingerpaint. Mount the paintings together for an explosion of color.

Math Center
Starstruck

Math is delicious when youngsters use tasty manipulatives to create patterns and then eat the manipulatives, too! Set a supply of JET-PUFFED® StarMallows® in your math center. Have a child use two different colors of marshmallows to form a pattern, such as *white star, blue star, white star, blue star*. Next, have her chant the pattern she sees. Encourage her to continue forming simple patterns in which each color of marshmallow is repeated one time. After children have completed the center, make sure to have individual bags of marshmallows for snacking. Patterning is mmm, mmm, good!

Math Center
Stars and Stripes Patterning

Patterning practice is easy when children create a path of stars and stripes! Cut at least ten each of red, white, and blue streamer lengths and ten each of red, white, and blue construction paper stars. Put the items in your math center. When a child visits the center, help him create a pattern using the stars and stripes (streamers). For example, his pattern might be *red star, blue stripe, red star, blue stripe*. To reinforce the pattern, clap a steady beat as the child walks along his path. Yeah! He's got the beat!

Cooking Center
Striped Ice

Looking for an easy way to help your little ones beat the heat? Then try these shivery treats as a cool addition to your tricolored celebration. In preparation, place a plastic bowl full of crushed ice; an ice-cream scoop; two squeeze bottles, one containing red juice and the other containing blue juice; and a class supply of clear plastic cups and flexible drinking stars in your cooking center.

To make a striped ice treat, a child fills his cup with one scoop of ice and then drizzles red juice and blue juice over the ice. Next, he places a straw in the ice and enjoys his slushy treat! Wow! Cool stripes!

Fine-Motor Center
Squishy Star Swirls

Give youngsters' fingers a workout with this shaving cream twist! To make one star swirl bag, use a black permanent marker to draw a few star-shaped outlines onto a large resealable, plastic freezer bag. Squirt a few dollops of white shaving cream along with either red or blue food coloring or tempera paint into the bag. If desired, add a sprinkle of glitter. Reinforce the seal of the bag with clear packing tape. Place several of the bags in a fine-motor center. Invite children at the center to explore the bags by squishing them and tracing the star outlines with their fingers. Ooh, squishy swirl fun!

Block Center
Building Blocks for Two

This patriotic partnering activity will encourage children to sort, count, and compare red, white, and blue blocks while also fostering creativity. Use red, white, or blue tape to create two large stars on the floor of your block area. (Make sure the stars are big enough for a child to build structures inside.) Put a matching set of either LEGO® or DUPLO® blocks in each center so that the two sets correspond in the number of each color of blocks.

Invite a pair of children to visit the block center. Help them sort the blocks by color and then compare their sets to see that they have the same number of each color. Then encourage each child to use her set of blocks to build a structure within her star shape. Help the partners realize that even though they have the same materials, they can use their creativity to build different structures. If desired, have children top off their structures with miniature American flags.

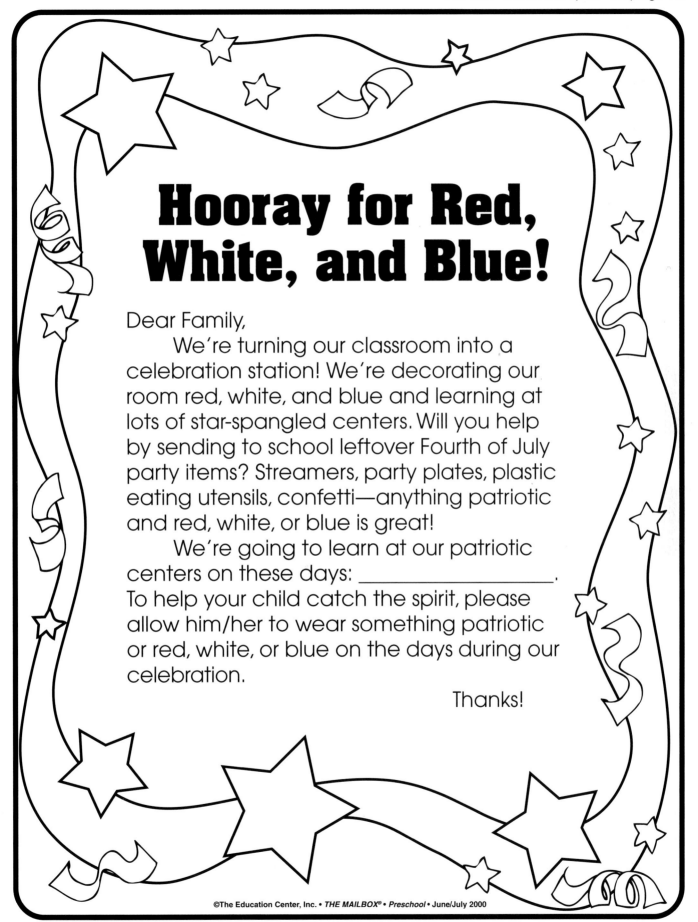

Hooray for Red, White, and Blue!

Dear Family,

We're turning our classroom into a celebration station! We're decorating our room red, white, and blue and learning at lots of star-spangled centers. Will you help by sending to school leftover Fourth of July party items? Streamers, party plates, plastic eating utensils, confetti—anything patriotic and red, white, or blue is great!

We're going to learn at our patriotic centers on these days: _____. To help your child catch the spirit, please allow him/her to wear something patriotic or red, white, or blue on the days during our celebration.

Thanks!

Count on

In honor of these eight-legged creatures, we give you eight great ideas to help your little ones get a leg up on math skills. One, two, three, four, five, six, seven, eight!

by dayle timmons—Special Education Inclusion, Alimacani Elementary School, Jacksonville Beach, FL

1
Spiders, Spiders, Everywhere!

Start off your number madness by asking children to bring to school arachnid toys they already own, such as stuffed or beanbag toys, puppets, or plastic spiders. As a group, count the legs on each spider to verify whether or not it has eight legs. Then sort the spiders in a variety of ways, such as whether or not they have eight legs, whether they are stuffed or plastic, and whether they are black or colorful. Each time you sort the spiders, count and record the number in each group. You can count on this activity to get youngsters caught up in spidery math fun!

2
Arachnid Antics

Invite youngsters to join in this activity to strengthen counting and to introduce the concept of adding one more. Seat your class in a circle (the web). Ask one child to walk around the web as the group chants the poem below. Pause to allow the child to select another spider to join him; then insert that child's name in the poem. Continue until every child has joined the chain of spiders walking in a circle.

[One] black spider went out to play
On a spiderweb one day.
He had such enormous fun,
He asked one more spider to come.
(Pause)
Spider [child's name], come out and play.
Spider [child's name], come out and play.

Spiders

3
Spiders Times Ten

Want to fill your classroom with spiders and learning fun? Multiply the number of students you have by ten; then start singing! For every child, use a fine-point permanent marker to draw a simple spider on each of his fingernails. Be sure to have the child count aloud with you as you add eight legs to each spider. When each child has a couple of handfuls of spiders, sing the following song. Have students hold up one finger for each numeral in the verse, then wiggle all their fingers during the chorus. At the end of the day, offer to remove the spiders with fingernail polish remover.

Spiders on My Hands
(sung to the tune of "Angels in the Band")

There was one,
There were two,
There were three little spiders.
There were four,
There were five,
There were six little spiders.
There were seven,
There were eight,
There were nine little spiders.
Ten little spiders on my hands!

Oh! Wasn't that a day, spiders on my hands,
Spiders on my hands, spiders on my hands?
Wasn't that a day, spiders on my hands?
Count them one to ten!

4
Weave a Story Web

Youngsters are sure to enjoy making these books that illustrate the verse of the previous song. To prepare, make spider printers by clipping one large pom-pom to each of several clothespins. Also fill a shallow pan with black paint. For each child, cut five sheets of paper in half; then program each half sheet with a different line of the song as shown. Help each child print the appropriate number of spiders on each of her pages. Then, when the paint is dry, direct the child to use a black marker to add eight legs to every spider. Bind the pages together sequentially. Let's all look at our books and sing along!

5
Colorful Cousins

Encourage youngsters to practice counting at this hands-on *and* legs-on play dough center. Provide a variety of colors of play dough and a number of pipe-cleaner halves. Invite little ones at the center to make a play dough spider body, then add eight pipe-cleaner legs. Creepy!

6
Spider Counting Games

Get your students involved in making these spider counting cards for use with several activities. Begin by having each child make a spider mask. To make one, cut a half circle out of the center of a paper plate as shown. Paint the plate black. When the paint is dry, glue on eight black paper legs that have been accordion-folded. If desired, add a craft stick to the base of each mask. When every child has made a mask, take a photo of a child holding his mask. Next take a picture of two children holding their masks. Continue taking pictures in this manner until every child has been included in a photo and you have the highest number of children desired in a photo at one time. Also label index cards with different numerals from 1 up to the largest number of children in a photo. Use the photos and numeral cards with these games.

- Encourage children to count the spiders in a photo and then find its matching numeral card.
- Practice arranging the pictures in order from the smallest number of spiders to the largest.
- Play a game of more or less. To play, two players sort the photos facedown into two stacks. Each player takes a card from the top of a stack, then counts the number of spiders shown. The player with the photo showing more spiders keeps both cards. After all of the cards have been chosen, the player with more pictures wins.

7
Web Sight

Your little web watchers will love getting caught using this spider's web. On a clear overhead transparency, use a black marker to draw a web. Put the web transparency on an overhead projector that has been placed on the floor. Also provide a number of plastic spiders and numeral cards. Turn on the projector. Encourage a child to select a card and then count the corresponding number of spiders onto the overhead projector. Have him invite friends to count the spiders as they are projected onto the wall.

8
Drop the Spider in the Bucket

To prepare this game, put a bucket, a number of plastic spiders, and a set of numeral cards in a center. To play, a child selects a card and identifies the numeral. He then stands over the bucket and counts as he drops the corresponding number of spiders into it. As a challenge, have a child toss the spiders into the bucket.

FIELD TRIP UNITS

OFF TO THE HOSPITAL!

These ideas are just what the doctor ordered for a fun, informative field trip to the hospital!

ideas by LeeAnn Collins—Director, Sunshine House Preschool, Lansing, MI

HOSPITAL BOUND AND BACK AGAIN

Read aloud Fred Rogers's *Going to the Hospital* (Paper Star) as a way to introduce your little ones to some of the things that happen at a hospital. Allow time for your children to discuss their feelings about this very large and somewhat strange place. Also encourage children who have been to a hospital (perhaps to see a relative or new baby) to share their experiences. Make a list of things children may see at the hospital, such as beds with wheels, doctors and nurses, X-ray machines, big sliding doors, lots of computers, and more. Then sing the following song so that it includes things from your list.

When you return from your trip, review the list for things your group saw and then add new things that students observed during the visit. Sing the second verse of the song in the same manner as the first verse.

TO THE HOSPITAL
(sung to the tune of "For He's a Jolly Good Fellow")

Off we go to the hospital.
Off we go to the hospital.
Off we go to the hospital,
To see [the doctors work].

When we went to the hospital,
When we went to the hospital,
When we went to the hospital,
We saw [the doctors work].

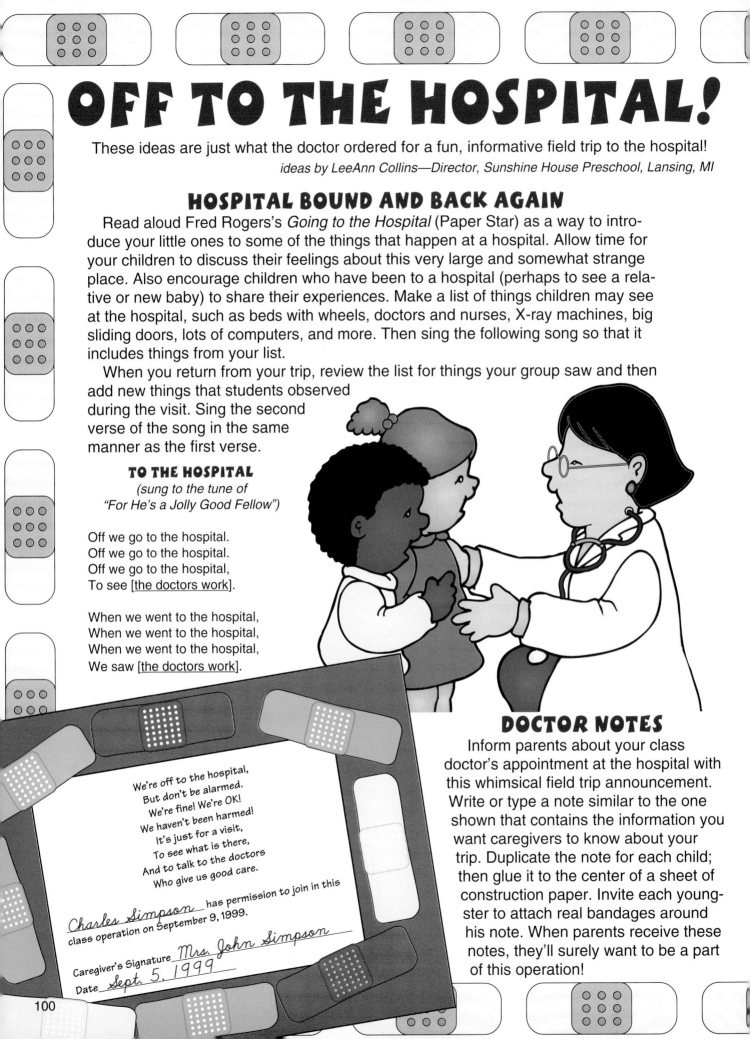

We're off to the hospital,
But don't be alarmed.
We're fine! We're OK!
We haven't been harmed!
It's just for a visit,
To see what is there,
And to talk to the doctors
Who give us good care.

Charles Simpson has permission to join in this
class operation on September 9, 1999.

Caregiver's Signature *Mrs. John Simpson*

Date *Sept. 5, 1999*

DOCTOR NOTES

Inform parents about your class doctor's appointment at the hospital with this whimsical field trip announcement. Write or type a note similar to the one shown that contains the information you want caregivers to know about your trip. Duplicate the note for each child; then glue it to the center of a sheet of construction paper. Invite each youngster to attach real bandages around his note. When parents receive these notes, they'll surely want to be a part of this operation!

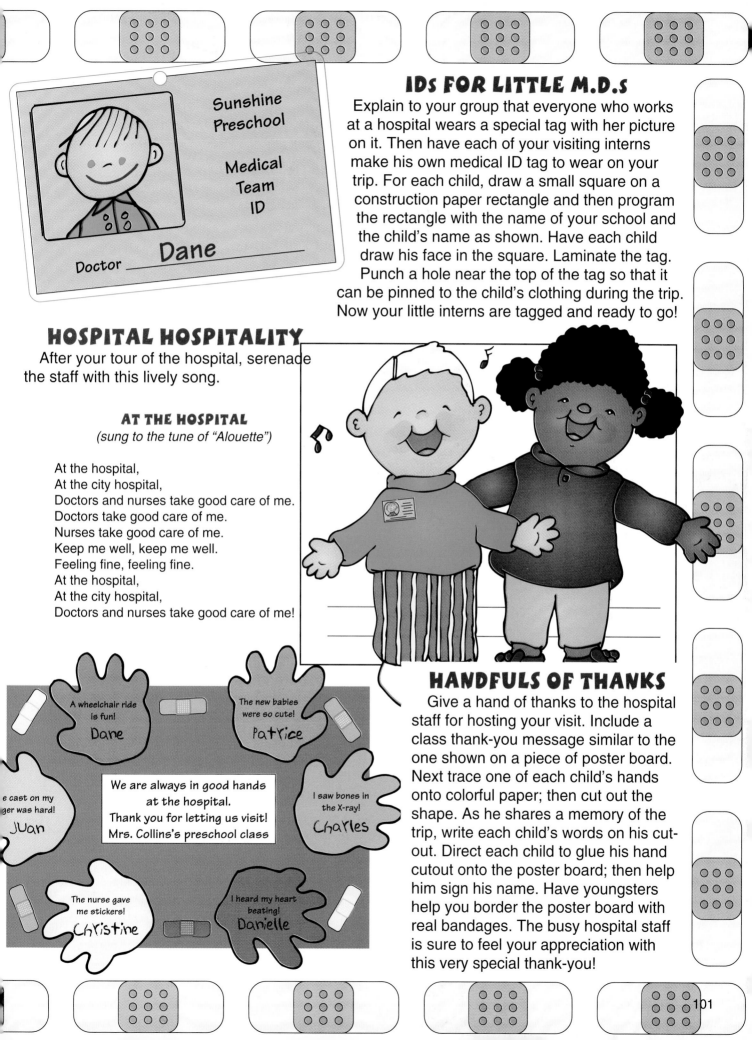

IDs FOR LITTLE M.D.s

Explain to your group that everyone who works at a hospital wears a special tag with her picture on it. Then have each of your visiting interns make his own medical ID tag to wear on your trip. For each child, draw a small square on a construction paper rectangle and then program the rectangle with the name of your school and the child's name as shown. Have each child draw his face in the square. Laminate the tag. Punch a hole near the top of the tag so that it can be pinned to the child's clothing during the trip. Now your little interns are tagged and ready to go!

Sunshine Preschool

Medical Team ID

Doctor __Dane__

HOSPITAL HOSPITALITY

After your tour of the hospital, serenade the staff with this lively song.

AT THE HOSPITAL
(sung to the tune of "Alouette")

At the hospital,
At the city hospital,
Doctors and nurses take good care of me.
Doctors take good care of me.
Nurses take good care of me.
Keep me well, keep me well.
Feeling fine, feeling fine.
At the hospital,
At the city hospital,
Doctors and nurses take good care of me!

HANDFULS OF THANKS

Give a hand of thanks to the hospital staff for hosting your visit. Include a class thank-you message similar to the one shown on a piece of poster board. Next trace one of each child's hands onto colorful paper; then cut out the shape. As he shares a memory of the trip, write each child's words on his cut-out. Direct each child to glue his hand cutout onto the poster board; then help him sign his name. Have youngsters help you border the poster board with real bandages. The busy hospital staff is sure to feel your appreciation with this very special thank-you!

A wheelchair ride is fun!
Dane

The new babies were so cute!
Patrice

e cast on my ger was hard!
Juan

We are always in good hands at the hospital.
Thank you for letting us visit!
Mrs. Collins's preschool class

I saw bones in the X-ray!
Charles

The nurse gave me stickers!
Christine

I heard my heart beating!
Danielle

Down at the

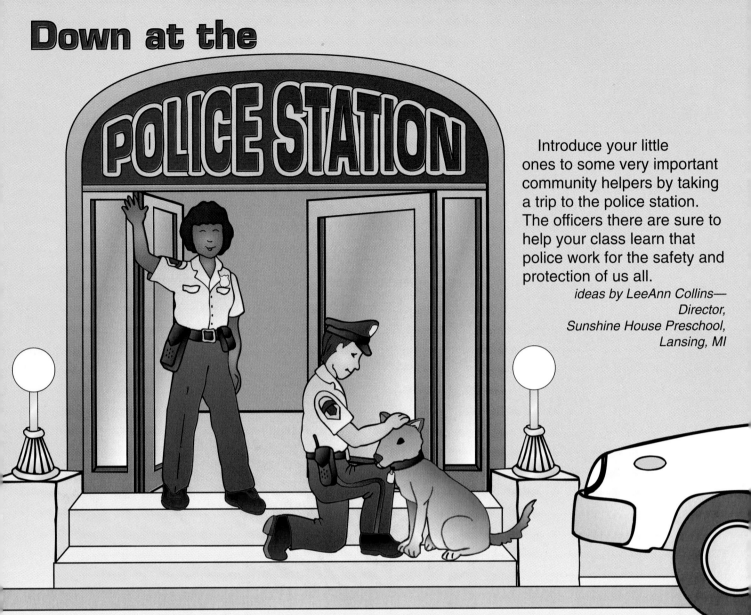

POLICE STATION

Introduce your little ones to some very important community helpers by taking a trip to the police station. The officers there are sure to help your class learn that police work for the safety and protection of us all.

ideas by LeeAnn Collins—
Director,
Sunshine House Preschool,
Lansing, MI

Help!

That's right, a police officer's job is to help! Share the following books about police officers with your children. Then ask them to contribute to a class list of the many ways police officers help the citizens in a community.

Police take care of lost dogs.

Police help kids cross the street at school.

Police help people in accidents.

I'm Going to Be a Police Officer
Written by Edith Kunhardt
Published by Cartwheel Books

Police Officers: A to Z
Written and Photographed by
   Jean Johnson
Published by Walker and
   Company

Police Officers
Written by Dee Ready
Published by Children's Press®

Order books online. www.themailbox.com

What'll We See at the Station?

Now that youngsters know what police officers do, it's time to take a look at where they work when they are not out and about helping people in the community. Sing the first verse of this song before visiting the station. Each time you repeat the verse, replace the word *police* with things youngsters think they will see such as *police dogs, police cars, whistles,* and *badges.* When you return, sing the second verse, varying it to include those things youngsters remember from the trip.

What's at the Station?
(sung to the tune of "Skip to My Lou")

What's at the station?
What'll we see?
What's at the station?
What'll we see?
What's at the station?
What'll we see?
We'll see [police],
Yes sirree!

What was at the station?
What did we see?
What was at the station?
What did we see?
What was at the station?
What did we see?
We saw [police],
Yes sirree!

Calling All Parents

These notes will signal parents about your trip so they can give the green light for all of your junior officers to go to the police station. Duplicate the note on page 104 to create a class supply. Have each child cut out a red, a yellow, and a green paper circle. Then have him glue the circles and a copy of the note to a black paper rectangle. Finally, have him "light up" the green light by gluing on green glitter. It's a go!

A Badge Makes It Official

Identify each visiting junior officer with a badge nametag. For each child, cut a badge shape pattern (on page 104) from lightweight cardboard (cereal boxes work well). Have each child cover a badge with a piece of aluminum foil. Use a black marker to personalize each child's badge; then have him decorate it with star stickers. Punch a hole near the top of each child's badge; then tie on a length of yarn to complete the nametag.

Meeting the Officers

While you're down at the station, invite your class to perform this fingerplay for the officers. They're sure to be impressed with your squad's knowledge of the job!

Five Police Officers

Five police officers in the city's streets,
They're the nicest people you'd ever want to meet.
The first officer helps the children get to school.
The second officer makes sure you follow the rules.
The third officer makes the traffic slow down.
The fourth officer drives the car around town.
The fifth officer helps when you've lost your way.
Thank you, officers, for helping people every day!

It's a green light to the police station!

Mrs. Collins's class will be visiting the
Greensboro Police Station on
Oct. 20, 1999.

Please sign below if your junior officer _____
will be a member of our visiting squad.

Parent's Signature_____ Date_____

Thanks for Letting Us Stop By!

The officers at the police station are sure to stop and take notice of this personalized thank-you message. Cut out a red paper octagon; then glue it onto the center of a piece of poster board. Label the poster board and octagon with the message shown. Next have each child color a paper person shape to resemble himself. Ask each child to add his shape and name to the poster. Thanks for the visit!

Parent Note

Use with "Calling All Parents" on page 103.

It's a green light to the police station!

_____'s class will be visiting the

_____ Police Station on

_____
(Date)

Please sign below if your junior officer

_____
(Name)

will be a member of our visiting squad.

Parent's Signature _____ Date _____

©The Education Center, Inc. • THE MAILBOX® • Preschool • 2000

It's a green light to the police station!

_____'s class will be visiting the

_____ Police Station on

_____
(Date)

Please sign below if your junior officer

_____
(Name)

will be a member of our visiting squad.

Parent's Signature _____ Date _____

©The Education Center, Inc. • THE MAILBOX® • Preschool • 2000

Badge Pattern

Use with "A Badge Makes It Official" on page 103.

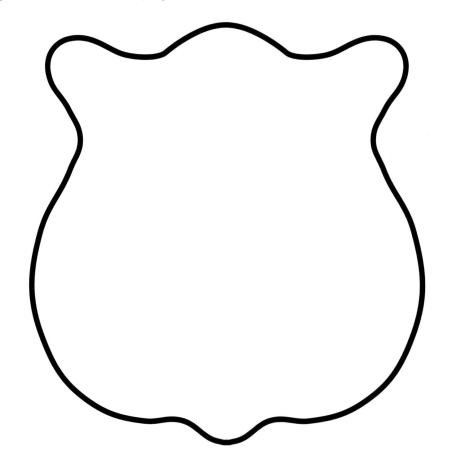

Nametag Pattern
Use with "Earning Your Wings" on page 106.

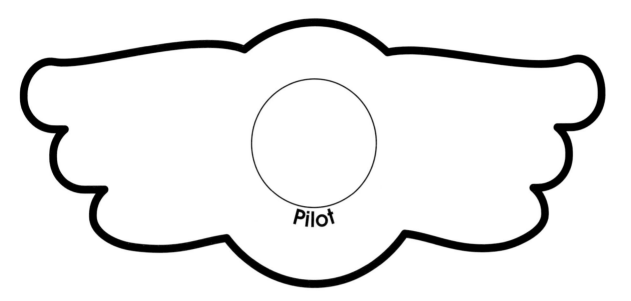

Pilot

Ticket Pattern
Use with "Round-Trip Ticket" on page 107.

Ticket for Airport Fun

Fly to the Airport!

Take a direct flight to the airport with these field trip ideas. You're sure to have a smooth flight!

ideas by LeeAnn Collins—Director, Sunshine Preschool, Lansing, MI

Pack Your Bags

This suitcase field trip announcement is sure to hold all of the information you need to relay to parents. For each child, fold a sheet of construction paper in half; then trim it as shown to resemble a suitcase. Type or write a field trip note similar to the one shown that contains information about your trip. Duplicate a class supply of the note, trim each one, and then glue one to the inside of each suitcase. Before taking his suitcase note home, have each child pack it with cutout magazine pictures of clothing. Don't forget to tag each piece of luggage with the owner's name!

Earning Your Wings

Your precious little ones have no doubt already earned their wings for the trip. Now help them prepare nametags before your class takes flight. For each child, duplicate the pattern on page 105 on heavy paper. Personalize each tag with a different child's name and your school's name; then have each child draw his face on his tag. If desired, laminate the tags for durability; then punch holes through each one and add a yarn loop to make a necklace. Or simply attach each child's tag to his clothing with a safety pin. Now your preschool pilots can be easily identified as members of your visiting airport crew.

Victoria

In-Flight Field Trip

Final destination: Piedmont Triad International Airport

Departure date and time: 8:00 A.M. Monday, Dec. 13, 1999

Your child has earned his/her wings and will take flight with your permission. Please sign below.

Like to go? Pack your bags and let Mrs. Collins know!

_____
Parent's signature

Sunshine

Preschool

Pilot
Laura

Airport Crew

It takes a lot of workers to help an airplane take off. Use this song to introduce your class to some of the folks they'll see at the airport.

Workers at the Airport

(sung to the tune of "Skip to My Lou")

Workers at the airport,
Whom will we see?
Workers at the airport,
Whom will we see?
Workers at the airport,
Whom will we see?
[Ticket agents giving tickets to me].

Substitute the underlined phrase with these endings:

Luggage carriers taking bags for me.
Pilots flying the plane for me.
Attendants bringing food to me.
Controllers watching planes for me.

First-Class Reading

Get your ground crew geared up with these books and a video about airports, airplanes, and flying. Check your library for these titles or visit our Web site to order available titles: www.themailbox.com.

Airplanes
Written & Illustrated by Byron Barton
Published by HarperCollins Children's Books

Flying
Written & Illustrated by Gail Gibbons
Published by Holiday House, Inc.

Let's Fly From A to Z
Written by Doug Magee
Published by Cobblehill Books

First Flight
Written & Illustrated by David McPhail
Published by Little, Brown and Company

Angela's Airplane
Written by Robert Munsch
Published by Firefly Books

Cleared for Takeoff (video)
by Fred Levine Productions

Round-Trip Ticket

Your students are sure to have so much fun on their trip that they'll want to return to the airport as soon as possible. In the meantime, have youngsters make this field trip thank-you to send to the airport's coordinator of your trip. Duplicate the ticket pattern on page 105 for each child; then cut out the tickets. Write each child's name on her ticket; then record her description of her favorite part of the trip. Include the tickets in a package along with a message, or display them on a piece of poster board around a message.

Ticket for Airport Fun

I like the plane's cockpit and all the computers.

CHRIS

Smile! We're Going to the Dentist!

Want a field trip that's perfectly polished? The ideas in this unit are sure to make you grin!

ideas contributed by LeeAnn Collins—Director, Sunshine House Preschool, Lansing, MI

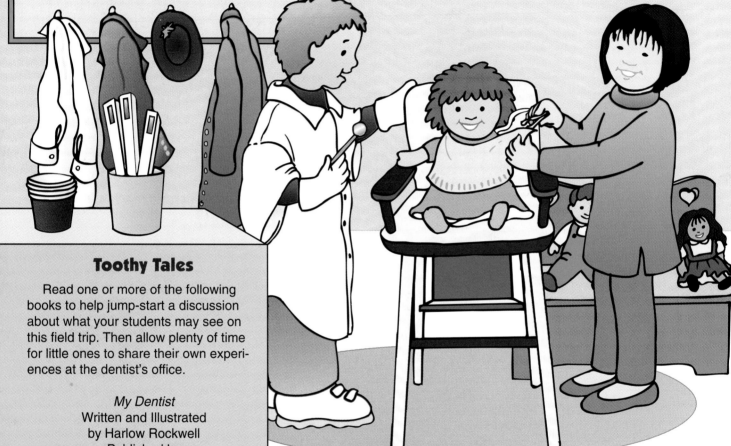

Toothy Tales

Read one or more of the following books to help jump-start a discussion about what your students may see on this field trip. Then allow plenty of time for little ones to share their own experiences at the dentist's office.

My Dentist
Written and Illustrated
by Harlow Rockwell
Published by
William Morrow and Company, Inc.

Going to the Dentist
Written by Anne Civardi
Illustrated by Stephen Cartwright
Published by EDC Publications

Dr. Kanner, Dentist With a Smile
Written by Alice K. Flanagan
Photo-illustrated by Christine Osinski
Published by Children's Press

Dental Dramatics

After reading about the dentist's office and sharing some of their own experiences, little ones will have fun working in a make-believe dentist's office right in your classroom. Set up the furniture in your dramatic-play area to resemble a dental office setting, using a doll's high chair as a dentist's chair and dolls as dental patients. Provide some or all of the following props: new children's toothbrushes, small cups, nonbreakable mirrors, white shirts, and rubber gloves. Make a dental bib by tying the two ends of a length of white yarn to separate spring-type clothespins and then clipping the clothespins to a white or blue paper napkin. Also set up a waiting room with chairs and children's magazines. When all is ready, encourage your youngsters to role-play dentists, hygienists, and other office staff. Be sure to leave this center in place after your field trip, as well, so that youngsters can incorporate what they learn on the trip into their dramatic play.

The Dentist Says

No visit to the dentist is ever complete without some sage advice on good dental care from your friendly dentist or hygienist! Remind little ones of the basics for proper dental health with this tune.

(sung to the tune of "Jimmy Crack Corn")

The dentist says,
"[Please brush your teeth.]"
The dentist says,
"[Please brush your teeth.]"
The dentist says,
"[Please brush your teeth.]
And you'll have a healthy smile!"

Repeat the song, each time substituting one of these phrases for the underlined words:

Please floss your teeth.
Please eat good foods.

We Have an Appointment!

Send home these reminder postcards before your field trip. Make one copy of the postcard pattern on page 110, and then fill in the date and time of your trip. Copy the postcard onto tagboard for each child. Invite each of your little ones to cut out her postcard along the bold lines and then decorate the blank side of the card with drawings or stickers of teeth and toothbrushes.

Pearly White Nametags

These sparkling nametags will really make your youngsters shine on their trip! For each child, copy the tooth patterns on page 110 onto manila paper. Set out cups of white tempera paint and clean toothbrushes. Have each child dip a toothbrush into paint and then gently "scrub" the paper tooth until it's pearly white! Before the paint dries, sprinkle on some iridescent glitter. Laminate the nametags before labeling each one with its creator's name. Punch a hole at the top and thread through a length of dental floss to make the nametag into a necklace.

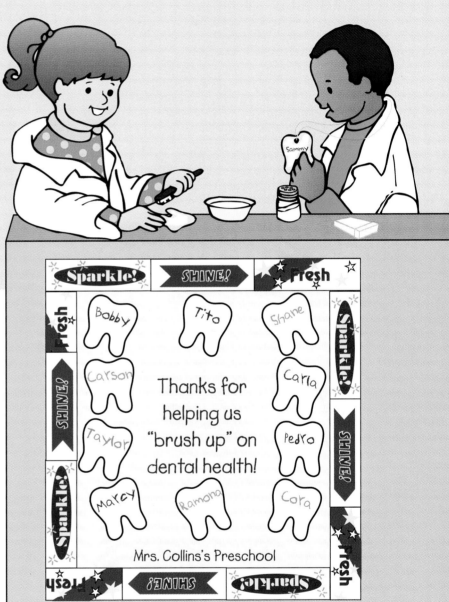

Thank You!

This giant thank-you note is sure to bring toothy grins to any dental office staff! In advance, ask parents to send in empty toothpaste boxes. Cut the panels apart on each box and then ask youngsters to help you glue the panels around a sheet of poster board to make a border. In the center of the poster board, write a message similar to the one shown. Then have each child personalize a white construction paper copy of the tooth pattern on page 110. Scatter the teeth around the message and glue them in place. The recipients are sure to love this note. That's the "tooth"!

Field Trip Reminder Postcard

Use with "We Have an Appointment!" on page 109.

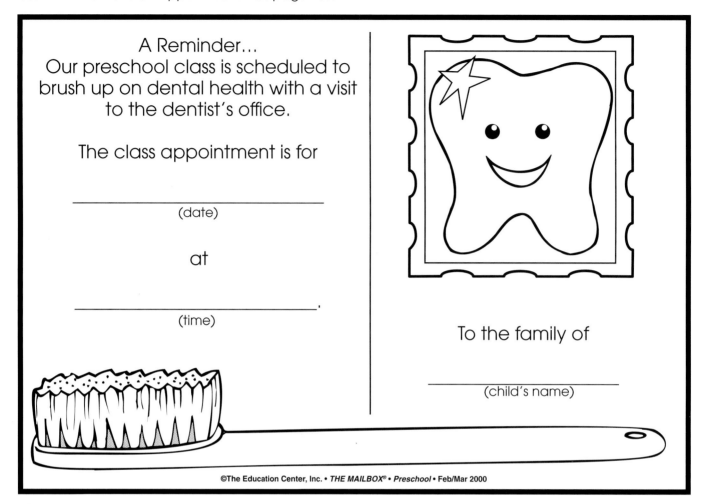

A Reminder...
Our preschool class is scheduled to brush up on dental health with a visit to the dentist's office.

The class appointment is for

_____
(date)

at

_____ .
(time)

To the family of

_____
(child's name)

Tooth Patterns

Use with "Pearly White Nametags" and "Thank You!" on page 109.

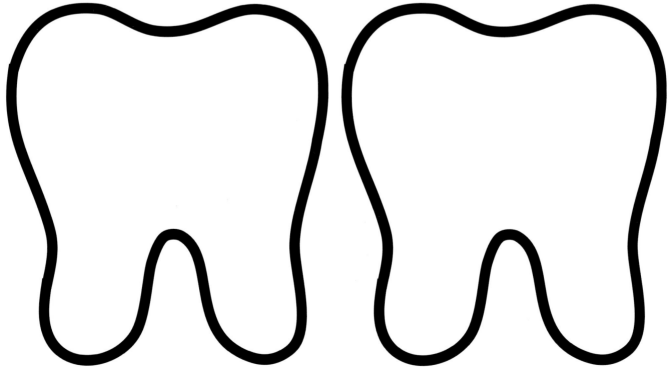

We're going to the farm—hooray!
It's going to be a super day!
_____ is the date
We'll arrive at the barnyard gate.
We'll meet the animals and then
We'll come "baa-ck" to school again!

Cow Pattern
Use with "Here a Cow, There a Cow…" and "'Hay!' Thanks!" on page 113.

Fun at the Farm

The Farm in Photos

Prepare your preschoolers for your field trip by sharing some photo-illustrated books about the farm. Before showing the books to your little ones, ask them to brainstorm a list of farm animals. Then read one or more of the books on the list below. If there are animals in the pictures that little ones didn't mention earlier, add them to your list. Then have youngsters list other items they saw in the books, such as foods grown on a farm or tools used by a farmer. Post the lists in your classroom. After your trip, revisit the lists and circle the animals or items your class saw on its trip.

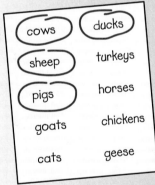

cows   ducks

sheep   turkeys

pigs   horses

goats   chickens

cats   geese

Farm Alphabet Book
Written and Illustrated by Jane Miller
Scholastic Inc.

Farm Animals
Eye Openers Series
Aladdin Paperbacks

I'm Going to Be a Farmer
Written and Illustrated by Edith Kunhardt
Cartwheel Books

Order books online.
www.themailbox.com

Farm Trip Announcement

Let parents know about your upcoming farm visit with these adorable announcements. To prepare, make one copy of the announcement pattern on page 111. Fill in the date of your trip on the blank line and add any additional information (such as the name of the farm you'll be visiting) on the silo; then photocopy a class supply onto red construction paper. Cut out the barns; then encourage each child to use cotton balls, glue, and a thin black marker to create a woolly sheep in the barn doorway on his announcement. We're off to the farm—but we'll be "baa-ck" soon!

We're going to the farm—hooray!
It's going to be a super day!
_____May 10_____ is the date
We'll arrive at the barnyard gate.
We'll meet the animals and then
We'll come "baa-ck" to school again!

These ideas for a field trip to the farm will get you "moo-ving" towards a memorable barnyard visit.

ideas contributed by LeeAnn Collins and Ada Goren

Here a Cow, There a Cow...

These dotted cows will serve double duty during your farmyard frolic—as nametags and as part of a thank-you note. First duplicate the cow pattern on page 111 twice for each child. Cut out all the cows; then write each child's name on two. Set out shallow containers of black and brown tempera paint at your art center. Encourage each child to find the two cows with her name on them. Then have her dip a fingertip into her choice of paint and make fingerprints on each of her cows. When the paint is dry, laminate one cow from each pair and punch a hole in the top. Set the other cow in each pair aside for use on a class thank-you note (see " 'Hay!' Thanks!"). On the day of your trip, your little ones will be easily spotted by the cow nametags pinned to their shirts!

"Hay!" Thanks!

Send your host farmer a giant thank-you for showing your class around his barnyard. To make a thank-you note, write the message shown in the center of a sheet of green poster board. Glue the second set of cows made for "Here a Cow, There a Cow…" all around the message. Your farm friends are sure to be "moo-ved" by this thank-you gesture!

Have You "Herd"? Mrs. Collins's class had a great time on its trip to the farm! Thanks so much!

A Farm Follow-Up

After returning from your trip, use this pocket-chart poem to review some of the jobs a farmer does. Write the poem on sentence strips as shown. Also gather a school photo of each child. Teach little ones the poem; then have your future farmers list other farm chores as you record each of their ideas on a separate sentence strip. Add a simple picture cue to help nonreaders decode each phrase. Then have each child take a turn personalizing the poem. Slip a child's photo into the pocket chart; then have the child select a chore to place on the third line of the poem. (If a pocket chart is not available, arrange the strips on the floor.) Invite the class to recite the new version of the poem on each child's turn.

If [photo] were a farmer,
There'd be lots to do!
Like | milking the cows | [cow]
And having fun, too!

113

A TRIP TO THE ZOO

Lions and tigers and bears...oh, my! Relax—a field trip to the zoo doesn't have to be scary. Use the ideas in this unit to make your safari a cinch!

ideas contributed by LeeAnn Collins—Director, Sunshine Preschool, Lansing, MI

We're preparing for our field trip to Central Zoo on June 7, but we need your help! We've made these binoculars as a reminder to please help your child search through old magazines to find some pictures of zoo animals. Please send at least one picture (more are welcome!) to school by Monday.

Thanks! You're "zoo-rific"!

ANIMALS ALL AROUND

Once you've collected a supply of zoo animal pictures, put them to good use. Show them to youngsters during circle time and discuss which animals they'd like to see during your field trip. Place some in your writing center to spark some imaginative zoo stories. Or use them for sorting activities. For even more wonderful pictures, check out these photo-illustrated books from the zoo animals series below. These books have a day at the zoo covered, from breakfast to bathtime!

Mealtime for Zoo Animals
Mother and Baby Zoo Animals
Noisytime for Zoo Animals
Playtime for Zoo Animals
Sleepytime for Zoo Animals
Splashtime for Zoo Animals
Written by Caroline Arnold
Illustrated by Richard Hewett
Published by Carolrhoda Books

Order books online. www.themailbox.com

PICTURES, PLEASE

This crafty prop will remind parents about your upcoming trip to the zoo *and* ask for their help with your preparations. To prepare, type up a short note similar to the one shown. Photocopy the note onto colorful tagboard to make a class supply; then punch a hole in the top of each note. String each note onto a 24-inch length of yarn. Then set these aside.

Next, have each child use toilet tissue tubes to make a pair of binoculars. To make one, simply cut a tissue roll in half. Hold the two short tubes side by side and then staple the pieces together. Decorate the outside of the binoculars with watercolor paints. When they are dry, punch holes as shown. Then tie the two ends of one of the prepared yarn lengths to the two holes. Send each child's binoculars home to help remind his parents to be on the lookout for zoo animal pictures!

THE ZOO'S THE PLACE TO BE

Teach little ones this catchy tune about the animals they may see on your trip. Use your picture collection to help youngsters think of other animal names to substitute in the third line of the song.

(sung to the tune of "The Addams Family Theme Song")

The zoo's the place to be,
If ever you want to see
A [lion] family.
So come along with me!

To the zoo! (clap, clap)
To the zoo! (clap, clap)
To the zoo, to the zoo, to the zoo! (clap, clap)

MAKE 'EM EASY TO SPOT

These giraffe nametags will have your group standing tall at the zoo! Photocopy the giraffe pattern (page 116) onto yellow construction paper to make a class supply. Write a different child's name on each nametag; then cut them out. Set out shallow containers of paint in a variety of colors, as well as a bowl of Cheerios® cereal. Have each child dip a cereal piece into her choice of paint and then press it onto her nametag to make a spot. Encourage little ones to cover these whimsical giraffes with spots of many colors. (Replace the Cheerios as needed.) When the paint is dry, laminate the nametags. Then punch a hole in the top of each one and thread a 30-inch length of yarn through the hole. Tie the ends to create a necklace. Ready to wear it? Just stick out your neck!

STICKER SAFARI

Did you see that tiger? How about the big snake? Help youngsters remember the animals they see on your field trip with some animal search cards. To prepare, photocopy the animal card (page 116) onto heavy paper to make a class supply. Personalize one for each child; then staple a sheet of sticky dots to the top of each animal card. Have each chaperone hold her group's cards during your tour of the zoo. Occasionally, have the chaperone give out the cards so that the children can put sticky dots over the pictures of the animals they've seen. Later, during discussions about the trip, have youngsters refer to their animal search cards to remind them of the animals they saw.

Kaye Sowell, Pelahatchie Elementary, Brandon, MS

ZOO MEMORIES

Making a memory book after your zoo trip will be a snap—just remember to bring along your camera! Be sure to have enough film to take one photo of each child, plus a few extras. As you tour the zoo, zoom in on each child as she stands near the enclosure of her favorite animal (perhaps getting a sign in the picture if getting the actual animal in it is impossible). Take a couple of group shots near the zoo entrance as well. Have the film developed. Encourage each child to glue her photo to a half sheet of construction paper, write her name above the photo, and then dictate a sentence or two about the photo or the zoo trip for you to write below the picture. Create a cover that reads "Our Zoo Review" and use one of the group photos as cover art. Laminate the cover and pages; then bind them together. After sharing the finished memory book, give each child an opportunity to take it home to share with her family. We just love the zoo—don't you?

Giraffe Nametag

Use with "Make 'em Easy to Spot" on page 115.

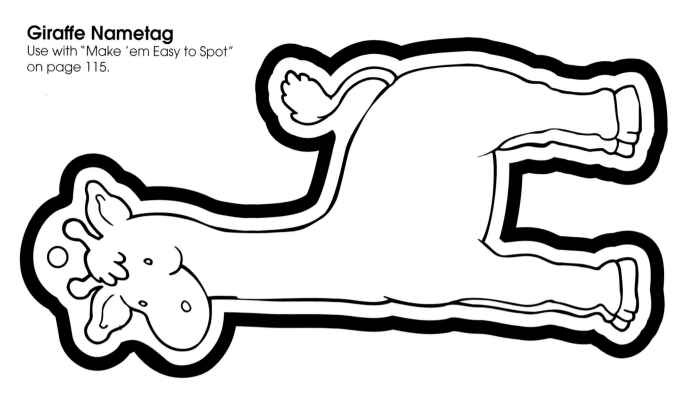

Animal Search Card

Use with "Sticker Safari" on page 115.

Name: _____

elephant	snake	giraffe	monkey
tiger	bear	parrot	zebra

BOOK FEATURES

The Itsy Bitsy Spider

Cover of *The Itsy Bitsy Spider* by Iza Trapani. ©1993 by Iza Trapani. By permission of Whispering Coyote Press.

As Told and Illustrated by Iza Trapani Published by Whispering Coyote Press

The itsy-bitsy spider climbed up the waterspout, but that's *not* the end of the story! Read (or sing) aloud this book to find more places the brave spider dared to go. At the end of the book, you'll find out why that teeny tiny climber never gave up!

ideas contributed by Lucia Kemp Henry

A Little Bit of Singing

It's easy to spin a wonderful story web that will catch the attention of your little listeners. Begin by asking them to join you in singing "The Itsy Bitsy Spider." Next prompt the children to use their "smallest" voices to help you sing the verse three more times, substituting the phrase *itsy-bitsy* with *itty-bitty, teeny-weeny,* or *eensy-weensy* each time. Then just keep right on singing as you introduce your group to the new verses and whimsical illustrations in Trapani's version.

Spot the Spider

Invite your little ones to play a find-the-spider game when you take a second look at the story. To give this seek-and-find challenge a spin, recite the teacher's line of the chant below as you open the book to each new spread of pages. When a number of the children have spotted the spider on a page, have them reveal the location by reciting the second line of the chant.

Teacher: Where is the spider? Can you spy her?
Children: We spy the spider. She's [in the waterspout].

Fuzzy-Wuzzy Fellows

Now that your little ones are big experts at spotting a spider, extend their search for the itsy-bitsy critter beyond the pages of the storybook. Prior to this activity, make a spider by hot-gluing two wiggle eyes to a one-inch-wide felt circle. To the back of the circle, glue four three-inch pieces of yarn.

During a group time, hide the spider in one hand. Ask youngsters to close their eyes. Put the spider on your body; then repeat the first line of the chant in the previous idea. When the students open their eyes, have them repeat the second line, inserting the location of the spider. Model this body-part review several times; then give each child a chance to hide the spider in her hand and then put it on her body. We spy the spider. She's on your foot!

Where Did That Spider Climb?

Make this story web to help youngsters recall the adventures that the spider had along the way. In advance, copy page 120 onto construction paper. Color the pictures, cut them out, and then laminate them. On a piece of tagboard, draw a web, similar to the one shown, that has five lines and two concentric circles.

During a group time, look again at the illustrations. As you reread each verse, have your youngsters name the place the spider went and what made her fall each time. Then tape the corresponding pair of picture cards on one section of the web. Complete the remainder of the story web in a similar manner; then review each situation the spider was in. Later, remove the picture cards from the web; then put the cards and the web in your reading center along with the book. Remind youngsters that because the spider had a goal (building her web), she climbed back up every time she fell down.

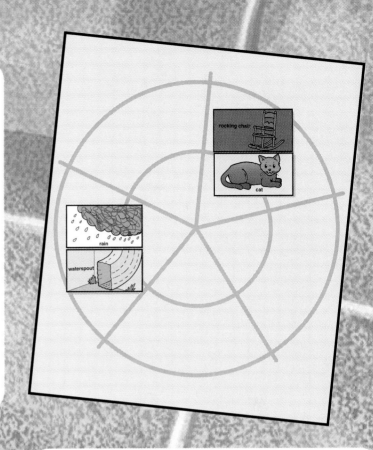

Wash That Spider Out!

There's no chance that this center will be a washout! Just add plastic spiders, a piece of plastic gutter or plastic pipe, and pouring items to your water table. Encourage visitors to the center to sing as they put a spider in the gutter or pipe and pour down the "rain" to wash him right out!

Watercolors and Webs

Invite youngsters to take a closer look at the pictures of the web that the spider finally got to weave. Point out that the illustrator used watercolor paints to create the colorful backgrounds behind the webs. Then invite each child to use watercolors to paint a sheet of white construction paper. When the paint is dry, have her use glue to squeeze a web onto her paper. Before the glue dries, have her sprinkle on clear glitter. Have youngsters rest in the sun, just like the spider did, when their webs are done.

Barry Slate

Patterns
Use with "Where Did That Spider Climb?" on page 119.

waterspout

rain

kitchen wall

fan

pail

mouse

rocking chair

cat

tree

dew

The Apple Pie Tree

Written by Zoe Hall
Illustrated by Shari Halpern
Published by Scholastic Inc.

Now here's a tasty tale! And since the season is autumn, the time is just "ripe" for reading it aloud. Invite your children to listen as a young girl describes her and her sister's apple tree from winter to fall and then explains the steps for making an apple pie. Sound delicious? It is! And so are the easy-as-pie learning activities that follow!

by Lucia Kemp Henry

Order this book at our Web site: www.themailbox.com.

Apple Tree Seasons

Watch your youngsters' understanding of the seasons blossom as they take part in this flannelboard activity. To prepare, cut flannelboard pieces similar to the ones shown so that you have a tree, small light green leaves, pink flowers, large dark green leaves, small light green apples, and large red apples. Read the story aloud. Afterward, look through the illustrations again and ask students to describe how the tree is different in each season. Next put the tree on the flannelboard and give the students the other flannelboard pieces. Use the pieces to create an apple tree in the winter, spring, summer, and then fall. Later put the flannelboard, the pieces, and the book in a reading center for students to use independently.

Winter

Spring
Tear light green paper leaves. Sponge-paint pink flowers.

Summer
Cut out light green paper leaves. Use small Styrofoam® ball halves to print green apples.

Fall
Cut out dark green paper leaves. Use large Styrofoam ball halves to print red apples.

"Tree-mendous" Art Project

Now that your little ones have taken a close look at the book's illustrations of an apple tree's seasons, invite them to branch out and display what they've learned through this class project. To prepare tree posters, label each of four large pieces of construction paper or strips of bulletin board paper with the name of a different season. Cut out four brown paper trees; then glue one to each poster. For each poster, discuss how the tree would look during that season. Invite the students to decorate the trees' branches (excluding winter) as suggested. Then display the four posters together along with a sign that notes the title of the book and lists the poster artists' names.

Sing a Song of Seasons

This "apple-tizing" song reinforces the seasonal sequence of an apple tree's changes.

(sung to the tune of "Have You Ever Seen a Lassie?")

An apple tree in winter, in winter, in winter—
An apple tree in winter is just brown and bare.
In winter it's sleeping, it's sleeping, it's sleeping.
An apple tree in winter is just brown and bare.

An apple tree in springtime, in springtime, in springtime—
An apple tree in springtime is sprouting new leaves.
In springtime it blossoms, it blossoms, it blossoms.
An apple tree in springtime is sprouting new leaves.

An apple tree in summer, in summer, in summer—
An apple tree in summer has apples that grow.
In summer they're growing and growing and growing.
An apple tree in summer has apples that grow.

An apple tree in autumn, in autumn, in autumn—
An apple tree in autumn has apples to pick.
In autumn they're ready, they're ready, they're ready.
An apple tree in autumn has apples to pick.

"Apple–tizing" Pies

After several readings of the story, it's likely that every mouth will be watering for a juicy bite of apple pie! Use this recipe so that each youngster can make a small apple pie and eat it too! Before making the pies, read again the part of the story that describes how the sisters make their pie. Ask the class which step is not named (adding the top crust). Then list all the steps on chart paper. Proceed to apple pie baking, explaining to the class that you'll be adding some extra steps when making your minipies.

Peel and dice enough large red apples so that you have a spoonful for each child (about one apple for every 12 children). To make one pie, a child flattens one refrigerator biscuit, then puts it on a personalized piece of aluminum foil. Next he puts a spoonful of apples on the center of the biscuit, topping the apples with a sprinkle each of cinnamon and sugar. Finally, he flattens a second biscuit, puts it on the apples, and then pinches the edges of the biscuits together. Use a fork to poke holes in the top of each pie. Bake the pies according to the biscuit package directions. "Apple-licious!"

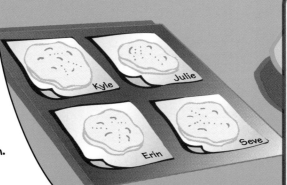

Peel the apples.
Cut the apples.
Pile them into the shell.
Sprinkle on cinnamon and sugar.
Put on the crust.
Put the pan in the oven.

Bake a Pie!
Bake a Pie!

Pass the time while the apple pies are baking by learning this chant.

Bake a pie, bake a pie, apple pie!
Roll out the dough in the wink of an eye.
Apples and sugar and cinnamon too.
Put it in the oven for me and you!

Pies Aplenty

Invite your little bakers to your dramatic play center to practice their sequencing skills making pretend pies. To put your center in order, stock the area with cooking items including aprons, pot holders, a rolling pin, an empty cinnamon container, spoons and bowls, a kitchen timer, an oven (made from a cardboard box), and pie pans in several sizes. Also provide the "ingredients" by cutting brown felt sized to match the tops of the pans to represent the top crusts. Cut a supply of apple slices from white craft foam. Invite a child to the center to bake a pie, bake a pie, apple pie!

Pie Tart Art

Top off your book activities with this project that's deliciously tempting! To make one paper apple pie, cut two four-inch circles from brown construction paper. Glue one circle (bottom crust) to the center of a small paper plate. Tear white construction paper into pieces (apples); then glue them onto the brown circle. Drizzle glue over the paper apples; then sprinkle on real cinnamon. Allow the glue to dry. Punch holes in the second brown circle (top crust); then staple it onto the plate so that it can be lifted to sniff the pie's contents. If desired, glue a copy of the "Bake a Pie!" poem (page 122) to the inside of the top crust. Encourage each child to share the chant and serve up his pie at home.

Bushels of Apple Books

Hankering for more great apple books for your storytime? Pick any of these!

The Seasons of Arnold's Apple Tree
Written & Illustrated by Gail Gibbons
Published by Harcourt Brace

I Am an Apple
Written by Jean Marzollo
Illustrated by Judith Moffatt
Published by Cartwheel Books

Picking Apples & Pumpkins
Written by Amy Hutchings
Photographed by Richard Hutchings
Published by Cartwheel Books

Order books online. www.themailbox.com

Time for Bed

Written by Mem Fox
Illustrated by Jane Dyer
Published by Harcourt Brace & Company

"The stars on high are shining bright" in this story by Mem Fox, sweetly illustrated by Jane Dyer. Tuck your little ones around you and snuggle them in tight as you share this cozy, sleepytime story of animal parents and their babies. To order this book, visit our Web site: www.themailbox.com.

ideas contributed by Lucia Kemp Henry

Sleepytime, Storytime

Since bedtime is well known for its calming rituals, why not introduce *Time for Bed* in an atmosphere that duplicates a good-night mood? Give your story area a sleepytime feel by covering the floor with cozy quilts and plump pillows. Turn off the overhead lights, draw the shades, and light the area with a lamp set on a small table. Play soft lullaby music as your little ones gather around you. Then sing the following song to set the mood. To sing additional verses, replace the underlined words with the other animal names as they are shown in the story: cats, cow; foals, fish; sheep, bird; bees, snake; dogs, deer.

(sung to the tune of "Rock-a-Bye Baby")

Come hear a story. Come sit with me.
Where do [mice] sleep? Let's all look to see.
Where does a little [goose] lay his head,
When stars fill the sky and it's time for bed?

Bedtime Babies

After sharing this soothing tale with your little ones, take a closer look at the illustration of each animal parent and young one. Have youngsters identify the resting place or name a possible resting place for each pair of animals.

Next reread the book and have your little ones listen carefully to the name given to each baby. Lead students to discover that some animals, such as mice and fish, use the same name for both parent and baby, while other animals use different names, such as the cow, horse, and dog. Finally, look through the book once more and have students recite the chant below as you display the corresponding page of the book. Each time you repeat the chant, substitute the animal names for the underlined words. Good night!

It's time for bed. Lay down your head,
[Mama/Daddy mouse] and little [mouse].

Becky Saunders

"The Stars Are Out and on the Loose"

Your classroom will shine with this star-studded bedtime display. Have your little ones examine pages from the book that show a star-filled sky, such as the pages with the geese, cows, and birds and the inside cover. To create the display, invite youngsters to sponge-print yellow stars on a length of purple bulletin board paper. When the paint is dry, mount the paper on a wall or bulletin board. In turn, send a disposable camera home with each child along with a note asking the parent to take a picture of the child in bed getting ready to go to sleep. When all the bedtime pictures have been developed, mount each child's photo on the bulletin board paper and add the title "Time for Bed." What a dreamy display!

Pass the Pillow

Transition your youngsters into naptime with this adaptation of Hot Potato. Have students sit in a circle and quietly pass a small pillow. As the pillow is passed, start playing lullaby music. The child holding the pillow when the music *starts* leaves the circle to rest. Have youngsters bid the child good night by reciting the phrases from the story, "It's time for bed, little Sam, little Sam." Continue playing until all of the children have left the circle to rest.

Stories for Sweet Dreams

Send your little ones into a sweet slumber with these books that are also about animals at bedtime. If desired, drop one or more of the books into a pillowcase to send home with a different child each night. Include a note to parents inviting them to read the tales when tucking in their little ones.

A Child's Good Night Book
Written by Margaret Wise Brown
Illustrated by Jean Charlot
Published by HarperCollins Children's Books

Little Donkey Close Your Eyes
Written by Margaret Wise Brown
Illustrated by Ashley Wolff
Published by HarperTrophy

When I'm Sleepy
Written by Jane R. Howard
Illustrated by Lynne Cherry
Published by Dutton Children's Books

Asleep, Asleep
Written by Mirra Ginsburg
Illustrated by Nancy Tafuri
(Check your library for this title.)

BARNYARD

Written & Illustrated by Denise Fleming
Published by Henry Holt and Company, Inc.

moo moo moo

mew mew mew

cock-a-doodle-doo

cluck cluck cluck

coo coo coc

muck muck muck

squeal squeak sque

Cover of Barnyard Banter by Denise Fleming. ©1994 by Denise Fleming. By permission of Henry Holt and Company, Inc.

There are so many animal sounds to be found in the hubbub of this colorful barnyard chorus! Each time you read aloud Denise Fleming's bright and lively book, students will enjoy the rhyming words and entertaining pictures more and more! Check out this book from your library or order it from our Web site: www.themailbox.com.

ideas contributed by Lucia Kemp Henry

BOISTEROUS BARNYARD

Before rereading the text, label 13 index cards, each with a different animal from the story. Then consider taking the class out to your own barnyard (playground), because this activity could get noisy! Give each card to a child or group of children to assign them parts. Review with each child or group of children the sound that each animal makes. Then, as you reread the story, invite the children to provide the barnyard banter for the animals. Moo, chirp, burp, squeak, HONK!

WITH A CLUCK, CLUCK HERE AND A MUCK, MUCK THERE

Now that you've introduced youngsters to some fun sound words that might be new to them, reinforce the new vocabulary by singing the traditional "Old MacDonald" with the sound words from the book. Old MacDonald had some pigs...with a muck, muck here and a muck, muck there! Afterward, if it is appropriate for your children, help them identify the animals in the story with similar rhyming sounds.

WHERE'S THE GOOSE?

Who's really the main character of this story? The only animal who's not where he's supposed to be—the goose! As you look at the story with a small group of children, invite them to point out where the goose is on each page as well as what he is doing. It won't take them long to discover that the reason he is causing such a hullabaloo is that he's after the butterfly!

To play a simple game of tag with the small group, designate one child to be the goose while the remainder of the children pretend to be butterflies. While the butterflies fly around in an outside area, the goose waddles around trying to tag them. When he tags a butterfly he loudly says, "Honk!" He then becomes a butterfly and the tagged child becomes the new goose. Continue playing until the children change roles a number of times.

BANTER

THE QUIET ONE IN THE BUNCH

Revisit the story so that the children can find the one animal in the book who is on every spread of pages (except one), but never makes a sound. After children discover the yellow butterfly, encourage them to use position words to describe the butterfly's location on each page. For the remainder of the day, continue to reposition a yellow paper butterfly in different locations in your room. When a child spots the butterfly, encourage him to use position words to tell you and his classmates where he found it.

BARNYARD COLLAGE

Your students might be surprised when you put the book in a painting center with a magnifying glass. And they'll really wonder what's up when you add birdseed, coffee grounds, and small pieces of hay (look for hay at a craft store). Invite a child to look closely at the illustrations (using the magnifying glass if desired) to find that the illustrator added real items to her pictures. Then encourage the child to paint a picture and then sprinkle his choice of the items onto the wet paint. When the paint is dry, have the child examine his painting with the magnifying glass.

CLASSROOM CLATTER

Wrap up your study of *Barnyard Banter* by adapting the rhythm of the story to fit a more familiar preschool setting. Encourage your little ones to chant the rhyme along with you as they perform the actions in each line.

Kids in the classroom, **yak, yak, yak.**
Kids in the block corner, **stack, stack, stack.**

Open and close hands.
Clap hands, one atop the other.

Kids in the clay center, **mash, mash, mash.**
Kids at the water table, **splash, splash, splash.**

Palms together, twist hands back and forth.
Cross hands back and forth.

Kids in the music center, **drum, drum, drum.**
Kids in the cooking center, **yum, yum, yum.**

Pat thighs.
Rub tummy.

Kids in the group circle, **clap, clap, clap.**
Kids in the sleeping place, **nap, nap, nap.**

Clap.
Put head on hands as if sleeping.

Planting a Rainbow

Written and Illustrated by Lois Ehlert
Published by Harcourt Brace & Company

Introduce your little ones to the colorful world of a flower garden with the rainbow of words and pictures in this book by Lois Ehlert. The science is simple, the colors are vivid, and the flower names are music to the ears! Before you know it, your youngsters' knowledge about flowers will grow…and grow…and grow! To order this book, visit our Web site at www.themailbox.com.

by Lucia Kemp Henry

Cover of *Planting a Rainbow* by Lois Ehlert. ©1988 by Lois Ehlert. By permission of Harcourt Brace & Company

From Seed to Flower

Cultivate an interest in flower growth by following an initial reading of *Planting a Rainbow* with this flannelboard activity. In advance, cut flannelboard pieces similar to the ones shown below, including a seed, a sprout, a small plant with a bud, and a flower with leaves. After reading Ehlert's story, review the first few pages and talk about the three different ways the flowers were started in the garden: as bulbs, as seeds, and as seedlings. Explain that different flowers are grown in different ways. Flip back through the pages again to follow the stages of growth for various flowers. Next, place the prepared pieces on your flannelboard in random order. Ask student volunteers to place them in sequential order to illustrate the growth stages of a flower grown from a seed. Later, put the book, the flannelboard, and the pieces in your reading center for students to use independently. You may also choose to use the pieces to help little ones learn the poem (right).

A Poem for Your Little Sprouts

Watch language skills blossom when your youngsters learn to chant this rhyme inspired by the sprouting seeds and beautiful blooms in the story. If desired, display the flannelboard pieces you prepared for "From Seed to Flower." Point to each piece as you and your students recite the lines of the poem. Once they have learned the poem, teach them the accompanying actions.

Teacher: Little flowers, little flowers, how do you grow?
Children: We start as seeds in the soil below.
(Kneel and touch forehead to floor.)

Teacher: Little flowers, little flowers, how do you come out?
Children: We wait a little bit and then we sprout!
(Sit up with bottom on heels.)

Teacher: Little flowers, little flowers, then what do you do?
Children: We stretch up to the sun and grow a leaf or two.
(Get up on knees; stretch arms out partway.)

Teacher: Little flowers, little flowers, how do you bloom?
Children: We open our petals and give off sweet perfume!
(Stand up with palms together in front; raise hands above head, then lower to sides with palms up.)

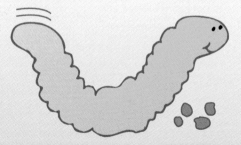

Sand Table Flower Garden

Wouldn't your budding gardeners love to actually plant a rainbow? Well, stock your sand table with the right materials, and they can do just that! Provide some small shovels, plastic flowerpots, empty plastic six-pack flower trays from a garden center, and a variety of artificial flowers and greens (in all the colors from the story). Before introducing youngsters to this center, review the graduated pages of the book and talk about the order of the colors in a rainbow: red, orange, yellow, green, blue, and purple. Then show little ones their garden-to-be and encourage them to plant the flowers in rows to make a rainbow. After they've made a rainbow garden, invite visitors at this center to design flower gardens of their own. Just watch those fertile imaginations grow!

Glorious Garden Colors

Use more artificial flowers and greenery for this color-sorting center where youngsters can pick and display flowers in a multitude of colors. Or make your own flowers and greenery by cutting simple shapes from felt and stapling each one to a drinking-straw stem. Insert all the artificial or felt flowers and greenery into a large block of green florist's foam to make a garden. Next, wrap a piece of construction paper around each of six tin cans so that you have a vase for each color of flower, plus the greenery. (Tape over the cut edges of each can for safety.) Place the flower garden and the vases in a center.

To use this center, a child picks all the flowers (or greenery) in a particular color and then sorts them into the corresponding vase. When all the blooms are sorted, she can have fun "replanting" them in the garden!

Painting a Rainbow

Invite your young artists to paint a rainbow brimming with fanciful leaves and flowers! In advance, cut sponge printers in simple leaf and flower shapes. Prepare shallow pans of red, orange, yellow, green, blue, and purple tempera paint. Then ask each child to print several shapes in each color on a large sheet of white construction paper. When the paint is dry, have each child cut around her shapes and then sort them by color into labeled containers. Once all the shapes are sorted, arrange and staple them onto a bulletin board to create the arches of color that make up a rainbow. Just for fun, put a few leaves and flowers in the wrong color in some sections of the rainbow. Ask youngsters to check out your design and see if they find anything out of place! Place extra leaf and flower shapes in your art area and encourage students to arrange the shapes on the tabletop to create their own miniature versions of your rainbow garden display.

129

THUMP, THUMP, Rat-a-Tat-Tat

by
Gene Baer

Illustrated by
Lois Ehlert

Written by Gene Baer
Illustrated by Lois Ehlert
Published by HarperCollins Publishers

Your youngsters will march right to the reading circle when you parade this colorful, noise-filled story before their eyes. Read this thumping, piping, squawking selection to your little ones; then invite them to play around with the band-themed activities that follow.

by Lucia Kemp Henry

Story Full of Sound and Flurry

Before you share the story, show the cover of the book to your students and read the title. Ask youngsters what they think the book might be about. Ask children to share if they have seen marching bands at parades or ball games. Read the story, discussing the marching band's movement and sound descriptions.

Prepare for a rambunctious second reading by seating the children at tables. Have them practice patting the tables with their hands palms down when you say, "Thump, thump," and tapping the tables with their fingers when you say, "Rat-a-tat-tat." Then read the story again. There's no doubt that this tuneful tale will be a hit with your little band of sound-effects experts!

Colorful Drums

Thump, thump, rat-a-tat-tat! Being a drummer is where it's at! Have each child decorate her own drum so she can join the band for the activities on page 131. For each child, cover a clean, empty powdered-drink canister with colorful construction paper. Have each child add colorful stickers to her can. Punch two holes on opposite sides of the can, just below the rim. Thread a length of ribbon through the holes, tie the ends together to create a neck strap, and then put the lid on the canister. Give each child two craft sticks or two pieces of a wooden dowel to use as drumsticks. Get ready to drum up some learning fun!

Order this book at our Web site:
www.themailbox.com

A-thumping We Will Go

Since your little ones have marched through the story more than once, they've probably developed an ear for how sounds can change. Help your students tune in to the way the sounds in the story changed by asking them to recall how the volume of the band varied throughout the tale. Look at the size of the words on each page and prompt students to remember that the band's sound started out soft, became louder, and then became softer again. To visually reinforce this idea, write the word *THUMP* on three different sentence strips: once in small letters to indicate a soft sound, again in medium-sized letters to indicate medium volume, and a third time in large letters to indicate a loud sound. Seat the students on the floor with their drums (see "Colorful Drums" on page 130). Prompt them to play their drums, changing the volume as you hold up each strip to indicate a change to soft, medium, or loud.

Strike Up the Band

It's time for your preschool players to go on parade. Arrange your youngsters in parade formation; then play some marching music at a moderate volume. As your little ones move around the room, encourage them to play their drums (see "Colorful Drums") to the rhythm of the march. After a few minutes, turn the volume of the marching music to a soft level. Prompt the children to match this level with softer drumming. Next turn the volume to a loud level as you encourage the drum corps to play loudly. Continue to vary the volume as long as students are interested in the activity. Your preschoolers won't let this parade pass them by!

Quiet as a Mouse

By this time, each of your sound-savvy students are probably adept at demonstrating the difference between loud and soft sounds. Set this cut-and-paste activity up in a center to promote more listening and literacy practice. Visually divide a piece of bulletin board paper into two sections, labeled "soft sounds" and "loud sounds." Put the paper in a center along with magazines, scissors, and glue. Encourage a child who visits the area to cut out a picture and then decide if the object makes a loud or soft sound. Have her glue the picture on the appropriate side of the chart. Label the picture.

To use the poster during a group time, ask a volunteer to pick a picture. Have her imitate the sound that object makes so that the group can guess which picture the child selected.

Blow, Toot, Thump...
Loud Reading Aloud

Here are more noisy books about bands for your storytime.

The Happy Hedgehog Band
Written by Martin Waddell
Published by Candlewick Press

Meet the Marching Smithereens
Written by Ann Hayes
Published by Harcourt Brace & Company

Snake Alley Band
Written by Elizabeth Nygaard
Published by Doubleday & Co., Inc.

Animal Music
Written by Harriet Ziefert
Published by
Houghton Mifflin Company

Order books online. www.themailbox.com

Instrumental to Learning

Have your group look closer at Lois Ehlert's illustrations to find the different types of instruments in the band. Make a list of those instruments. Then ask an upper-school band teacher to assist you in collecting some of the instruments for your children to look at. Or, if possible, ask several band students to visit your class to demonstrate how the instruments are played. Find out which instruments your little ones take a liking to by lining the instruments up on the floor. Ask each child to select the instrument he is most interested in by standing next to it. Count the results. Then ask the band students to give the children mini music lessons on how each instrument is played.

Once Upon a Story...

$\mathcal{O}$nce Upon A Story...

Brown Bear, Brown Bear, What Do You See?

This classic children's book by Bill Martin, Jr., and Eric Carle (Henry Holt and Company, Inc.) is the perfect way to introduce your youngsters to various painting techniques while reinforcing color recognition. After reading the book, discuss the difference between an author and an illustrator; then examine Carle's illustrations. Next focus on a different color each day as you have students use different techniques to paint outlines of animals that correspond to those in the book. For example, when you focus on yellow, have each child use a feather to paint a simple duck outline yellow. Or, when you focus on red, have each student paint liquid starch on a bird outline and then cover it with red tissue-paper squares. Other ideas include spatter-painting a frog outline green, sponge-painting a bear outline brown, fingerpainting a horse outline blue, or using small carpet squares to paint a cat purple. When a child has painted an animal to represent each one in the book, bind his pages together with a cover. If desired, add text similar to the book's to complete each child's own colorful book.

Betty Kabis Bissot—Pre-K
St. Anthony Cathedral School
Beaumont, TX

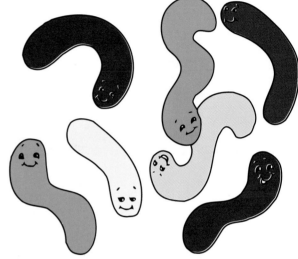

Count!

Count on having some fun with this lively counting book by Denise Fleming (Henry Holt and Company, Inc.). Read the book a second time and invite your youngsters to perform the actions described on each page. Or designate the appropriate number of children to perform the animal actions for each number up to ten as you read.

When your little ones are familiar with the story, place the book in a center along with a flannelboard and felt cutouts that correspond to the animals and their quantities as shown in the book. Invite students to use the cutouts for counting, sorting, or retelling the story. Your youngsters' early math skills are guaranteed to improve by leaps and bounds!

Carmen Carpenter—Pre-K
Highland Preschool
Raleigh, NC

See the corresponding book notes on page 146.

Pass the Fritters, Critters

What's the magic word? Please! Your youngsters are sure to be pleased with this delightful rhyming book on table manners by Cheryl Chapman (Simon & Schuster). After reading the story, have students practice some mealtime etiquette with this activity. Direct each child to make her own place setting by gluing a paper plate, a napkin, and plastic utensils on a sheet of colored construction paper. Next have her cut out one or more magazine pictures of food and then glue them to her plate. Encourage her to use polite words in a sentence; then write the sentence on her paper. For example, under a picture of pizza, a child's dictation may read, "Please pass the pizza" or "Thank you for the pizza!" Mount the completed place settings on a wall or bulletin board to create a dashing display of mealtime manners.

Joan Tietz—Pre-K
St. James Lutheran
Lafayette, IN

wonderful flowers

What a Wonderful World

This vibrant, multicultural book was inspired by Louis Armstrong's familiar rendition of the song by the same title and is illustrated by Ashley Bryan (song by George David Weiss and Bob Thiele, book published by Sundance Publishers & Distributors). After sharing the book, make a class "Wonderful World" book. To make the simple pages, ask each child to cut out her choice of "wonderful" pictures from magazines. After she glues her pictures to a circular piece of construction paper, have her dictate words or phrases to be written about the pictures. Bind the pages together behind a circular cover of the same size that has been colored to resemble Earth. What wonderful things can we find in your world?

Lucia Kemp Henry

Please pass the pizza.
Meghan

See the corresponding book notes on page 146.

Once Upon A Story...

The Pumpkin Blanket

Are you planning a class trip to a local pumpkin patch or farmer's market so that each child can select his own harvest pumpkin? Follow up the trip by reading Deborah Turney Zagwÿn's *The Pumpkin Blanket* (Tricycle Press). Your older preschoolers will enjoy this heartwarming story of a girl who uses her baby blanket to keep a crop of pumpkins from freezing. After reading the book, give each child a personalized square of cotton fabric; then have him use fabric paints, iron-on fabric cutouts, or felt shapes to decorate it. Instruct him to drape the fabric over his pumpkin for the night. Before your students return the next morning, sew all the squares together into a quilt; then display it in your classroom. At the end of the next day, allow students to take their pumpkins home. To create a cozy home-school connection, place the quilt and a copy of the book in a large bag. Have each student take the bag home to share the story and the quilt with his family.

Charlotte Thompson—Four-Year-Olds
Highland Plaza United Methodist Preschool
  and Kindergarten
Hixson, TN

Owl Babies

Follow up a reading of *Owl Babies* by Martin Waddell (Magi Publications) by having your class make these enchanting owls. To make one, dip a handled dish-washing sponge into black paint; then tap the paint onto a brown piece of construction paper. In the same manner, tap white paint onto the paper. When the paint is dry, cut out an owl shape. Create the owl's face by gluing on a yellow construction-paper beak and two flattened minimuffin-liner eyes. Then place a round black sticker in the middle of each liner to complete the owl's eyes. Hang these fine-feathered friends in your classroom for an "owl-standing" display!

Rose Semmel—Pre-K
Stanton Learning Center
Stanton, NJ

See the corresponding book notes on page 147.

Parade

Thanksgiving and Christmas parades are right around the corner! Help your class catch the spirit of the season with *Parade* by Donald Crews (Mulberry Books). After reading the story and discussing parades, toss a parade trinket or party favor to each child; then make this book-related display. Direct each student to trace his arm and hand along the bottom edge of a sheet of bulletin board paper. Then have him color in the outline using skin-toned crayons or markers. Label each arm with the child's name; then have him glue his trinket onto the drawing of his hand. If desired, top off the scene by asking students to glue confetti to the paper. After displaying this class creation, allow each child to choose an extra party favor to take home.

Robyn Tadda and Lorie Hebert—Speech Therapy
Donaldsonville Elementary
Donaldsonville, LA

Barnyard Banter

Your youngsters will hoot and holler over this fun farmyard story and activity! After reading *Barnyard Banter* by Denise Fleming (Owlet Publications), review the different sounds the animals made. Then, to make story recall props, cut out pairs of same-size barn shapes, one of each pair from red construction paper and the other from white construction paper. Cut several flaps in each red barn. Open the flaps; then glue each red barn to a white barn. Under each flap, draw or glue a picture of a different animal mentioned in the story. Also write the animal sound from the story in the box; then close the flap. Invite pairs of children to take turns opening the flaps and making the appropriate animal sounds such as "muck, muck, muck" for the pig. Your little ones will have fun recalling the story and making the silly noises. They may also begin to recognize some of the words. Now that's something to crow about!

Patty Welsh Cox
Austin Elementary School
Abilene, TX

Order books online.
www.themailbox.com

See the corresponding book notes on page 147.

Once Upon A Story...

Cookie's Week

Cookie the cat just can't seem to stay out of trouble! Read aloud this story by Cindy Ward (Paper Star) describing Cookie's antics on each day of the week. Suggest to your group that although the text on the final pages hints that Cookie might rest on Sunday, the kitty may still be up to more trouble. Make sure students look carefully at the illustrations to catch the mischievous twinkle in Cookie's eyes. Then invite them to create new endings for the story by predicting Cookie's next move.

Next have your class help you describe their antics on each day of the week. Record text (similar to that shown) for each day on a separate large sheet of paper. Then ask students to help illustrate the pages before you bind them together. Now that's a book they'll want to read every day of the week!

Stephani Sanzo
John Paterson School
Newington, CT

On Mondays we have crafts.

There is glue everywhere!

Jesse Bear, What Will You Wear?

This popular story by Nancy White Carlstrom (Aladdin Paperbacks) gives youngsters a glimpse into Jesse Bear's day. After reading the book, create this story kit for youngsters to take home. To prepare, cover a large coffee can with Con-Tact® paper. Label the can with the title of the story and then decorate the can with teddy bear stickers. Next cut out a bear shape from felt and a variety of felt clothing shapes sized to fit the bear. Place these pieces in the can along with a copy of the book and an audio tape of the book, if desired. Send the can home so that youngsters can enjoy the story with a caregiver and use the felt clothing to dress the bear.

adapted from an idea by Caroline Hotaling
Davenport Head Start
Davenport, NY

See the corresponding book notes on page 148.

Barnyard Song

Ahh-choo! One little sneeze brings the flu to a barnyard full of animals in *Barnyard Song* by Rhonda Gowler Greene (Atheneum). Follow up a reading of this delightful tale by inviting students to participate in some classical "moo-sic"! Have your youngsters name one animal from the story and then practice making that animal's sound. Next challenge them to sing a common tune, such as "Twinkle, Twinkle, Little Star," using only the animal sound. Direct students to stop singing when you say "Ahhhh-choo!" Have them silently pretend to eat a bowl of soup and then finish singing the song. Have students name another farm animal and repeat the activity. How about that barnyard singing! Oink, oink, baa, baa, moo, moo, moo!

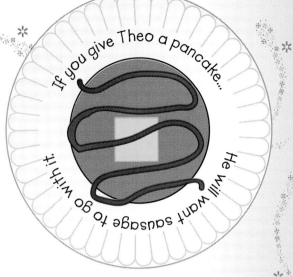

If You Give a Pig a Pancake

Your little piggies will squeal with delight over this craft and language activity! After reading *If You Give a Pig a Pancake* by Laura Joffe Numeroff (HarperCollins Juvenile Books), have each child make a pretend pancake that smells good enough to eat! In preparation, cut out a class supply of five-inch circles from tan construction paper (pancakes) and one-inch squares from yellow paper (pats of butter). Next mix a four-ounce bottle of glue with approximately two teaspoons of imitation maple flavor. Provide each child with a large white paper plate, a paper pancake, and a pretend pat of butter. Have him glue the pancake onto the plate and then glue the butter onto the pancake. Finally, have him squeeze the maple-scented glue onto his pancake to resemble syrup. When the glue is dry, program the plate with the phrase "If you give [child's name] a pancake…" and the child's response. Mmmm, something smells yummy!

Laurie Hanmer—Early Intervention Teacher, Toddlers
United Cerebral Palsy
Utica, NY

Order books online.
www.themailbox.com

See the corresponding book notes on page 148.

Once Upon A Story...

The Snowy Day

If your area is having more than its fair share of snowy precipitation (or even if you only get glimpses of blizzards on the evening news), your little ones can enjoy some chilly wintry fun. In advance, set up snow-related activities in several centers. Then stamp several footprint cutouts with white or pastel snowflake-shaped prints and sprinkle them with clear glitter. Arrange for a colleague to attach the footprints to the floor leading from your coat area to the center areas. When the snow is piling up (or you wish it would), delight your students by reading aloud Ezra Jack Keats's *The Snowy Day* (Viking Press). Discuss the tracks Peter makes in the snow; then help your children bundle up and encourage them to make real or imaginary snow tracks on your playground. When it's time to come back inside, encourage your snow buffs to hang up their coats and follow the tracks to more snowy fun!

adapted from an idea by Cindy Lawson—
   Toddlers and Preschool
Certified Family Daycare
Shell Lake, WI

The Crocodile and the Dentist

During February, National Children's Dental Health Month, a timid crocodile with an aching tooth may be just what you need to help your youngsters see the wisdom in good brushing habits. Prior to reading Taro Gomi's *The Crocodile and the Dentist* (Millbrook Press), fit a large laminated crocodile cutout with a set of egg-carton teeth. Place the crocodile on a tabletop along with two soft toothbrushes and some nonmenthol shaving cream (imitation toothpaste). Read the story aloud; then encourage pairs of students to take turns brushing your crocodile's pearly whites. Don't forget to brush!

Sheri Dressler—Pre-K
Woodland School
Carpentersville, IL

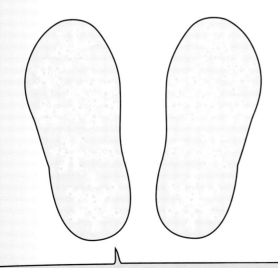

See the corresponding book notes on page 149.

Put Me in the Zoo

For decades, an overgrown yellow critter has been lobbying his way into the zoo. Share the classic *Put Me in the Zoo* by Robert Lopshire (Random House) with your little ones, and he'll lobby his way right into your color and shape practice too. In advance, obtain a yellow lunch bag for yourself and each of your students. Photocopy the face pattern (page 150) onto yellow construction paper and the tongue pattern onto pink paper for each bag. Prepare only your bag by cutting out and attaching a face pattern and a tongue; then attach clear Con-Tact® covering to the lower front and entire back panels. Ask parent volunteers to cut out ten 1 1/2-inch paper circles for each child and another ten for you. Prior to students' arrival on the day you'll read *Put Me in the Zoo*, use loops of tape to attach ten of the circles around the room at your students' eye level. When the time is right, read the story and show the plain yellow puppet to your students. Ask children to help you find the critter's spots around the room. As each one is found, have the finder identify its color and attach it to your puppet. When your puppet is covered in spots, help each of your youngsters create his own spotted yellow critter using the patterns and remaining circles. Reuse your puppet and its spots each time students ask to have the story reread.

Anita Edlund—Three-Year-Olds
Cokesbury Children's Center
Knoxville, TN

Freight Train

Take your students on a ride they won't soon forget! Read Donald Crews's *Freight Train* (Mulberry Books) aloud. For the follow-up activity, give each child a sheet of construction paper in one of the colors from the story, making sure that at least two children have a black sheet and that at least one child has each of the colors red, orange, yellow, green, blue, and purple. Reread the story. This time, as you mention a color, have each child holding that color step forward to become a part of the train. As the train in the book begins to chug along, have your children do the same. It's going to be great fun to see your train clickety-clacking through tunnels, by cities, on trestles, in darkness, and in daylight. But be sure the engineer knows just when to pull into the station, too. Whew!

Jan Brennan
Avon, CT

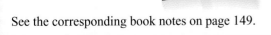

Order books online. www.themailbox.com

See the corresponding book notes on page 149.

Once Upon A Story...

In the Small, Small Pond

Introduce the topic of pond life to your youngsters with a frog's-eye peek at life in a small pond. Share *In the Small, Small Pond* by Denise Fleming (Henry Holt and Company). After a first read-through, ask students to name animals that use the pond as their home. Encourage students to name animals from the story as well as any others they might know. Record their responses on a sheet of chart paper. Next reread the story outside where students will have plenty of room to move. As you read, stop after each animal's action, and invite your students to act out the movements of the pond creatures. Your youngsters will be swimming like fish, hopping and diving like frogs, crawling and climbing like insects, and slithering like snakes!

The bunny could become a cat and run out in my yard.

Tanja

The Runaway Bunny

Every mother bunny knows that no matter where her little bunny goes and no matter what he becomes, she will find him and love him. Read to your class this comforting story written by Margaret Wise Brown about a mother's steadfast love (published by Harper Trophy). Then make this class book that is also bound to become a classic. To make each page, ask a child to think of something the bunny could become and where he could run away to. Record the child's idea; then have her illustrate the page. Laminate the pages; then bind them together. To one end of a laminated paper bunny shape, tape a length of yarn. Tie the other end of the yarn to the binding of the book or tape it inside the front cover. As a child enjoys the book, she can move the bunny to each page of the book, pretending he is running away to all of the imaginary places.

Tanja Stone
Springdale, AR

There Was an Old Lady Who Swallowed a Fly

Now *why* did that old lady swallow a fly? Nobody knows why she swallowed a fly, but everyone knows what happened after she swallowed the fly, spider, bird, cat, dog, cow, and horse. She died, of course! Share this famous poem with your class by reading aloud either the book by Simms Taback (Viking Children's Books) or the book by Pam Adams (Child's Play [International] Ltd.). Then use the patterns on pages 14 and 15 to make story props that promote reading comprehension and sequencing skills. Duplicate the patterns onto white construction paper to make a class supply. Have each child color a copy of the lady and the animals; then have him cut out the animal patterns and the lady's stomach. To assemble one child's prop, glue a seven-inch square of waxed paper or clear cellophane to the back of the lady's stomach; then glue the side and bottom edges of the page to another piece of construction paper. When the glue is dry, the child slides the animal patterns into the lady's stomach as he retells the story.

Danette Jones—Preschool
Lakewood School
Buchanan, TN

See the corresponding book notes on page 151.

The Seed Bunny

What happens when a rabbit loses a tooth? He gets a visit from the Seed Bunny! The Seed Bunny leaves carrot seeds to plant and watch grow while the little bunny waits for a new tooth to grow in. Share *The Seed Bunny* by Jennifer Selby (Harcourt Brace & Company). After sharing the story, take another look at the note that the Seed Bunny left for Sam. Then try his suggestion to plant a carrot top. Just put a carrot top on a saucer of warm water. Replenish the water when it dries up. After several weeks in a bright, warm place, the carrot top will sprout leaves!

Once Upon A Story...

The Day Jimmy's Boa Ate the Wash

Your older preschoolers will get a laugh out of the antics that take place when Mrs. Stanley's class takes a trip to the farm. Before you know it, they'll be asking you for a field trip that promises as much adventure! After reading the story by Trinka Hakes Noble (E. P. Dutton), ask the children if they think that all of the events described actually happened or if the girl telling the story has a great imagination. Look back through the pictures to help youngsters decide. Follow up the story with some of these fun ideas. Set up the laundry center described in "Setting the Stage" on page 224. Then provide a long snake cut from bulletin board paper for youngsters to color and hang on the clothesline or drying rack. For outdoor fun, transform a large refrigerator box to look like a school bus. Put the box outside with another long paper boa and clothes to hang on a clothesline or fence. Encourage students to act out the events in the story, or have them make up new adventures during free play.

Angelia Dagnan—Preschool
Royal Childcare and Learning Center
Knoxville, TN

Who Hops?

Who hops and who *doesn't?* Who flies, slithers, swims, and crawls… and who doesn't? Read this colorful book with fun repetitive text by Katie Davis (Harcourt Brace & Company), and your students will not only find out how animals move but that kids can move many ways, too! Have your students move or pretend to move in the ways suggested. Then, for another story extension, try this activity that promotes literacy. Have each child cut out a picture of an animal from a nature magazine and then glue it onto a piece of construction paper. Help the child decide how the animal moves; then write text on the page similar to the text in the book. As a class, look at the pictures and read the words. Group together the pictures of animals who move similarly. Frogs hop. Cows walk. We read!

See the corresponding book notes on page 154.

The Grouchy Ladybug

The grouchy ladybug is as grouchy as she was over 20 years ago when Eric Carle first created her. Her story (HarperCollins Publishers) is also just as good for teaching manners, time, and size as it was 20 years ago! Introduce your class to the grouchy ladybug; then talk about what might have been bugging her and caused her to be grouchy. Follow up by making this class book about bothersome things and the appropriate ways to react to them. For each child, cut a simple ladybug shape (as shown) from white construction paper and a red paper circle that is the same size as the center of the ladybug's body. Cut the circle in half; then use a brad to attach the circle halves to the ladybug. On the center of each ladybug, write as a child dictates her completion to the sentence shown. Have the child draw a picture to match her sentence and color her ladybug as desired. During a group time, share each child's ladybug. As a class, discuss the best ways to react to each bothersome thing.

adapted from an idea by Catherine McCann
St. Stephen School
Hamden, CT

The Lady With the Alligator Purse

Miss Lucy called the doctor, Miss Lucy called the nurse, and it's a good thing Miss Lucy called the lady with the alligator purse, because *she's* the one who brought the pizza! Youngsters will fall over in giggles when you share Nadine Bernard Westcott's zany version of this famous nonsense rhyme (Little, Brown, & Company). Afterward, offer to let each child, in turn, take home an "alligator purse" (green gift bag with a paper alligator glued to the front). Ask each child to return to school with something in the alligator purse that can either be enjoyed by the entire class (like cookies or party treats) or something that will make them laugh (like mom's curlers, big shoes, or one of dad's ugly ties). It's time to be silly, and it all starts with what's in the alligator purse!

It bugs me when... it rains and we can't go outside!

Book Notes

After reading each of the books mentioned below and on pages 134 and 135, send home copies of the corresponding note.

Have you seen the book

Brown Bear, Brown Bear, What Do You See?

It was written by Bill Martin, Jr. and illustrated by Eric Carle.

Let's go to the library to find more books with pictures by Eric Carle.

There are a lot!

1-2-3-4-5! Today we read

Count!

by Denise Fleming.

Let's count to ten together!

Pass the Fritters, Critters,

by Cheryl Chapman, is a polite story about table manners.

Say the magic word and I'll tell you all about it!

What a Wonderful World,

illustrated by Ashley Bryan, is a wonderful book!

Let's name some of the wonderful things in my world.

You're one of them!

Book Notes

After reading each of the books mentioned below and on pages 136 and 137, send home copies of the corresponding note.

Today we read
The Pumpkin Blanket
by Deborah Turney Zagwÿn.

Ask me how a baby blanket saved a crop of pumpkins!

Our story today was
Owl Babies
by Martin Waddell.

"Whoooo" wants to go to the library and find more books about owls?

Oom-pah-pah!
Today we read
Parade
by Donald Crews.

Let's pretend we're in a parade. Follow me as I march!

Cock-a-doodle-doo!
Today we read
Barnyard Banter
by Denise Fleming.

I'll make a sound from the story. Can you guess which animal I'm pretending to be?

Book Notes

After reading each of the books mentioned below and on pages 138 and 139, send home copies of the corresponding note.

One little kitty makes a big mess every day in **Cookie's Week** by Cindy Ward.

Ask me what fun things I like to do on each different day of the week.

©1999 The Education Center, Inc.

Today we read **Jesse Bear, What Will You Wear?** by Nancy White Carlstrom. Let's pick out some clothes for me to wear tomorrow!

©1999 The Education Center, Inc.

Moo, ahh-choo!

That's the sound a sick cow makes in **Barnyard Song** by Rhonda Gowler Greene. I'll make the sound of another sick animal. Can you guess which one I am?

©1999 The Education Center, Inc.

Oink, oink, oink! We read **If You Give a Pig a Pancake.**

Let's go to the library and find another book by Laura Joffe Numeroff.

©1999 The Education Center, Inc.

Book Notes

After reading each of the books mentioned below and on pages 140 and 141,
send home copies of the corresponding note.

Today we read
The Snowy Day
by Ezra Jack Keats.

Let's talk about
the things we
like to do
in the snow.

©2000 The Education Center, Inc.

Today we read
**The Crocodile
and the Dentist**
by Taro Gomi.

The crocodile promises
to do something. Ask
me what it is. Then let's
go brush our teeth.

©2000 The Education Center, Inc.

Clickety-clack,
Clickety-clack,
Clickety-clack!
Woo-wooooooooooo!

We read
Freight Train
by Donald Crews.

Let's make a train and chug
around in our house.

©2000 The Education Center, Inc.

We read
Put Me in the Zoo
today.

I can pretend to be an
animal with spots. Ask
me to name five
different colors
my spots could be.

©2000 The Education Center, Inc.

Patterns

Use with *Put Me in the Zoo* on page 141.

face

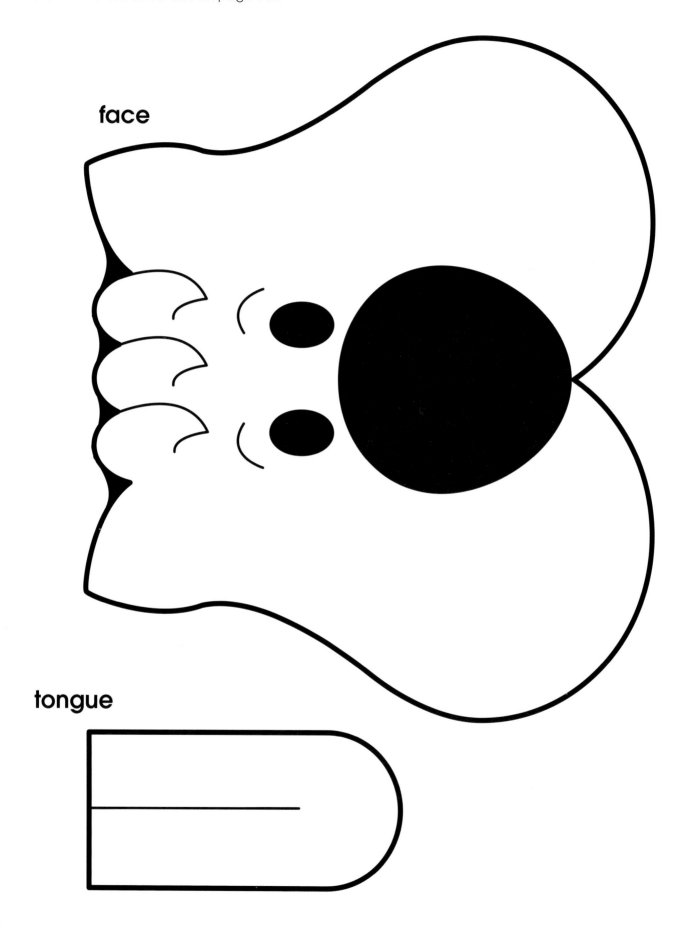

tongue

Book Notes

After reading each of the books mentioned below and on pages 142 and 143, send home copies of the corresponding note.

Today we acted out
the story
In the Small, Small Pond
by Denise Fleming.

Ask me to
wiggle like a tadpole
waddle like a goose
quiver like a dragonfly
doze like a turtle
dip like a duck

Everywhere the little
bunny goes in
The Runaway Bunny
by Margaret Wise Brown,
the bunny's mother finds him!

Let's play hide-and-seek.
I'll hide. Can you find me?

Today we heard a silly
story called
There Was an Old Lady Who Swallowed a Fly.

She also swallowed a spider,
bird, cat, dog, cow,
and horse!

Let's think of lots of
other animals she
could swallow.

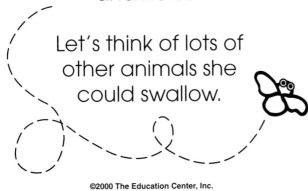

Ask me what happens
when Sam the bunny
loses his tooth.
The answer is in
The Seed Bunny
by Jennifer Selby.

What will
happen when
I get older and
start to lose my
baby teeth?

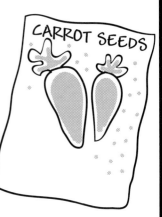

CARROT SEEDS

Pattern

Use with *There Was an Old Lady Who Swallowed a Fly* on page 143.

Patterns

Use with *There Was an Old Lady Who Swallowed a Fly* on page 143.

fly

spider

dog

cow

cat

horse

bird

Book Notes

After reading each of the books mentioned below and on pages 144 and 145, send home copies of the corresponding note.

The Day Jimmy's Boa Ate the Wash

by Trinka Hakes Noble

is a silly story about a field trip!

Let's make up a silly story about going somewhere.

Once upon a time we went to…

We did a lot of moving today after we read **WHO HOPS?** by Katie Davis.

Ask me to name animals who

We read
The Grouchy Ladybug
by Eric Carle.

The ladybug was grouchy and wanted to fight. Let's talk about things I can do to make myself feel better when I get grouchy.

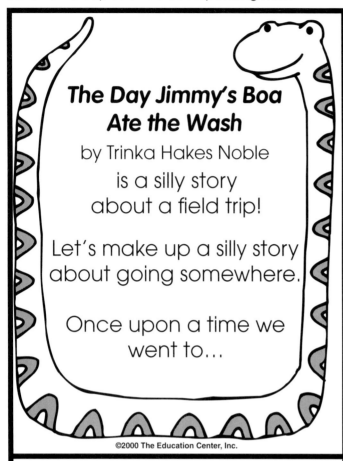

Guess what! We read a story called

The Lady With the Alligator Purse
by Nadine Bernard Westcott.

The doctor came, the nurse came, and then the lady with the purse came. Do you know what she brought? Ask me!

NURSERY RHYME UNITS

Wee Willie Winkie

Wee Willie Winkie is running around again, but this time he's not checking to see if the children are in bed. He's peeking in on their counting, sorting, and problem-solving skills. Just take a look at these ideas and you'll see!

ideas contributed by Lucia Kemp Henry

**Wee Willie Winkie runs through the town,
Upstairs and downstairs in his nightgown,
Rapping at the window, crying through the lock,
"Are the children all in bed?
For now it's eight o'clock."**

Flannelboard Bed Check

Prepare flannelboard pieces to introduce your class to Wee Willie and his unusual bedtime routine. In advance, duplicate the gameboard (page 158) and the game cards (page 159) onto heavy paper. Color the pieces; then cut them out. Cut along the dotted lines on the bed; then prepare all of the pieces for use on a flannelboard. Recite the rhyme; then use the pieces with the following extension activities during several of your group times to improve youngsters' problem-solving, sorting, and counting skills.

- Hide the characters in your hand; then put one to three characters in the bed. Recite the rhyme again before asking, "Are the children all in bed? Which are not?"

- As a variation, hide the characters in your hand; then put zero to three characters in the bed. Ask, "How many are in bed? How many are not?"

- Give each of six children in the group a character. Then give directions such as, "Wee Willie says, 'Put the children with blue pajamas in the bed,'" "Wee Willie says, 'Put three children in the bed,'" or "Wee Willie says, 'Put some children in the bed, but keep four awake.'"

Through the Town

Send Wee Willie running through the town and into your children's homes with this take-home kit that reinforces your group-time flannelboard activities. To make one for a child to take home, duplicate pages 158 and 159. Have a child color the pages. Cut out the pieces, cutting a slit along the dotted line of the gameboard. Glue the edges of the gameboard to a piece of construction paper. Slide the game pieces and parent note inside the gameboard; then put the items in a resealable plastic bag.

A Bedtime Song

Getting ready for bed may not always be easy for your little ones. Ask children to share some of the things they do to get ready for bedtime. Then include their suggestions in this song, acting out the motions as you sing. Try substituting the phrase *get ready for bed* with tasks such as *wash your face; read a story; brush your teeth; change your clothes; say, "good night"; close your eyes;* and *go to sleep.*

Get Ready for Bed

(sung to the tune of "London Bridge")

Can you please [get ready for bed, ready for bed, ready for bed]?
Can you please [get ready for bed]? Yes, we can!

The Ins and Outs of Bedtime

Here's a lively activity to help youngsters focus on classifying. Use masking tape to outline a large rectangle on the floor to represent a bed. Seat the class in a circle around the bed. Play some bedtime or lullaby music. Then recite the rhyme below to designate children who should get in bed (lie down in the rectangle). Suggest groupings such as all boys, all girls, children with blue shirts, and more.

Wee Willie Winkie said,
"Children with [blond hair] get in bed!"

Wee Willie Recommends

Piggy Washes Up
Written & Illustrated by Carol Thompson
Published by Candlewick Press

Time for Bed
Written by Mem Fox
Illustrated by Jane Dyer
Published by Harcourt Brace & Co.

Ten, Nine, Eight
Written & Illustrated by Molly Garrett Bang
Published by Mulberry Books

Bedtime Pretending

Reinforce youngsters' bedtime routines with a bit of dramatic play. To get your housekeeping center ready for bedtime, stock the area with items such as a child-sized cot and quilt, a small plastic washtub and washcloth, bathrobes, stuffed animals, a tape player with a tape of lullabies, a bedside table, an alarm clock, and plenty of sleepy-time stories (see the list on this page). Encourage children to reenact their bedtime routines while singing the previous song. One child will want to be Wee Willie Winkie to make sure everyone is in bed by eight o'clock!

Order books online.
www.themailbox.com

157

Gameboard

Use with "Flannelboard Bed Check" and "Through the Town" on page 156.

Wee Willie Winkie runs through the town,
Upstairs and downstairs in his nightgown,
Rapping at the window, crying through the lock,
"Are the children all in bed?
For now it's eight o'clock."

Game Cards

Use with "Flannelboard Bed Check" and
"Through the Town" on page 156.

Parent Note

Use with "Through the Town" on page 156.

Dear Parent,

Ask your child to help you recite the nursery rhyme on the gameboard. Then use the gameboard and cards to reinforce your child's problem-solving, sorting, and counting skills. Try these activities:

- Ask your child to put a number of animals in the bed. How many are left?
- Put a number of animals in the bed. Can your child remember who's not in the bed?
- Help your child sort the animals by the colors of their pajamas.
- Encourage your child to tell stories with the animals. For example, "The monkey and the cat went to bed. Then one of them had a dream and jumped out of bed! Now there's only one left in the bed."

Mary had a little lamb;
Its fleece was white as snow.
And everywhere that Mary went
The lamb was sure to go.

It followed her to school one day.
That was against the rule.
It made the children laugh and play
To see a lamb at school.

Mary Had a Little Lamb

Make your little ones laugh and play when you try these lamb-themed lessons at school!

ideas contributed by Lucia Kemp Henry

Mary Had a Little Lamb and a Little Piggy and...

Begin your group time by asking youngsters to join you in singing "Mary Had a Little Lamb." Ask the children to offer reasons why the lamb might have followed Mary to school. Also ask why they think it was against the rule to have a lamb at school. Next suggest to the group that the lamb wasn't the only animal interested in learning! Then modify the traditional song to include the names of other animals.

Mary had a little lamb,
Little lamb, little lamb.
Mary had a little lamb and a
[piggy], too!

The [piggy] followed Mary's lamb,
Mary's lamb, Mary's lamb.
The [piggy] followed Mary's lamb
All the way to school!

Mary's Famous Poem

School children began reciting the poem "Mary Had a Little Lamb" way back in 1830 when it was written by Sarah Hale. It was first published in a book of poems for children and then put to music in 1834. Explain to your students that this means that their parents, grandparents, great-grandparents, and even great-great-grandparents knew and sang the song! The famous song is featured in these lamb tales. Be sure to use them with your unit!

Mary Had a Little Lamb
Written by Sarah Josepha Hale
Photo-illustrated by Bruce McMillan
Published by Scholastic Inc.

This book places the traditional verses in a contemporary setting with photographs that wonderfully illustrate the different ways that Mary cares for her lamb. After looking at the pictures of Mary brushing, feeding, and playing with her lamb, ask the animal owners in your group to tell how they care for their pets at home.

Mary Had a Little Lamb
Written by Sarah Josepha Hale
Illustrated by Tomie dePaola
(Out of print. Check your library.)

Mr. dePaola's book also emphasizes the lesson of kindness to animals. However, his illustrations depict life in days of long ago. Have your little ones look carefully at the pictures to find ways (such as the clothes, school, houses) that life is different today.

Mary Had a Little Lamb
As told and illustrated by Iza Trapani
Published by Whispering Coyote Press

What would happen if the lamb *didn't* follow Mary everywhere she went? Find out about the lamb's adventures when you read aloud Iza Trapani's version of the story. Then ask your little ones to make up new adventures for the lamb, dictating and illustrating their stories if desired.

A Lamb for "Ewe"

Mary had a little lamb, and now Johnny, Sally, and Kaitlyn can have one, too! Duplicate the patterns (page 162) onto white construction paper for each child. To make one lamb puppet, a child cuts out the patterns. Next he glues the patterns to a white paper bag as shown so that the head is on the flap of the bag and the poem is on the back. Finally, he colors the nose pink and then glues cotton balls onto his lamb. Have each child help his puppet sing the traditional song. Then use the puppets with the activity below.

Follow the Leader Lamb

None of your little lambs will be unruly when they play this follow-the-leader game. Ask youngsters to line up, one behind the other, with their lamb puppets (see "A Lamb for 'Ewe' "). In turn, ask each child to move to the front of the line and be the leader lamb. Direct the leader to move around the room or outdoor area as his classmates follow. As the group moves, modify the traditional song substituting the leader's name for Mary's name. Micah had some little lambs, little lambs, little lambs!

What's Against the Rule?

If a lamb followed one of your children to school, what would it learn about good behavior? To reinforce the rules of your classroom, sing this song (right) to the traditional tune. Include phrases such as *listen close, walk in line, watch and learn, play with friends, share the toys,* and more as you sing the second verse.

[Teacher's name] had some little lambs,
Little lambs, little lambs.
[Teacher's name] had some little lambs,
That followed her to school.

The lambs learned how to [say kind words],
[Say kind words], [say kind words].
The lambs learned how to [say kind words]
When they came to school.

Order books online. www.themailbox.com

Lamb Patterns

Use with "A Lamb for 'Ewe'" on page 161.

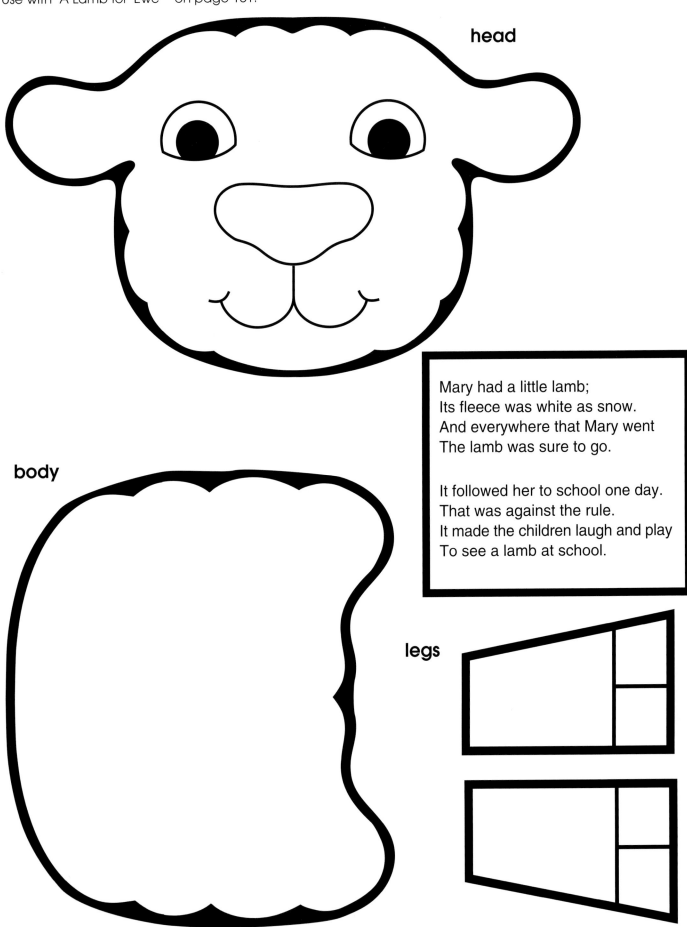

head

body

Mary had a little lamb;
Its fleece was white as snow.
And everywhere that Mary went
The lamb was sure to go.

It followed her to school one day.
That was against the rule.
It made the children laugh and play
To see a lamb at school.

legs

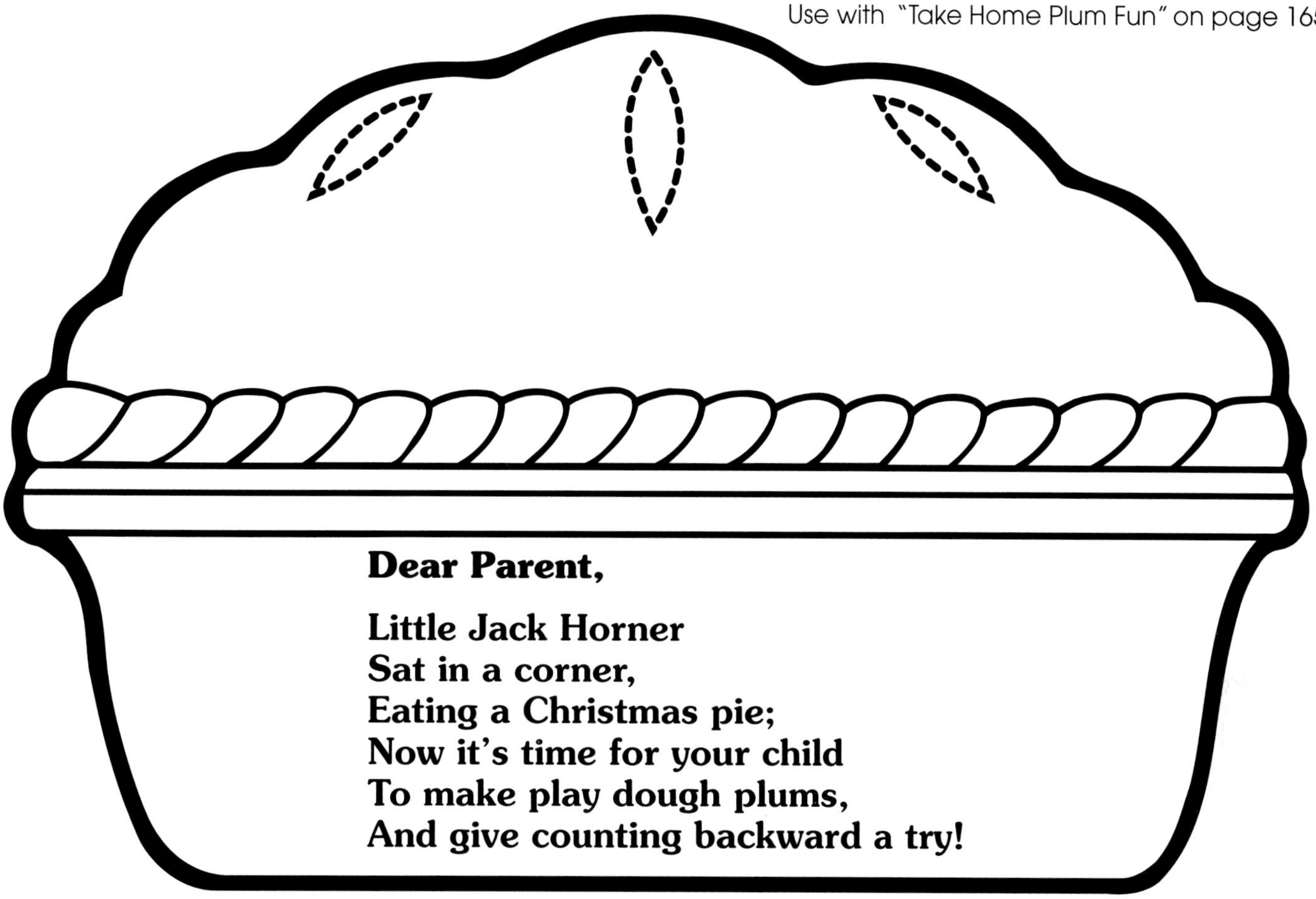

Dear Parent,

Little Jack Horner
Sat in a corner,
Eating a Christmas pie;
Now it's time for your child
To make play dough plums,
And give counting backward a try!

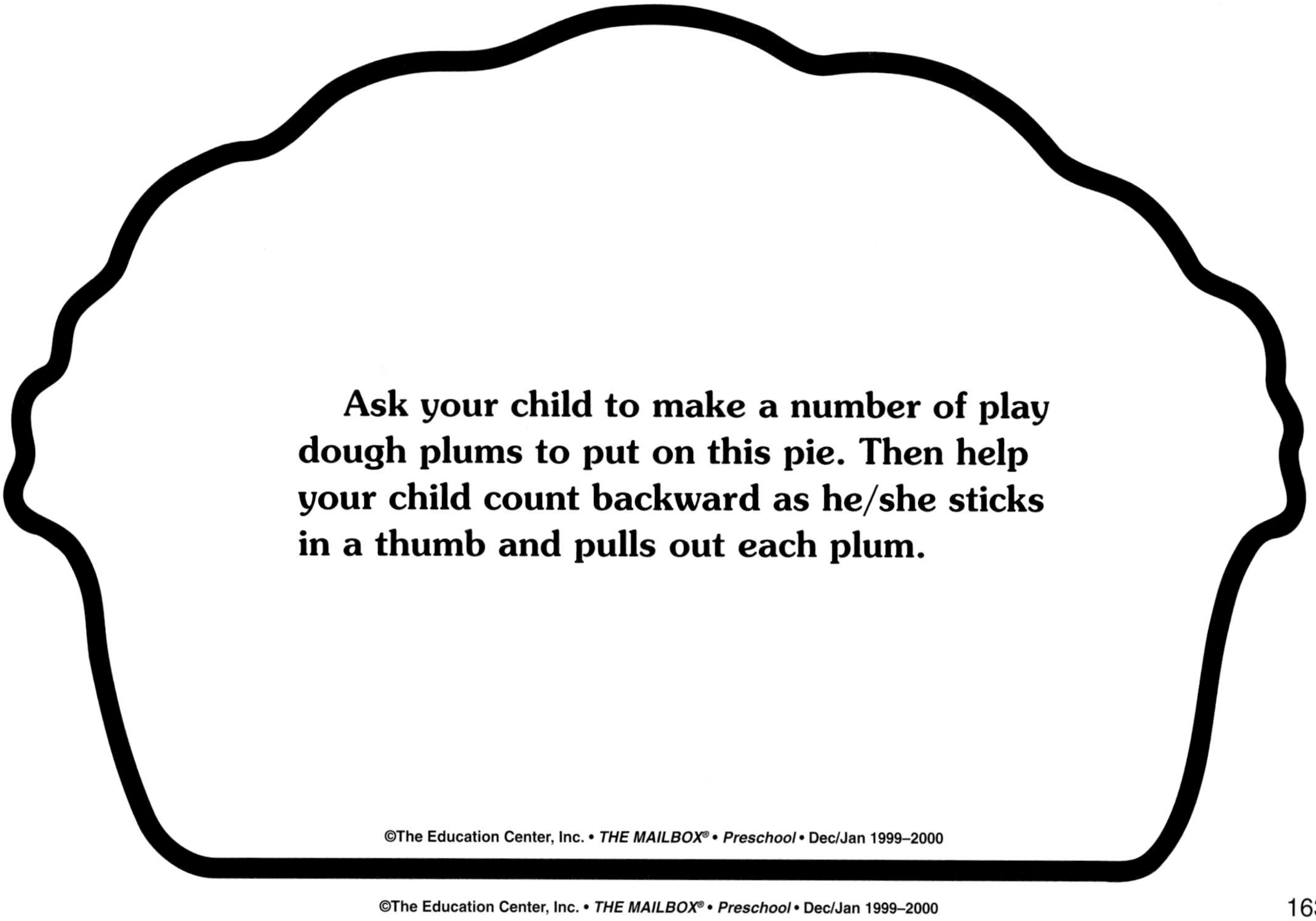

Ask your child to make a number of play dough plums to put on this pie. Then help your child count backward as he/she sticks in a thumb and pulls out each plum.

©The Education Center, Inc. • *THE MAILBOX®* • *Preschool* • Dec/Jan 1999–2000

Little Jack Horner

Serve up these easy-as-pie counting, language, and tactile activities to provide each child with a heaping helping of sweet learning success!

by Lucia Kemp Henry

Little Jack Horner
Sat in a corner,
Eating a Christmas pie;
He put in his thumb
And pulled out a plum
And said, "What a good boy am I!"

A Plumb Good Rhyme

In advance, cut a number of plum shapes from purple felt. During a group time, introduce the rhyme. Then ask some questions. Why was Jack in the corner? What might grown-ups say if you put your thumb in a pie? Next ask a volunteer to come to the board and to close her eyes. Place a number of the plums on the board. Have the volunteer open her eyes, count the plums she finds, and then say, "What a good girl am I!" After each child's turn, have the group modify the rhyme (see below) to include the child's name and the number of plums she counts.

> Little [child's name] Horner
> Sat in the corner,
> Eating a Christmas pie;
> [He/She] put in [his/her] thumb
> And pulled out [number] plums,
> And said, "What a good [boy/girl] am I!"

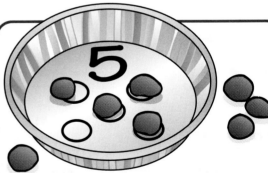

Play Dough Plums

Your little ones are sure to give this counting center the thumbs-up! To prepare the center, use a permanent marker to label each of ten aluminum pie pans with a different numeral and matching dot set. Next use your favorite recipe to make a batch of purple play dough. Place the pans and the play dough in a center. A child visiting the area makes a number of small play dough balls (plums) and then fills each pan with the corresponding pieces of fruit.

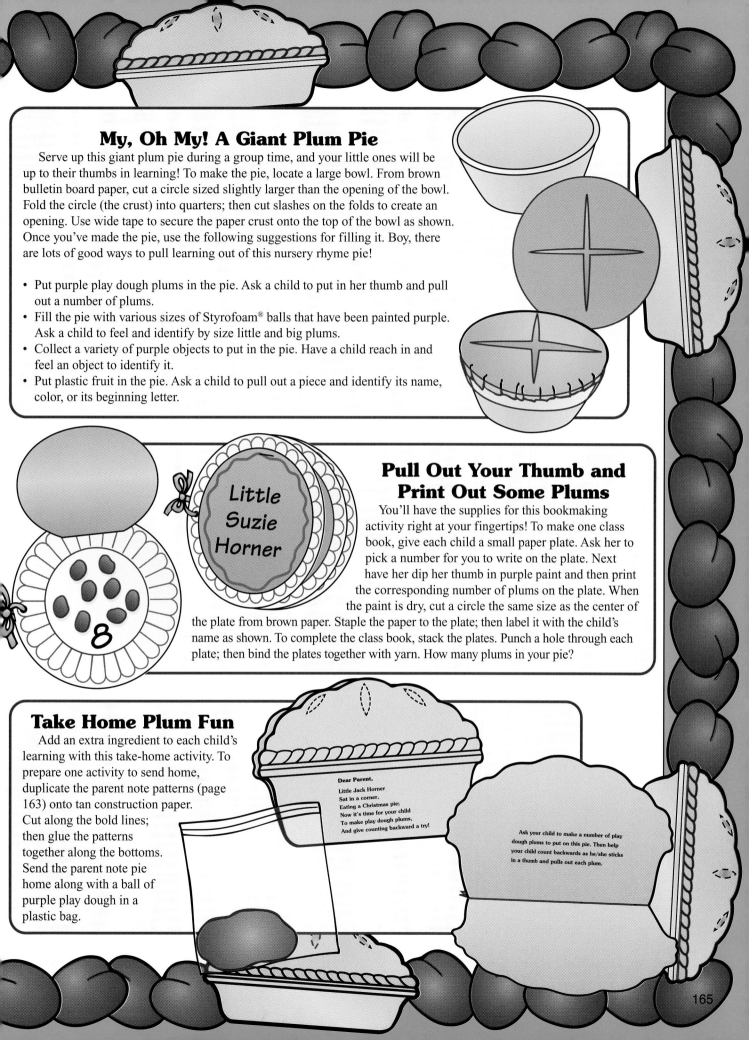

My, Oh My! A Giant Plum Pie

Serve up this giant plum pie during a group time, and your little ones will be up to their thumbs in learning! To make the pie, locate a large bowl. From brown bulletin board paper, cut a circle sized slightly larger than the opening of the bowl. Fold the circle (the crust) into quarters; then cut slashes on the folds to create an opening. Use wide tape to secure the paper crust onto the top of the bowl as shown. Once you've made the pie, use the following suggestions for filling it. Boy, there are lots of good ways to pull learning out of this nursery rhyme pie!

- Put purple play dough plums in the pie. Ask a child to put in her thumb and pull out a number of plums.
- Fill the pie with various sizes of Styrofoam® balls that have been painted purple. Ask a child to feel and identify by size little and big plums.
- Collect a variety of purple objects to put in the pie. Have a child reach in and feel an object to identify it.
- Put plastic fruit in the pie. Ask a child to pull out a piece and identify its name, color, or its beginning letter.

Little
Suzie
Horner

8

Pull Out Your Thumb and Print Out Some Plums

You'll have the supplies for this bookmaking activity right at your fingertips! To make one class book, give each child a small paper plate. Ask her to pick a number for you to write on the plate. Next have her dip her thumb in purple paint and then print the corresponding number of plums on the plate. When the paint is dry, cut a circle the same size as the center of the plate from brown paper. Staple the paper to the plate; then label it with the child's name as shown. To complete the class book, stack the plates. Punch a hole through each plate; then bind the plates together with yarn. How many plums in your pie?

Take Home Plum Fun

Add an extra ingredient to each child's learning with this take-home activity. To prepare one activity to send home, duplicate the parent note patterns (page 163) onto tan construction paper. Cut along the bold lines; then glue the patterns together along the bottoms. Send the parent note pie home along with a ball of purple play dough in a plastic bag.

Dear Parent,
Little Jack Horner
Sat in a corner,
Eating a Christmas pie;
Now it's time for your child
To make play dough plums,
And give counting backward a try!

Ask your child to make a number of play dough plums to put on this pie. Then help your child count backwards as he/she sticks in a thumb and pulls out each plum.

The Queen of Hearts

Invite your youngsters to use their problem-solving skills to help the
Queen of Hearts find the tarts stolen by that naughty Knave!

ideas contributed by Lucia Kemp Henry

A Royal Group of Sleuths

Encourage your sweet little sleuths to join the search for the
missing tarts with this flannelboard activity. In advance, cut out
a number of felt hearts to represent tarts. Hide the tarts around
your classroom. During a group time, recite the rhyme. Ask
youngsters to tell you what they think a *knave* is; then explain that
a knave is a dishonest, tricky person. Next, read the extension of
the rhyme (below). Then ask little ones to try to find the hidden
tarts in your classroom and place them on the flannelboard. (Give
clues as necessary.) When all the tarts have been located, grant each
of your youngsters the title "Royal Detective"—by proclamation of
the Queen of Hearts, of course!

> That Knave of Hearts,
> He hid those tarts,
> So they could not be seen;
> Please find those tarts
> That look like hearts,
> And give them to the Queen.

The Queen of Hearts,
She made some tarts,
All on a summer's day;
The Knave of Hearts,
He stole those tarts
And took them clean away!

Which Heart Is Missing?

For further flannelboard fun using the felt tarts, prepare
this visual memory game that your youngsters will heartily
enjoy! Use a permanent marker to label the tarts with different
letters or numbers. Ask your young detectives to close their
eyes as a student volunteer—playing the part of the naughty
Knave—removes one heart from the flannelboard. Then have
students open their eyes and guess which tart is
missing.

Increase the challenge of this activity by adding
more tarts to the lineup.

Who Has the Heart?

The one who holds the Queen's heart is a secret in this game that's sure to become the craze of your classroom castle! Before playing, personalize a white paper bag for each child. Provide crayons, valentine stickers, die cut hearts, and glue, and encourage little ones to decorate their bags as they wish. Then gather youngsters in a circle, stand in the center, and have them hold their decorated bags in front of them. Show the children one of the heart-shaped tarts from "A Royal Group of Sleuths"; then put the tart between both hands to conceal it. Walk around the circle, stopping in front of each child to place your hands inside her bag. Secretly place the heart tart in one child's bag; then continue around the circle until you have reached into each child's bag once. Return to the center of the circle and say, "The Queen has asked you to decide. In whose bag does her little heart hide?" Have volunteers take turns guessing whose bag contains the heart tart. After the holder of the heart is correctly named, play another round. If desired, set the decorated bags aside for use with "Puzzling It Out Together."

The Mystery of the Hidden Heart

More mystery-solving sessions are in store with this activity that focuses on listening and following directions. To prepare, fill a heart-shaped box with a class supply of candy conversation hearts. Tie a ribbon around the box to secure the lid and then hide the box somewhere in your classroom. Tell students that you want them to use their detective skills to find a mystery box that's hidden in the room. Give clues and invite a pair of children to follow your directions to move them into the vicinity of the box. Give progressively more specific clues, such as "The box is somewhere in the front of the room. The box is near the block area. The box is behind a shelf." Once the detective pair has located the hidden heart-shaped box, ask them to shake it and have your class guess what might be inside. Open the box to check their guesses; then pass out a treat to each child. Hold another hunt on a subsequent day with a different treat in the box, such as valentine M&M's® candies or heart-shaped chewable candies.

Puzzling It Out Together

The Queen of Hearts has proclaimed that each of her preschool sleuths is ready to work with a parent in puzzling out the problems posed by this take-home activity! For each child, duplicate the parent note and heart puzzles on page 168 onto pink construction paper. Cut out the note and puzzles on the bold and dotted lines. Tuck the note and puzzle pieces into the paper bag the child decorated for "Who Has the Heart?" or into a zippered plastic bag. Send the materials home so that parent and child can turn time together into a royal learning experience!

Dear Parent,
    Use these heart-shaped puzzles, inspired by the nursery rhyme "The Queen of Hearts," to build your child's problem-solving skills. Tell your child that it looks as though the Knave of Hearts broke the tarts in his attempt to steal them! Lay all the puzzle pieces out on a table and have your child assemble them. Next play the part of the Knave, "stealing" the pieces and hiding them around the room. Have your child locate all the pieces (with or without clues from you) and then assemble the puzzles.

The Queen of Hearts,
She made some tarts,
All on a summer's day;
The Knave of Hearts,
He stole those tarts,
And took them clean away!

Parent Note and Puzzles

Use with "Puzzling It Out Together" on page 167.

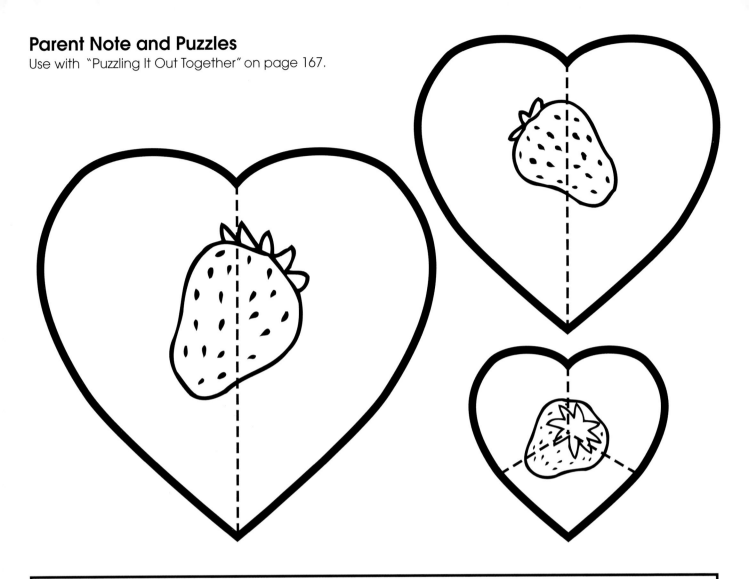

Dear Parent,

Use these heart-shaped puzzles, inspired by the nursery rhyme "The Queen of Hearts," to build your child's problem-solving skills. Tell your child that it looks as though the Knave of Hearts broke the tarts in his attempt to steal them! Lay all the puzzle pieces out on a table and have your child assemble them. Next play the part of the Knave, "stealing" the pieces and hiding them around the room. Have your child locate all the pieces (with or without clues from you) and then assemble the puzzles.

The Queen of Hearts,
She made some tarts,
All on a summer's day;
The Knave of Hearts,
He stole those tarts
And took them clean away!

Little Bo-Peep

Invite youngsters to join Bo-Peep in her search for some wandering sheep and they'll find some math, language, and motor skill fun along the way!

ideas contributed by Ada Goren and Lucia Kemp Henry

**Little Bo-Peep has lost her sheep,
And can't tell where to find them.
Leave them alone, and they'll come home,
Wagging their tails behind them.**

Finding Bo-Peep's Sheep

Create flannelboard pieces (centerfold) to involve your students in a search for Bo-Peep's sheep. Duplicate the sheep on page 171. Cut out the pieces and prepare them for flannelboard use. Before students arrive, hide the five flannelboard sheep around your classroom. During a group time, recite the traditional rhyme. Then ask for student volunteers to locate the missing sheep. As students search, give them some clues involving positional words and phrases, such as "Look *under* that chair," or "Look *on top of* the bookcase." Add each found sheep to the flannelboard. Then recite the rhyme below to congratulate your students on their shepherding skills. Leave the flannelboard pieces available for youngsters to use at free-choice time. This is one game of Hide-and-Seek they'll want to play again and again!

Little Bo-Peep has all her sheep;
They're back home safe and sound!
They were hiding, it's true, but thanks to you,
All of them now are found!

Where Can the Little Sheep Be?

To further emphasize positional words, try this scaled-down search for sheep on the move. Ask five youngsters at a time to stand in front of the group. Give each child one of the flannelboard sheep (from the centerfold). As you recite the rhyme below, have the five students pose their sheep as indicated. Then repeat the rhyme as another five children take their turns with these shifting sheep!

Little sheep, little sheep, where can you be?
I am **on** your hand, just look and see.   *Set sheep on back of hand.*
Little sheep, little sheep, where can you be?
I am **in** your hand, just look and see.   *Put sheep in cupped hand.*
Little sheep, little sheep, where can you be?
I am **behind** your hand, just look and see.   *Hide sheep behind hand.*
Little sheep, little sheep, where can you be?
I am **next to** your hand, just look and see.   *Hold sheep next to hand.*
Little sheep, little sheep, where can you be?
I am **in front of** your hand, just look and see.   *Place sheep in front of hand.*
Little sheep, little sheep, where can you be?
I am **under** your hand, just look and see.   *Hide sheep under cupped hand.*

Wagging Their Tails Behind Them...

Little ones will love making these crafty sheep whose tails really wag! To make one, fingerpaint swirly designs with white tempera paint on a square of waxed paper. Next, press a puffy shape cut from black construction paper (about six inches in diameter) onto the paint; then lift it up and allow the print to dry. Glue small wiggle eyes and some cotton-ball wool onto a precut black construction paper circle. Cut two ears from black paper scraps and glue them in place. When the glue is dry, add a chalk smile; then glue the sheep's finished face onto the front side of the body. Cut two 2-inch pieces of thick black pipe cleaner; then tape these to the back of the sheep's body to make legs. To make a wagging tail, bend and twist one end of a white pipe cleaner half to make a small loop. Tuck a cotton ball into the loop; then staple the pipe cleaner to the back side of the sheep, positioning the staple just in front of the loop, as shown. Just wiggle the straight end of the pipe cleaner to make the sheep's tail wag!

Five in a Flock

Add a mathematical twist to a fun dramatization of the traditional rhyme. To prepare, make a copy of the sheep patterns on page 171. Cut out the patterns, laminate them, and punch a hole in the top of each one. Thread a length of yarn through each hole to create a necklace. Create a crook for Bo-Peep by twisting together two chenille stems as shown. Designate one child to be Little Bo-Peep and have five other youngsters wear the sheep necklaces and play the part of her wandering flock.

Have Bo-Peep turn her back as the five sheep hide somewhere in your classroom. Then invite Little Bo-Peep to turn around. Have the rest of the class help you recite the rhyme. At the rhyme's end, have the five sheep emerge from their hiding places and wag their tails as they happily return to Bo-Peep. Encourage Bo-Peep to be sure that all of her flock have come "baa-ck" by lining the sheep up in front of the group in numerical order. Then begin again by naming a new Bo-Peep and five new sheep. Continue until every child has had a turn to play a part.

Send the Flock Home

Those silly sheep—they just can't stay put! They're lost again as part of the take-home activity on page 171. To prepare it, mask the pattern names and page number directions on page 171; then duplicate the page for each child to take home. Your young shepherds will be rounding up the flock again—this time with a little help from Mom and Dad!

Little Bo-Peep has lost her sheep,
And can't tell where to find them.
Leave them alone, and they'll come home,
Wagging their tails behind them.

Dear Parent,

Little Bo-Peep has lost her sheep, but your child is sure to find them! First have your child cut out the five sheep below. Then have your child close his or her eyes as you hide the five sheep somewhere in the room. Recite the traditional nursery rhyme together; then have your child hunt for the sheep. Have your child count to determine when he or she has found all five. Then have him or her place the five sheep in numerical order. Little Bo-Peep will be *so* grateful for your help!

Sheep Patterns
Use with "Finding Bo-Peep's Sheep" on page 169 and "Five in a Flock" and "Send the Flock Home" on page 170.

Jack and Jill

Jack and Jill went up the hill
To fetch a pail of water;
Jack fell down and broke his crown,
And Jill came tumbling after.

Fetch your youngsters and invite them to meet Jack and Jill, a dependable duo who only want to perform a simple chore: to put some water in their pail!

ideas contributed by Lucia Kemp Henry

The Flannelboard Adventure of Jack and Jill

What was it that set Jack and Jill out on their adventure? The independent pair simply set out to fetch some water! Introduce the story of Jack and Jill's water-fetching fiasco and get your youngsters thinking about cause and effect. Afterward, ask youngsters some questions to get them thinking about this simple story.

—Where did Jack and Jill go?
—What did they want to get? Why do you think they needed water?
—What happened to Jack and Jill? What do you think made them fall down?
—What do you think happened to the water when they fell?
—What would you do differently if you were Jack or Jill?

Will It Hold Water?

Jack and Jill didn't get much (if any) water in their pail. Will your little ones be able to fetch some water with these pails made from Styrofoam® cups? Test them and see! To prepare, make four small pails from Styrofoam cups by securing a pipe cleaner handle to each one as shown. Then cut a dime-sized hole in the bottom of one cup, poke three holes around the base of a second cup, and poke one hole about a half inch from the top of a third cup. Leave the fourth cup as is.

Gather a small group of students around your water table; then pass around the pail with the hole cut in the bottom for each child to inspect carefully. Ask if they believe this pail will do a good job of holding water. Have a volunteer scoop up some water and hold the pail where the group can observe what happens. Continue the predicting and testing with the other three pails until your little ones have discovered which pails hold water. Then extend this activity by placing bowls, colanders, sieves, slotted and solid serving spoons, berry baskets, and plastic cups in the water table. Invite youngsters to study the containers, make water-holding predictions, and then test the containers. It'll be a "hole" lot of fun!

More or Less?

Just how much water was in that pail, anyway? Place a variety of containers in your water table, including a few sand pails, a few containers that hold less than the pails, and a few containers that hold more. If possible, include a container or two that hold an equal amount to the pails. Visit the table during center time to get little ones thinking and talking about *more* and *less* as they "pour" over this question of volume!

Emilie and Jacob went to the art area to fetch a pail of crayons.

Fill 'er Up!

Which container is best in a water-fetching quest? Invite your youngsters to find out! Move your water table outdoors (since spills and splashes are bound to happen); then place a big bucket several feet away from the table. Tell a small group of children that you need them to fetch some water from the water table to fill the bucket. Give each child a tablespoon and set everyone to work. After a few minutes, stop and ask if the tablespoons are working well to fill the bucket. Show your students an assortment of ladles, plastic cups, and sand pails; then challenge them to discover which container will help them fill the bucket in the fewest trips. Do they have any ideas for filling the bucket even *faster*? Invite them to try out their ideas!

What Can We Put in a Pail?

Jack and Jill wanted water in their pail, but your youngsters probably have more interesting ideas for things to fetch! Make this class book to chronicle their ideas for packing a pail and to help with early reading skills, too! To begin, take along a child's sand pail as you walk around your classroom. Ask students to help you look for things that will fit inside the pail. Test some of their suggestions. Then gather in your group area and pair up your students. Provide a sand pail for each pair. Ask the pairs to act the parts of Jack and Jill as they fill the pail with the object(s) of their choice and then return to the circle. Snap a photo of each pair as they share what they've fetched. Then recite a line similar to the traditional rhyme, such as "Scott and Kevin went to the art center to fetch a pail of crayons." Then have one child from each pair return the items to the appropriate location.

When the photos are developed, mount each one on a separate sheet of construction paper and add a line of text as shown. Bind the pages together into a class book. Your preschoolers will enjoy success as they read classmates' names and the names of familiar centers!

To Fetch a Pail of... Lemonade?

Why did Jack and Jill fetch a pail of *water*? Perhaps they wanted something to drink! Invite each of your little ones to fetch a pail of her favorite beverage with this activity that combines coordination skills and math. In advance make a "pail" for each child by attaching a pipe cleaner handle to a Styrofoam® cup as shown. Label each cup with a different child's name. Next, set out a variety of beverages on a table, making sure that each drink is in an easy-to-handle container with a pouring spout. Label an individual index card for each drink on the table. Then line up the cards across a table nearby. Ask each child to fetch her drink of choice by pouring a serving into her personalized pail. Then place her pail on the table nearby in a column above the corresponding index card. When every child has fetched her beverage and the graph is complete, help little ones analyze the results. Which drink is the class favorite? Then pass out the pails and invite youngsters to drink up!

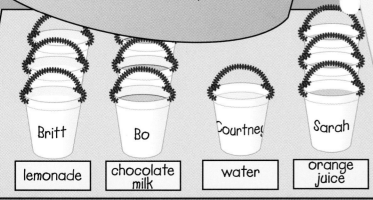

Britt — lemonade
Bo — chocolate milk
Courtney — water
Sarah — orange juice

173

It's Circle Time!

Living Christmas Trees

Need a little Christmas? Right this very minute? Bring on the holiday spirit with this "live-tree" trimming idea! In advance, gather various types of old garland. Then prepare a star headband. Also cut out a large supply of tagboard ornament shapes. Invite your little ones to use craft supplies to decorate the ornaments. Then punch a hole in the top of each ornament and attach a yarn loop for hanging. To do this activity, have a child don the star headband and pretend to be a Christmas tree. Then invite the remaining students to use the decorations to trim this little living tree. When the child is fully decorated, take a photo of the results; then remove the decorations. Repeat this process until each child has had a chance to be a Christmas tree.

Cindy Bormann—Three- to Six-Year-Olds
Small World Preschool
West Bend, IA

Counting on Christmas Trees

Get your older preschoolers on a counting roll with this small-group tree-decorating activity. To prepare, cut out several felt Christmas trees (pattern on page 184). Place each tree on a mat or tray. Next to each mat, position a small container of approximately 25 colorful craft items, such as sequins, beads, and buttons. To do this activity, invite a child to roll a die; then have each child in the group add that many craft items to her tree. Continue around the circle in the same manner until each child has had a chance to roll the die. After children admire one another's work, have them return the decorating items to the containers to prepare the activity for the next group of tree decorators.

Leora Olson—Three-, Four-, and Five-Year-Olds
Crayon Castle Preschool
Alton, IA

If This Is Your Name

Music and movement combine in this activity to reinforce name recognition. In advance, make name cards by writing each child's name on a theme-related cutout. As you sing the song below, show a child's name, encouraging that child to follow the directions in the song. As you repeat the song, substitute different action words, such as *stomp your feet, shout hooray,* and *take a bow.*

(sung to the tune of "If You're Happy and You Know It")

If this is your name, please stand up.
If this is your name, please stand up.
If this is your name, stand up and [wave hello].
If this is your name, please stand up.

Shelley Hoster—Pre-K, Jack and Jill Early Learning Center
Norcross, GA

Bunnies, Bears, Birds, and Bats

Scurry, scurry, little critters—winter's on the way! Your children will love their roles in this little rhyme that reinforces movement, colors, and simple science facts. In advance, collect large sheets of construction paper in white, black, blue, and gray. Arrange the sheets in random fashion on the floor of an open area. Divide your children into four groups. Assign each group a different animal—bunny, bear, bird, or bat. As you say the rhyme below, encourage each animal (child) to move according to the words of the rhyme. When you say the last two lines, have everyone come back to greet the spring!

White bunny, white bunny, hop to white.
Hide in the snow, out of sight!
Black bear, black bear, crawl to black.
Sleep awhile; then hunt for a snack.
Little bird, little bird, fly to blue.

Fluff your feathers like little birds do.
Gray bat, gray bat, flutter to gray.
Hibernate the cold, cold winter away.
Come back, bunnies, bats, birds, and bears.
Winter is gone and spring is in the air!

Julie Koczur
Norman, OK

Chinese New Year Parade

What's a Chinese New Year parade without a few dragons for good luck? Invite each child to create his own original dragon puppet. To make one puppet, use colorful markers to color a dragon face on an old sock. Then decorate a tagboard wreath to slip over the dragon's head for a scaly effect. Have each child wear his dragon puppet on his hand as the class marches around in a Chinese New Year parade. Happy new year!

Patricia Moeser—Preschool, U.W. Preschool Lab, Madison, WI

177

IT'S CIRCLE TIME!

Great Groundhogs!

Great groundhogs! Spring is popping up with this song and puppet idea! To prepare the puppet prop, cut out the bottom from an empty cube-shaped tissue box. Cover the sides of the box with brown paper. Next transform a brown sock into a groundhog puppet by gluing on two wiggle eyes, felt ears, and a pom-pom nose. Ask a child to slip the puppet onto his hand and then slip his hand into the box. Instruct him to pop the puppet through the top of the box after the group sings the following song. Will the groundhog stay out or will he disappear back into his hole and hide? Let each child decide!

(sung to the tune of "Frère Jacques")

Mr. Groundhog, Mr. Groundhog,
Please wake up! Please wake up!
We heard your alarm ring!
Will we have an early spring?
Please wake up! Please wake up!

Patricia Moeser—Preschool, U. W. Preschool Lab Site One, Madison, WI

You've Got Mail!

Boost youngsters' alphabet recognition with this first-class song and activity. To prepare, program 26 sheets of paper each with a different letter of the alphabet. Fold each sheet and place it inside a business-sized envelope; then put the envelopes in a class mailbox. Have the class sing the following song, including a different child's name in the last line each time. Direct that child to take an envelope from the box, open the letter, and identify the alphabet letter. Continue the activity until each child has opened an envelope or until all of the envelopes have been opened.

(sung to the tune of "For He's a Jolly Good Fellow")

I'm sending you a letter!
I'm sending you a letter!
I'm sending you a letter!
This letter is for [Shonte].

Jeri H. Gardner—Pre-K
Reid Memorial Preschool
Augusta, GA

Tooth on the Loose

Youngsters will giggle and wiggle with this gross-motor activity similar to London Bridge. Select two children to face each other and hold hands and raise them. As the class sings, direct them to move in a line under the raised arms of the two children. The tooth that gets captured gets wiggled about!

(sung to the tune of "London Bridge")

Where's the tooth that's falling out,
Falling out, falling out?
Where's the tooth that's falling out?
Must be this one!

Children holding hands "capture" a child in line.

Wiggle, wiggle it right out,

Children holding hands gently rock child back and forth between their arms.

Wiggle out, wiggle out.
Wiggle, wiggle it right out,
Where's the next one?

Children holding hands release child.

adapted from an idea by Jan Steffenauer—Three- to Five-Year-Olds
Lutz Preschool
Bloomsburg, PA

Pass the Hat

Hats off to this idea that has youngsters singing, moving, and following directions! In advance, cut out a class supply of construction paper shamrocks. Program each one with a simple direction, such as "Leap like a leprechaun" or "Pretend to count five pieces of gold." Place the cutouts in a leprechaun hat. (Available at party supply stores.) Have youngsters stand in a circle and sing the song below. When the song ends, have the child holding the hat pull out a shamrock. Help him read the shamrock; then have him follow the given direction. Next have the class copy the child's actions. Continue passing the hat until every child has had a turn. Your little ones will enjoy this activity so much, you'll want to have a hat for every season!

(sung to the tune of "Jingle Bells")

Pass the hat! Pass the hat!
All around the ring.
When it stops, take a turn,
And do a special thing! Hey!
(repeat)

Leslie Madalinski—Four- and Five-Year-Olds
Weekday Children's Center
Naperville, IL

Leap like a leprechaun.

IT'S CIRCLE TIME!

Box of Sounds

Looking for a new way to introduce letter sounds? Then sound off with this twist on a popular teaching method. In advance, wrap a large box and its lid separately with alphabet paper. (Or use an ink pad to stamp letters onto paper; then use this paper to cover the box.) Next fill the box with objects that begin with the featured letter sound and replace the lid. During group time, invite a child to remove an item from the box. Have him identify the object. Then lead your little ones in singing the following song featuring the child's name, the object, and the letter sound. Continue until all of the items have been taken out of the box, each by a different child. Then announce the featured letter.

(sung to the tune of "Sally the Camel Has Five Humps")

[Justin], our friend, has a [football].
[Justin], our friend, has a [football].
[Justin], our friend, has a [football].
So, [/f/ football /f/]
[/f/, /f/, /f/, /f/].

Catherine Blankemeyer—Pre-K, Winston-Salem, NC

Read-and-Tell

Promote literacy skills and a love of books by using this variation of show-and-tell. In advance, ask a child to bring her favorite book on her designated read-and-tell day. During circle time, have the child share her book with the group. If the child needs prompting, you might ask her about the cover, her favorite page, and the story's ending or beginning. If the child is already familiar with her book, then have her "read" the story to her preschool friends. For a child who does not bring a book on her special reading day, consider having her choose a familiar classroom favorite; then spend a few moments helping her prepare for her reading.

Mary Epthimiatos
P.S. 180
Brooklyn, NY

Rainy-Day Umbrella

Make every rainy day fun when students spend time with you beneath a large umbrella. (A golf umbrella works well for this activity.) In advance, tape or cover any sharp spokes on the umbrella. Place the opened umbrella on a carpeted area. During a group time, invite a small group of children to sit with you beneath the umbrella; then share a rainy-day story or lead them in singing their favorite rainy-day songs. Rain, rain, come again another day!

Angelia Dagnan—Preschool
Royale Childcare and Learning Center, Knoxville, TN

Old MacDonald's Farmer Friends

Tweak a classroom favorite and build self-esteem with this variation of "Old MacDonald Had a Farm." Designate a child to be the farmer. Ask that child to name an animal she has on her farm. Then direct the group to sing a verse, substituting the child's name for "Donald" and including the animal of the child's choice. Repeat the verse until each child has been featured as the farmer. "Old MacJenna had a farm. E-I-E-I-O!"

Denise Harlor—Three-Year-Olds
Honeytree Daycare and Preschool
Minersville, PA

Windblown Clouds

The sky is the limit with this counting activity. Provide each child in a small group with a sheet of blue construction paper and a handful of cotton balls (clouds). Then tell a simple story problem and have each child place the corresponding number of cotton balls on his paper. For example, "One day I looked up and saw two clouds." (*Student places two cotton balls on his paper.*) "The wind blew two more clouds into the sky." (*Student places two more cotton balls on his paper.*) "How many clouds are in the sky?" (*Student counts total number of cotton balls.*) To introduce youngsters to the concept of taking items away from a set, adapt the story so that the wind blows the clouds away. Or have children take turns making up the counting stories. How many clouds? The answer, my friend, is blowin' in the wind!

Sharla Park—Three- to Five-Year-Olds
Friends and Neighbors Preschool
Lehi, UT

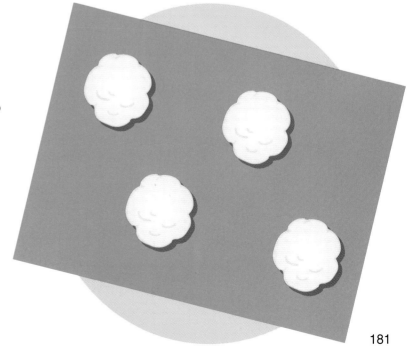

IT'S CIRCLE TIME!

Spin the Watermelon

Here's a fresh-off-the-vine idea for a summer circle time! Seat your class in a circle; then put an oblong-shaped watermelon on the floor in the center of the circle. Use a permanent marker to draw a face on one end of the watermelon. To play, invite a child to give the watermelon a spin. Invite the group to join in as you sing the song below. When the watermelon stops, the child at whom it is facing gets to take the next turn spinning the watermelon. Play the game, for several days if necessary, until every child has had an opportunity to spin the watermelon. Then slice the watermelon and give everyone a chance to eat it!

(sung to the tune of "Pease Porridge Hot")

Watermelon red, watermelon green,
Spin that watermelon so it smiles at me!

Patricia Duncan—Pre-K
American School for the Deaf
West Hartford, CT

Self-Portrait Bingo

This bingo game takes just a bit of time to prepare, but your children will feel so special when they play the game, the time spent will be well worth it! Ask each child to draw a self-portrait on a personalized 1½" square of paper. To prepare the bingo cards, draw an empty bingo grid (with 1½" squares) on a 9" x 12" piece of construction paper. Duplicate the blank card onto construction paper to make a class supply. Then duplicate the portraits so that you have enough pictures to fill each card's grid plus five extra sets. Cut out the portraits and then glue them onto the cards so that each card is different. Label the remaining five sets of pictures each with a different letter *B, I, N, G,* or *O.*

To play the game like bingo, give each child a card and a set of markers. Each time you select a picture, say the child's name and the letter. Or tell something special about the child and have the children guess the name. When a child gets five markers in a row on his card he says, "I'm special!" As a prize, he gets a group hug from his classmates!

Diane Dillow—Four-Year-Olds
Crown of Life Lutheran School
San Antonio, TX

Puzzle Pals

Teach your children the joy of working together by having them put together a large floor puzzle. In advance, assemble the puzzle. Then, working from left to right and top to bottom, sequentially number the back of each puzzle piece. During a group time, give each child a piece of the puzzle. (If there are more pieces than you have children in your class, sequence the pieces by number and give out the first of as many pieces as are needed. During following rounds give out the remaining pieces.) After you have distributed the pieces, guide the children with the pieces numbered 1 and 2 to put them together. Then have the children with pieces 3 and 4 add them to the puzzle. Continue in this manner until the puzzle is complete. We did it!

Karen Phillips—Pre-K
Pine Forest Day Care Center
Jonesboro, GA

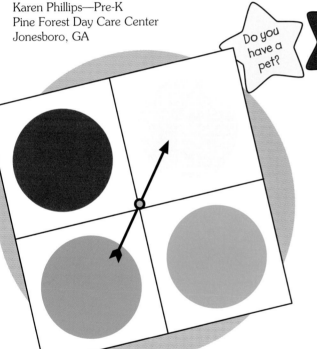

Getting to Know You

Get to know all about your children with this colorful time filler. To prepare, make a spinner with four different-colored sections. Cut out a number of shapes from the same colors of paper as used on the spinner. Program each shape with a different question, such as "Do you have a pet?" or "Name a food you *don't* like to eat."

To play, ask a child to spin the spinner and then select a shape that is a matching color. After reading the question, let the child who chose the shape be the first to answer it. Have each of the remaining children take a turn answering the question as the shape is passed from child to child around the group.

Ann Bovenkamp—Three- to Five-Year-Olds
Young Ideas Preschool
Newton, IA

What's Wrong With the Coconut Tree?

If your children love *Chicka Chicka Boom Boom* by Bill Martin Jr. and John Archambault (Aladdin Paperbacks), then they're sure to enjoy this flannelboard game that reinforces letter names and uppercase/lowercase matching and improves visual discrimination. To play, you'll need sets of uppercase and lowercase felt letters and a felt palm tree. To begin, arrange the tree and all or some of the letters on the flannelboard. Have children close their eyes while you take away one letter. Ask children to open their eyes and name the missing letter. Or pair some uppercase/lowercase letters correctly and some incorrectly. Ask children to find the mismatched pair. As a final option, turn some letters the wrong direction. Ask children to find the letters and place them correctly on the board. Chicka chicka boom boom—now that's one fun coconut tree!

Linda S. Wagner
West Lawn, PA

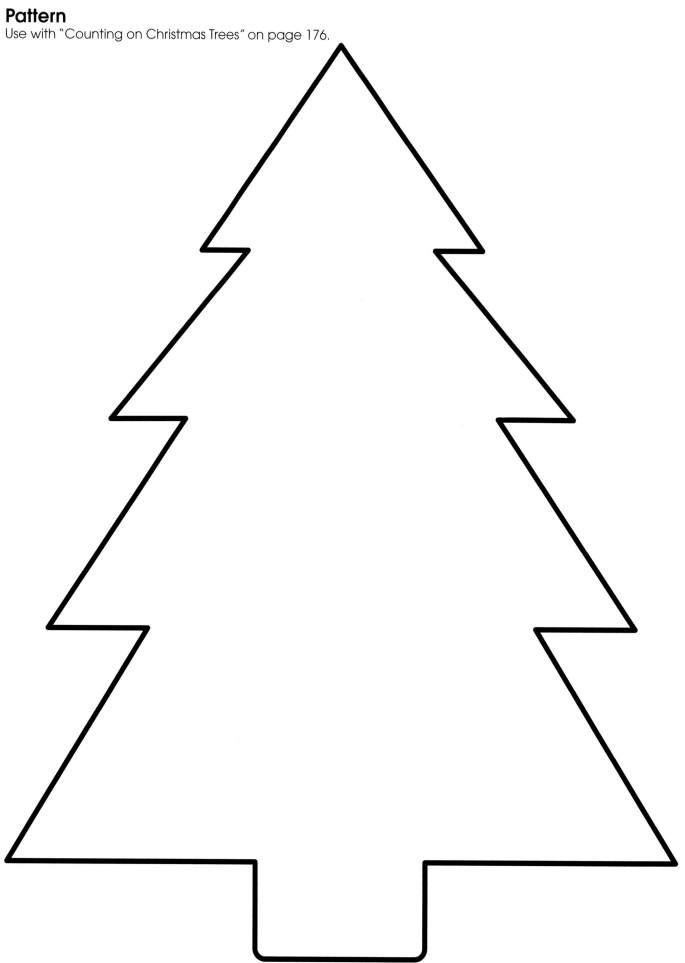

Songs & Such

SONGS & SUCH

Here We Go Round the Birthday Cake

This personalized birthday song will have your little ones huffing, puffing, and giggling! During a group time, lead children in circling around the birthday boy or girl as they sing the first verse of the following song. Then have them circle around in the opposite direction as they sing the second verse. Invite the honoree to pretend to blow out the "candles" (her classmates). Your preschoolers will giggle with delight as they fall to the floor!

(sung to the tune of "The Mulberry Bush")

Here we go round the birthday cake, the birthday cake, the birthday cake.
Here we go round the birthday cake.
Today is [child's name]'s birthday!

Make a wish and blow us out, blow us out, blow us out.
Make a wish and blow us out.
Today is [child's name]'s birthday!

Karen Eiben and Melinda Wilson—Preschool
The Kids' Place Child Development Center, LaSalle, IL

The Days of the Week

(sung to the tune of "Alouette")

Sunday, Monday,
Tuesday, Wednesday, Thursday,
Friday, Saturday; now we start again!

Sunday, Monday, Tuesday,
Wednesday, Thursday, Friday,
Saturday; now we're all done!

Pat Marr, Taft School, Ferndale, MI

It's Time To Say Good-Bye

Use this tune to help end each day on a happy note! As a variation, substitute a different child's name for the words "our friends" in the first, second, and last lines. Repeat the song until you've sung a good-bye to each child in your group.

(sung to the tune of "If You're Happy and You Know It")

Oh, it's time to say good-bye to our friends. *(Clap, clap.)*
Oh, it's time to say good-bye to our friends. *(Clap, clap.)*
Oh, it's time to say good-bye, so just smile and wink your eye!
Oh, it's time to say good-bye to our friends. *(Clap, clap.)*

Mark Pittelkow—Four- and Five-Year-Olds
Merrick Community Services Preschool, St. Paul, MN

A Wiggly Worm

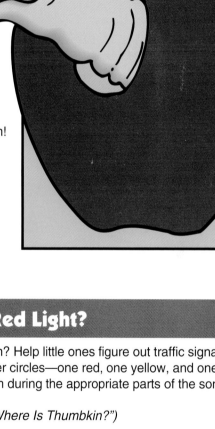

This happy apple tune is perfect for a fall day! Add some action by using your index finger to represent the worm, popping him out of the apple (your fist) at the appropriate point in the song. Or, if desired, make an apple-and-worm puppet. Simply cut a large apple shape from laminated red construction paper. Cut a hole in the apple large enough to slide a hand through. Glue two small wiggle eyes to the toe of a green sock. When you're ready to perform the song, slip the sock onto one hand and hold the apple in the other. Make the worm appear at just the right moment!

(sung to the tune of "Boom! Boom! Ain't It Great to Be Crazy?")

Chorus
Yum! Yum! Don't you know I love apples?
Yum! Yum! Don't you know I love apples?
Red and green and yellow, too…
Yum! Yum! Don't you know I love apples?

Verse 1
Way up high in an apple tree, I saw two eyes look at me.
I reached for an apple; it started to squirm…oops! I found a wiggly worm!

Chorus

Verse 2
That wiggly worm is a friend of mine. We eat apples all the time.
I let him crawl back to that tree…hey! I see that worm looking at me!

Chorus

Sandy Moons—Four- and Five-Year-Olds
Parkcrest E.C.E., Long Beach, CA

Where Is Red Light?

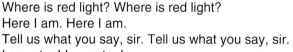

Red, yellow, green—what do all those lights mean? Help little ones figure out traffic signals with this song. Tape a craft stick handle to each of three paper circles—one red, one yellow, and one green. Ask three children to hold these light puppets up high during the appropriate parts of the song.

(sung to the tune of "Where Is Thumbkin?")

Where is red light? Where is red light?
Here I am. Here I am.
Tell us what you say, sir. Tell us what you say, sir.
I say stop! I say stop!

Where is yellow light? Where is yellow light?
Here I am. Here I am.
Tell us what you say, sir. Tell us what you say, sir.
I say wait! I say wait!

Sandy Moons

Where is green light? Where is green light?
Here I am. Here I am.
Tell us what you say, sir. Tell us what you say, sir.
I say go! I say go!

Red says stop, yellow says wait,
Green says go, green says go.
These are traffic signals, these are traffic signals,
That we know, that we know.

SONGS & SUCH

Up on the Treetop

As your little ones sing this fall tune, have them pretend to crunch, crunch, crunch through the leaves.

(sung to the tune of "Up on the Housetop")

Up on the treetop
Watch the leaves.
They are changing.
You can see.
Red and orange,
Yellow and brown.
Pretty soon they'll all fall down!

Crunch, crunch, crunch!
Walk through the leaves.
Crunch, crunch, crunch!
Walk through the leaves.
Up on the treetop
In the fall,
Leaves are changing.
Watch them all!

Laurel Jonas—Four-Year-Olds
Trinity Lutheran
Wisconsin Dells, WI

Pumpkin and Shakin'

Shake up some fall fun with these nifty milk-carton shakers. To make one, paint an empty half-pint milk carton orange. When the paint is dry, place a handful of dried beans inside the carton. Cut several lengths of green curling ribbon; then tape one end of each length inside the carton top. Curl the lengths of ribbon to resemble vines. Staple two construction-paper leaves to the top of the carton while stapling the top shut. If desired, glue black construction-paper features on one side of the carton to create a jack-o'-lantern face. Now get your youngsters shaking as they sing their Halloween favorites or the song below!

(sung to the tune of "I'm Bringing Home a Baby Bumblebee")

I'm picking out a pumpkin on a vine.
I want one big and fat and fine.
I'm picking out a pumpkin on a vine,
Oh, I see mine!

I'm pulling on a pumpkin on a vine.
It's so big and fat and fine!
I'm pulling on a pumpkin on a vine.
Snap! It's mine!

craft idea by Nancy K. Mazur—Preschool, St. Joseph Preschool, Wapakoneta, OH

Round Little Pumpkin

Here's a little tune, ripe for the picking!

(sung to the tune of "Five Little Ducks")

Round little pumpkin on the vine,
You look so orange.
You look so fine.
I think you're the one that I've plans for.
You will be the jack-o'-lantern by my door!

LeeAnn Collins—Director
Sunshine House Preschool
Lansing, MI

Did You Ever See a Turkey?

Reinforce color recognition with this turkey tune. In advance, cut out a class supply of red, brown, yellow, and orange construction-paper feathers. Give each child one feather. As the class sings the song below, have each student hold up his feather when its color is mentioned.

(sung to the tune of "Did You Ever See a Lassie?")

Did you ever see a turkey, a turkey, a turkey
As he struts around the farmyard with feathers so bright?
With red ones and brown ones and yellow ones and orange ones,
Did you ever see a turkey with feathers so bright?

Cele McCloskey and Brenda Peters, Dallastown, PA

I'm a Firefighter

(sung to the tune of "I'm a Little Teapot")

I'm a firefighter.	*Point to self.*
Here's my hose.	*Outstretch arm with finger pointed.*
I put out fires	
As everyone knows.	
When I see a fire	*Hand over brow.*
I douse it out.	*Outstretch arm with finger pointed.*
"Thank you! Thank you!"	
People shout!	

Linda Rice Ludlow
Bethesda Christian School
Brownsburg, IN

SONGS & SUCH

Santa Had a Christmas Tree

Add to the fun of this tune by preparing a few props. Gather the following items: a paper star covered with glitter, a jingle bell, a paper Christmas bulb covered with glitter, and a box wrapped in holiday paper. (Put a couple of marbles or blocks in the box, so it will rattle when shaken.) Ask four student volunteers to hold the items in front of the group as you sing. As each item is mentioned in the song, have the designated child hold it up or shake it to make a noise.

(sung to the tune of "Old MacDonald Had a Farm")

Santa had a Christmas tree,
Ho, ho, ho, ho, ho!
And on that tree he had a star,
Ho, ho, ho, ho, ho!
With a twinkle, twinkle here
And a twinkle, twinkle there.
Here a twinkle, there a twinkle,
Everywhere a twinkle, twinkle!
Santa had a Christmas tree,
Ho, ho, ho, ho, ho!

Continue with additional verses:

And on that tree he had a bell…With a jingle, jingle here…
And on that tree he had a light…With a sparkle, sparkle here…
And under that tree he had a gift…With a rattle, rattle here…

Diana Shepard—Toddlers, First Presbyterian Preschool, Wilmington, NC

We Are Christmas Lights

What would Christmas lights say if they could talk? They'd sing this happy song!

(sung to the tune of "Jingle Bells")

Verse:
We are Christmas lights,
And you know it's true—
We blink red and green
And sometimes white and blue!
We decorate your tree
To make your spirits bright.
Just look at all our colors when we
　sparkle every night!

Chorus:
We blink red; we blink green;
We blink white and blue!
Yes, we blink at Christmastime;
We do it just for you!
Oh, we blink red; we blink green;
We blink white and blue!
Have a Merry Christmas and a
　Happy New Year, too!

Jane Hosford—Four-Year-Olds, Crossgates Methodist Children's Center, Brandon, MS

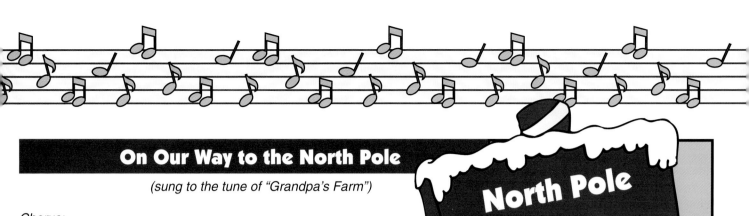

On Our Way to the North Pole

(sung to the tune of "Grandpa's Farm")

Chorus:
We're on our way, we're on our way, on our way to the North Pole.
We're on our way, we're on our way, on our way to the North Pole.

Verses:
At the North Pole, the elves are making toys.
At the North Pole, the elves are making toys.
The elves, they make a sound like this—tap, tap.   *Pretend to use a hammer.*
The elves, they make a sound like this—tap, tap.   *Pretend to use a hammer.*

At the North Pole is Rudolph the reindeer.
At the North Pole is Rudolph the reindeer.
Rudolph, he makes a sound like this—blink, blink.   *Tap nose with index finger.*
Rudolph, he makes a sound like this—blink, blink.   *Tap nose with index finger.*

At the North Pole is jolly, round Santa.
At the North Pole is jolly, round Santa.
Santa, he makes a sound like this—"Ho, ho!"   *Put both hands on belly.*
Santa, he makes a sound like this—"Ho, ho!"   *Put both hands on belly.*

Sue McClimans—Three-Year-Olds
Edwards School
Davenport, IA

Mr. Cloud

(sung to the tune of Raffi's "Mr. Sun")

Oh, Mr. Cloud, Cloud,
Mr. Fluffy Cloud,
Please snow down on me!
Oh, Mr. Cloud, Cloud,
Mr. Fluffy Cloud,
Snow is what I want to see!

These little children are asking you
To send some snow. Oh, please, won't you?
Oh, Mr. Cloud, Cloud,
Mr. Fluffy Cloud,
Please snow down on,
Please snow down on,
Please snow down on me!

Eileen Saad—Preschool
Meadowbrook Nursery School
Troy, MI

SONGS & SUCH

Animal Sounds Symphony

Your little ones will enjoy providing the animal sound effects in this song.

(sung to the tune of
"How Much Is That Doggie in the Window?")

How much is that [kitty] in the window?
[Meow, meow!]
The one with the [long, furry] tail.
[Meow, meow!]
How much is that [kitty] in the window?
[Meow, meow!]
I do hope that [kitty's] for sale!
[Meow, meow!]

Repeat the verse, substituting other animal names, sounds, and tail descriptions, such as
piggy…oink, oink…small, curly
horse…neigh, neigh…long, pretty
cow…moo, moo…long, skinny
snake…hiss, hiss…slithery
dinosaur…roar, roar…spikes on its

Veronica Tyler—Three-Year-Olds
Almost Angels Child Care Center, Sandston, VA

Hibernation Station

Teach little ones the concept of hibernation with this fun tune and activity. Drape a blanket or two over a long table. Invite youngsters to take their teddy bears along as they hide inside this makeshift cave during the first verse of this song. Then have them bring their bears out during the second verse. Hello, spring!

(sung to the tune of "Wheels on the Bus")

The bears in the woods are sleeping now,
Sleeping now, sleeping now.
The bears in the woods are sleeping now,
All winter long.

The bears in the woods are waking up,
Waking up, waking up!
The bears in the woods are waking up;
Springtime is here!

Deborah Garmon, Groton, CT

Toothbrush Cha-Cha

Invite youngsters to dance along to this lively tune. It's perfect for February—National Children's Dental Health Month.

(sung to the tune of "La Cucaracha")

We brush our teeth up.	*Stand and pretend to brush teeth.*
We brush our teeth down.	*Squat and pretend to brush teeth.*
We brush 'em, brush 'em, all around.	*Stand again and pretend to brush teeth as you turn around in a circle.*
We don't want cavities.	*Shake head no.*
Oh, no, no gum disease.	*Shake finger no-no.*
We tell those germs, "Get outta town!"	*Point thumb over shoulder.*

Leslie Madalinski—Preschool, Weekday Children's Center, Naperville, IL

A Rainbow of Colors

Transform a few sheets of construction paper into a bright rainbow when little ones act out this tune. First give each of six student volunteers a different color of construction paper—one red, one orange, one yellow, one green, one blue, and one purple. Arrange the children in front of your group from left to right in that order. Ask them to hold their papers in front of them and then turn around so that their backs are to the group. As each color is sung, tap the child holding it and have her turn around and hold her paper high. Look! It's a rainbow!

(sung to the tune of "Pop Goes the Weasel")

Let's all name our colors right now.
Red and orange and yellow.
Green and blue and purple, too.
Look! It's a rainbow!

Deborah Garmon, Groton, CT

Mr. Groundhog

Put some swing into spring when you teach youngsters this song!

(sung to the tune of "Mr. Sandman")

Mr. Groundhog, give us a sign.
Will it be winter or will the sun shine?
Will we be inside with the fireplace glowing?
Will we be outside with the flowers growing?

Mr. Groundhog, give us a sign.
Will it be winter or will the sun shine?
Oh, Mr. Groundhog, give us a sign!

Maryanelle Callaghan and Colleen Klickner—Three- and Four-Year-Olds
Tinley Park District, Tinley Park, IL

SONGS & SUCH

Puddle Play

Can your little ones think of animals that might like to splish and splash in a puddle? Maybe a worm would *slide* in a puddle. Or a bug could *jump* in a puddle! Sing about a different animal each time you repeat a verse of this song.

(sung to the tune of "Go In and Out of the Window")

What loves to splish in a puddle?
What loves to splash in a puddle?
What loves to **swim** in a puddle?
A **duck** loves a puddle, don't you?

What loves to splish in a puddle?
What loves to splash in a puddle?
What loves to **hop** in a puddle?
A **frog** loves a puddle, don't you?

Who loves to splish in a puddle?
Who loves to splash in a puddle?
Who loves to **play** in a puddle?
Oh, **I** love a puddle, don't you?

Lucia Kemp Henry

Do You Have an Egg for Me?

During a group time, seat your children in a circle; then ask one child to pretend to be the Easter bunny. Give that child a basket filled with a class supply of plastic Easter eggs. As the group sings the following song, the bunny hops around the circle and then gives an egg to a classmate. This child stands up, puts the egg on the floor to mark his space in the circle, and then takes the basket for his turn as the bunny. Play until each child has an egg.

(sung to the tune of "He's Got the Whole World in His Hands")

Easter Bunny [child's name] is hopping by.
Easter Bunny [child's name] is hopping by.
Easter Bunny [child's name] is hopping by.
Oh, do you have an egg for me?

LeeAnn Collins—Director
Sunshine House Preschool
Lansing, MI

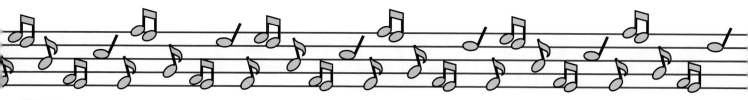

Cheep, Cheep!

Provide each child with a construction paper chick shape (pattern on page 198) to decorate with markers and feathers. Then have each child put his puppet on his fingers. Hold your chick in a different direction each time you repeat the song and encourage your little ones to copy as they sing (and cheep) along!

(sung to the tune of "If You're Happy and You Know It")

If you have a yellow chick, say, "Cheep, cheep!" (cheep, cheep)
If you have a yellow chick, say, "Cheep, cheep!" (cheep, cheep)
If you have a yellow chick,
Hold it [up] like this, real quick!
If you have a yellow chick, say, "Cheep, cheep!" (cheep, cheep)

puppet idea by Sue Jacobs, Shiloh U. C. C. Nursery School, York, PA

Old MacDonald Had a Song

If "Old MacDonald" is one of your class favorites, make these nesting cans for use when the group sings the song. Collect a number of cans that are different sizes. Cover the rims of the cleaned cans with tape. Next cover each can with Con-Tact® paper; then attach a picture of a different farm animal to each can. Label the cans. When you're ready to sing, stack the cans inside one another. At the beginning of each verse, have a child pull out the center can to indicate which animal to sing about next. Later put the cans in a music or games center. Sequencing skills are improved with a song!

Patti Moeser—Toddlers/Preschool, U. W. Madison Preschool Lab, Madison, WI

Flower Petal Countdown

Counting backward is a breeze with this song. Ask a child to stand in front of the class with his palm facing the group and his fingers spread apart. Explain that the child's hand is a flower with five petals. Instruct the child to bend down a finger each time the class repeats the verse. Get ready to blow the petals away!

(sung to the tune of "Sally the Camel")

[Child's name]'s flower has five petals,
[Child's name]'s flower has five petals,
So blow, wind, blow.
Blow, blow, blow…

[Child's name]'s flower has four petals…

Cheryl Sexton—Pre-K, First Baptist Day Care, Providence, OH

SONGS & SUCH

Guess What...Watermelon!

(sung to the tune of "London Bridge")

Guess what grows from small black seeds,
Small black seeds, small black seeds.
Guess what grows from small black seeds—
Watermelon!

Guess what grows with big green leaves...

What is round, and smooth, and green...

What's pink inside and full of juice...

What tastes sweet and makes me grin...

Leslie Ethington
Columbia, OH

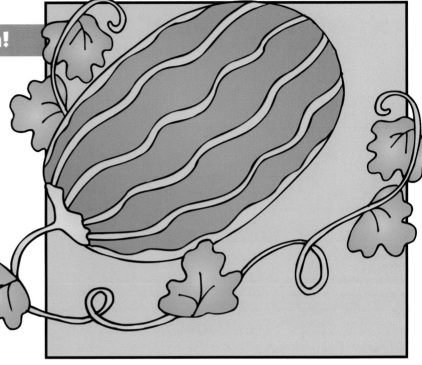

Ooo-eee! Slimy!

Do your little ones love slimy things? Ooo-eee! They'll love singing this slippery song full of similar sounds!

*(sung to the tune of
"I'm Bringing Home a Baby Bumblebee")*

I'm bringing home a slippery, slimy worm.
Won't my mommy wiggle and squirm?
I'm bringing home a slippery, slimy worm.
Ooo-eee! It slimed me!

I'm bringing home a slippery, slimy slug.
Won't my mommy shiver and shrug?
I'm bringing home a slippery, slimy slug.
Ooo-eee! It slimed me!

I'm bringing home a slippery, slimy snail.
Won't my mommy's face go very pale?
I'm bringing home a slippery, slimy snail.
Ooo-eee! It slimed me!

Lola M. Smith
Hilliard, OH

Sing a Song of Seasons

(sung to the tune of "Sing a Song of Sixpence")

Sing a song of seasons,
Something bright in all.
Flowers in the summer,
Leaves in the fall.
Snow in the winter,
Buds in the spring.
Aren't all these changes
A wonderful thing?

Joan Grohowski—Preschool, Posen Homebase
Headstart, Presque Isle, MI

Preschool Personalities

By now your children have probably gotten to know their classmates pretty well. Celebrate each child's uniqueness with this simple song. Just announce a child's name and a personality trait. Ask the special child to stand in front of the group, on a stool or stable chair if possible, while the class sings his praises!

(sung to the tune of "The Wheels on the Bus")

The [Zach] in our class [loves to sing,
Loves to sing, loves to sing].
The [Zach] in our class [loves to sing].
He's special that way!

Happy Trails

(sung to the tune of "Happy Trails to You")

Happy trails to you,
It's the end of our school year.
Happy trails to you,
Now summertime is here.
Next year we'll be in kindergarten,
But pre-k's the grade we left our heart in.
Happy trails to you,
It's time to say, "So long!"

Rhonda Leigh Dominguez
Oconee Pre-K at Downs Preschool
Bishop, GA

Pattern

Use with "Cheep, Cheep!" on page 195.

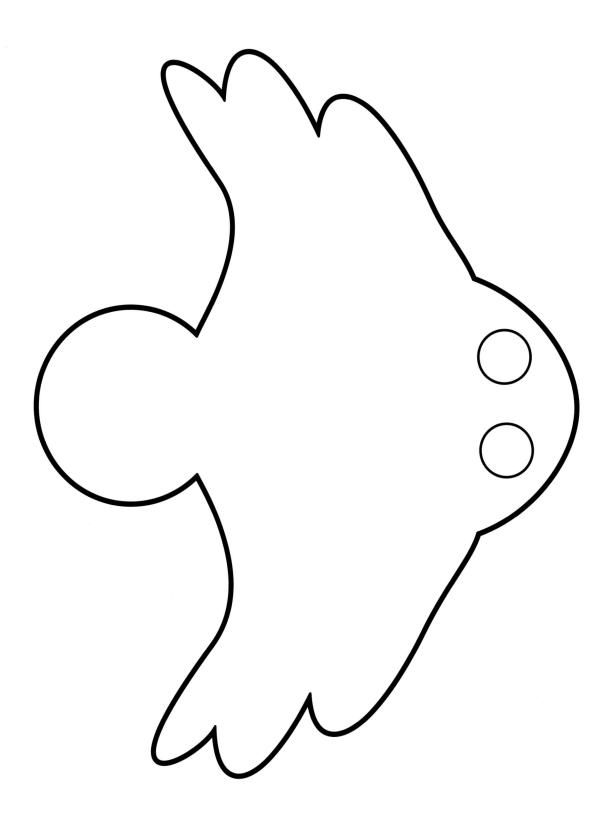

Fingerplays, Poems, & Rhymes

A Penny for Your Pumpkin

This fingerplay reinforces counting skills and coin recognition as well! To make this poem worth a lot of learning and fun, put five to ten felt pumpkin shapes on a flannelboard; then give each of the same number of children a coin. In turn, invite each child to show his coin. Identify the coin (penny, nickel, dime, quarter); then have him exchange it for a pumpkin as the class recites the rhyme.

[Five] orange pumpkins in a pumpkin patch.
You know, the kind that are big, and round, and fat!
Along came a child with a [penny] to pay,
He bought a pumpkin and took it away.

Sherry Hammons—Pre-K, Tunica Elementary, Tunica, LA

Poems, & Rhymes

Turkey Countdown

Invite ten children to stand in a row and pretend to be turkeys. (Be sure to encourage plenty of wing-flapping and gobbling from your little actors!) As a group, recite the following rhyme; then have the turkeys quickly trot off one by one as you count them down.

Ten fat turkeys standing in a row.
They spread their wings and tails just so.
They look to the left;
Then they look to the right.
When they strut their stuff, they're quite a sight!
But you won't see them on Thanksgiving Day,
'Cause one by one they'll run away! Ten, nine, eight…

Fingerplays,

Sleepy Little Groundhog

Take note of Groundhog Day (February 2) with this action poem.

Up through the ground,
Creep, creep, creep—

The sleepy little groundhog
Peek-peek-peeks.

If he sees his shadow
And the sun is bright,

He jumps down his hole
And ducks out of sight!

Up through the ground,
Creep, creep, creep—

The sleepy little groundhog
Peek-peek-peeks.

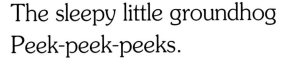

If there is no shadow
And the clouds hide the sun,

He jumps out of his hole
And he's ready for fun!

Roxie Summers—Three-Year-Olds
Jack and Jill Pre-school, Leavenworth, KS

Leprechaun, Leprechaun

Your little leprechauns will have a high time moving to this spritely chant!

(chanted to the rhythm of "Teddy Bear, Teddy Bear")

Leprechaun, leprechaun,
Turn around.

Leprechaun, leprechaun,
Touch the ground.

Leprechaun, leprechaun,
Point your ears.

Leprechaun, leprechaun,
Touch your beard.

Leprechaun, leprechaun,
Tip your cap.

Leprechaun, leprechaun,
Clap, clap, clap.

Leprechaun, leprechaun,
Dance a jig.

Leprechaun, leprechaun,
Smile so big!

adapted from a chant by Clara Hayes and Kathy Peterson
Integrated Language Preschool, Arlington Elementary School, Tacoma, WA

Tiny Apple Seed

After teaching youngsters this poem, put some apple seeds in a container at your sand center so that students can "plant" them under the ground.

I put a tiny apple seed

Underneath the ground.

I covered it with soft, brown dirt,

Then patted all around.

The sun shone down; the rain fell, too,

Upon my seed you see.

And now my tiny apple seed

Is a big apple tree!

—Deborah Garmon, Groton, CT

CRAFTS FOR LITTLE HANDS

Crafts For Little Hands

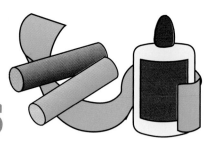

"A-peel-ing" Apples

For a colorful display, try these translucent apples. To make one apple, draw a simple apple and stem outline on a piece of white paper. Tape a piece of clear plastic wrap or a resealable plastic bag over the drawing. Squeeze white glue along the outline; then press yarn onto it, making sure to include the stem to create a loop. Allow the glue to dry. Next tint glue with red, yellow, or green food coloring. Use a paintbrush to paint a thick coat of the glue on the plastic, inside the dried yarn. Let the glue dry for a day. Peel the apple decoration from the plastic; then suspend it. Apples, apples everywhere!

The Apple of My Eye

Got your camera ready? These adorable apple frames make a great gift for someone special, such as a grandparent. Take a close-up picture of each child; then trim the developed pictures into circles sized to fit in the center of a small paper plate. To make one frame, sponge-paint a paper plate red. Next lightly sprinkle red or clear glitter on the wet paint. Program a construction paper leaf with "I'm the apple of your eye!" and the child's name. Glue the leaf, a paper stem, and the photo to the dry plate as shown. Complete the frame by attaching a strip of magnetic tape to the back of it. Smile!

Sunny Delight

Light up your classroom with a display of student-made sunflowers! In advance, cut several potatoes in half. Trim some of the halves to make petal-shaped prints and some to make square prints. To create a sunflower, dip a square printer into brown paint; then repeatedly press it onto a large sheet of art paper, creating a somewhat circular design. Outside this, use a petal-shaped printer and yellow paint to encircle the brown area. When the paint is dry, cut around the flower shape. To turn a bulletin board into a patch of sunny sunflowers, staple each student's blossom atop a green paper strip embellished with some green paper leaves. That's sunny all right!

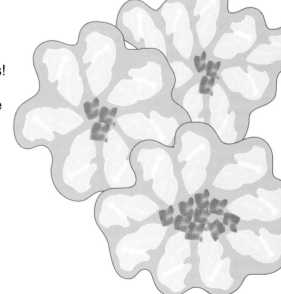

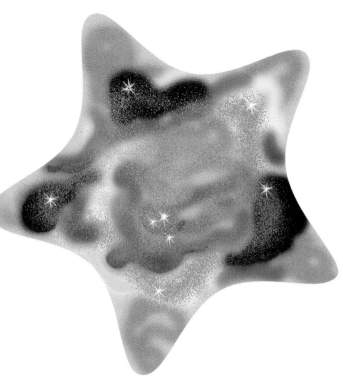

"Sense-ational" Starfish

This craft uses a fabulous textured paint with lots of sensory appeal! To prepare, mix several different colors of puff paint. For each color, combine two tablespoons of washable tempera paint and 1/3 cup of white glue. Fold in two cups of nonmentholated shaving cream until the color is well blended. (For best results, use the paint soon after mixing it.)

To make one starfish, fingerpaint a star-shaped tagboard cutout with several colors of the puff paint. Sprinkle glitter over the wet paint; then set the starfish aside to dry overnight. Youngsters will enjoy smelling, touching, and seeing this interesting paint—even when it's dry!

Beverly Folena—Pre-K
Creative Kids Preschool
Placerville, CA

3-D Jellyfish

Who's afraid of jellyfish? Certainly none of your youngsters after they make these unique projects! For every two children, use a serrated knife to cut a two-inch Styrofoam® ball in half. To make one jellyfish, paint a half with tempera paint. When the paint is dry, push a metal brad partway into the round part of the ball half. Thread a 16" length of yarn through the brad; then push the brad completely into the half. Tie the yarn to make a hanging loop. Next spread craft glue onto the flat part of the ball half. Press one end of each of a number of 6"x1" tissue paper strips onto the glue to resemble tentacles. Suspend these jellyfish around your classroom for a cool underwater effect.

Beth Costello—Pre-K
First Presbyterian Day School
Deland, FL

Handprint Crabs

Teach youngsters to crab-walk (walk on hands and feet with tummy facing up); then invite them to crab-walk right over to your art center to make these snappy crabs! To make one, a child dips her hands into washable red tempera paint. Then she presses them onto a sheet of construction paper so that the palm prints overlap and the fingerprints extend in opposite directions. When the paint is dry, she draws on a smile, then glues a wiggle eye onto each thumbprint. Finally she glues sand underneath the crab to complete the picture. These cute crustaceans can't be beat!

Kimberly Calhoun—Pre-K
Tutor Time Learning Center
Apex, NC

207

Crafts For Little Hands

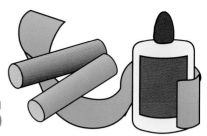

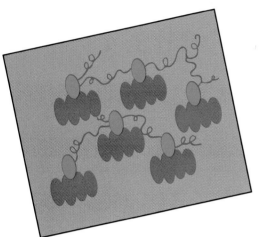

"Di-vine" Pumpkin Patch

Children will be making these precious pumpkins hand over fist! To make a pumpkin-patch scene, make a fist. Then paint the top of the fist (fingers and knuckles) orange. Press the fist onto a sheet of construction paper to resemble a pumpkin. Repeat until the paper has as many pumpkin prints as desired. Make a green fingerprint at the top of each pumpkin for a stem. When the paint is dry, use a green marker to add vines to the picture. What a handsome pumpkin patch!

Juli Clark—Preschool, Safari Street BDCH Kids Care, Beaver Dam, WI

Autumn Leaf Lantern

Take your class outdoors to collect leaves; then preserve the autumn foliage with these simply beautiful lanterns. To make one lantern, place two 18-inch sheets of waxed paper on a newspaper-covered table. Sandwich a number of leaves between the sheets of waxed paper. Cover the waxed paper sheets with a layer of newspaper; then use an iron on low heat to join the sheets. Next fold two 4" x 18" strips of fall-colored construction paper in half lengthwise. Slip a folded strip over each long waxed paper edge; then staple the strips in place. Staple together the short sides of the waxed paper to form a cylinder. Punch two equidistant holes in the top of the cylinder; then twist one end of a pipe cleaner through each of the holes to make a handle. Invite each child to take her lantern home to share with her family.

Karen Gremer—Three-Year-Olds
Walnut Creek Presbyterian Christian Preschool
Walnut Creek, CA

"Spider-ific" Webs

Put your round cake pans to creative use to make these painted spiderwebs. To make one web, cut a black construction paper circle to fit in a cake pan. Place the paper in the pan; then pour a spoonful of white tempera paint onto it. Next place a marble in the pan. Gently tilt the pan repeatedly to roll the marble through the paint, forming a web design on the paper. Remove the marble; then sprinkle silver glitter over the wet paint. Carefully remove the resulting web and let it dry. Glue a plastic spider onto the web. Or tie a length of white yarn to a spider, punch a hole near the edge of the web, and then thread the yarn through the hole and tie it off. Charlotte herself would be proud of these webs!

Sharla Park—Preschool, Friends and Neighbors Preschool, Lehi, UT

Jack-o'-Lantern Mobiles

Your preschoolers will be pleased to make this unique patch of jack-o'-lantern mobiles. To make one, cut out the center of a paper plate and discard it. Paint both sides of the remaining plate rim orange. To make the jack-o'-lantern face, cut three triangles and a zigzag smile from black construction paper. Cut two three-inch lengths and one six-inch length of black yarn. Glue the features to the yarn as shown. When the glue is dry, tape the yarn lengths to the back of the plate so that the shapes are positioned as desired. Punch a hole near the top of the plate; then tie on a length of yarn so the completed mobile can be suspended from the ceiling. These great pumpkins are on the rise!

Cathie Sarvis—Three-Year-Olds
Park Avenue School
Wilmington, NC

Mummy Madness

Your little ones will go mad for these marvelous mummies! To make one, trace a person shape onto sturdy white paper (a large gingerbread-man cookie cutter works well as a tracer). Cut out the shape. Using a glue mat to protect the tabletop, spread white glue that has been thinned with a small amount of water onto the cutout. Cover the glue with torn strips of white tissue paper or toilet tissue to resemble a mummy's wrappings. Cut two black eyes from construction paper; then glue them on the mummy's face. Mount the completed project on an orange background. Looks like Halloween decorating is all wrapped up!

Christa J. Koch—Pre-K
Circle of Friends
Bethlehem, PA

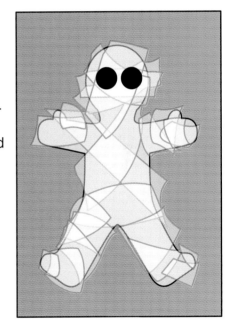

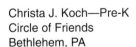

Fine-Feathered Holder

This fine-feathered Thanksgiving project holds plenty of treats! To make one holder, cut six inches off the top of a brown paper lunch bag. Cut six 2" x 5" strips of brown construction paper. Fringe each strip along one long side. To both the front and back of the bag, glue three strips (fringe down) so that they overlap slightly. Bend the fringe upward. Cut a head, a beak, a wattle, a tail, and two eyes from construction paper; then glue them in place as shown. Fill the completed holder with treats, such as pretzels or bags of candy corn. Gobble, gobble!

Renee E. DeAngelo—Director, The Rainbow School, Plains, PA

Crafts For Little Hands

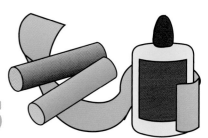

Guardian Angels

Have youngsters make these angels to keep watch over your classroom during the holidays. Prepare an angel tracer similar to the shape shown. Also make a circle tracer the same size as the angel's head. To make an angel, trace the pattern onto the front of a Christmas card that has religious-themed art. Trace a circle onto skin-toned construction paper. Cut out the shapes. Glue the circle onto the angel shape; then glue on wiggle eyes and a line of glitter for a halo. Use a cotton swab to rub on powder-blush cheeks. Finally, unwrap a five-inch length of paper twist; then retwist it once in the center before gluing it to the back of the angel to create wings.

Linda Shute—Four-Year-Olds, Grace Day Care, Lafayette, IN

Simple and Sweet

Even your little angels can make these sweet cherubs. To make one, use a glue stick to glue a four-inch round doily to the point of an upside-down six-inch heart-shaped doily. Cut another six-inch heart-shaped doily in half; then glue each half to the back of the first heart-shaped doily for wings. Attach star-shaped stickers for the angel's facial features and halo. To make the angel into an ornament, glue a 1" x 4" piece of heavy white paper to the top back of the angel. Punch a hole near the top of the strip; then tie on a length of white yarn for hanging.

Mary Anne Deik and Lynn McDowell—Four-Year-Olds
Reformed Church Weekday Nursery School
Poughkeepsie, NY

Rudolph Pendant

Round up some cardboard puzzle pieces to transform into reindeer pendants! To make one pendant, use craft paint to paint three puzzle pieces brown. When the paint is dry, glue the pieces together as shown. Also glue on two wiggle eyes and a pom-pom nose. Attach a self-adhesive pin to the back as shown. Rudolph with his nose so bright, on your clothes will look just right!

Karen Sheheane—Preschool, Killearn United Methodist Preschool, Tallahassee, FL

Decaf Santa

Ho! Ho! Ho! To make one of these Santas, cut a six-inch triangle from red construction paper. Glue the triangle to a flattened coffee filter as shown. Glue cotton balls onto the top and bottom of the hat. Use markers to add facial features to the filter; then trim around the edges to create Santa's beard. Jolly good work!

Shelly Wooldridge—Preschool, Smithville Elementary School
Smithville, WV

Foil Christmas Tree

Each of these trees is unique when decorated by your crafty youngsters. For each child, cover one side of a cardboard triangle with green floral foil (used to wrap pots) or foil wrapping paper (used to decorate doors). To complete his tree, a child glues a paper trunk to the back of the triangle and a star to the top. He then embellishes the tree with various art supplies, such as paper scraps, jewels, sequins, and stickers.

Lois Maiese—Two-Year-Olds to Five-Year-Olds
Camden County College Child Care Center
Blackwood, NJ

Tree Topper

Top off your tree with these ornaments. To make one ornament, cut a triangle from poster board. Stack and glue cardboard puzzle pieces onto the triangle. When the glue is dry, spray-paint both sides of the ornament green. When the paint is dry, glue glitter, small gems, or sequins onto the puzzle pieces. Tape a loop of ribbon to the back of the ornament for hanging.

Karen Sheheane—Preschool, Killearn United Methodist Preschool
Tallahassee, FL

Crafts For Little Hands

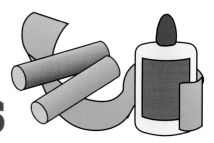

Lovebug Valentines

Few valentines have quite the personality of these student-made ones! Create a template for the bug body and wings as shown. To make one lovebug, trace the templates onto construction paper; then cut on the resulting outlines. Write a simple message on the larger area of the bug's body. Then use a brad to attach the wings. To bring the bug to life, attach paper reinforcer eyes and small sticker wing spots. Have each student deliver his buggy valentine to a friend or loved one.

Kathy Burrows—Toddlers and Preschool
Country Meadows of South Hills Child Care
Bridgeville, PA

Wait a Minute, Mister Postman

As the valentines begin to pour in or just after a visit to the post office, these giant envelopes are sure to come in handy. In advance, collect a cereal box for each child. Spray-paint each box white and allow it to dry completely. Next cut a U-shaped slit in one panel of each box, as shown, to resemble an envelope's opening. Give each child a box and have him paint it pink. When the paint has dried, punch holes above and below the slit. Assist the child in securing a pipe cleaner loop in the bottom holes and a long pipe cleaner strap in the upper one. Then write his name and address on the other side of the box. Encourage each child to decorate his envelope and attach an imitation stamp of his own design.

Jolene Schaeffer—Three- and Four-Year-Olds
Honey Tree Day Care and Preschool
Minersville, PA

Sealed With a Kiss—for Real!

For Valentine's Day, there's no better gift than kisses from a child. To make a self-standing frame, fold pink tagboard, trace a heart onto it (with the top of the heart near the fold), and then cut it out. Snip off the pointed area of the heart, creating a straight surface for the frame to rest on. Trim a child's photo into a heart shape; then have her glue it onto the center front of the frame. If the child wishes to add a kiss or two, use your finger to rub lipstick on her lips. (Wash your hands before and after each application to avoid the spread of germs.) Have the child plant a kiss or two on the frame. Then have her write her name inside the folded frame and date it. On the frame, write a message the child dictates before tucking the gift into a sandwich bag for delivery—special delivery, that is!

Bonnie McKenzie—Pre-K and Gr. K, Cheshire Country Day School, Cheshire, CT

Magic Clovers

Just in time for St. Patrick's Day, help your students create this artwork that's a touch Irish. In advance, cut a green clover shape for each student. Also mix together an amount of green and yellow tempera paint. To make one project, use pieces of rolled tape to secure a clover to a large sheet of yellow construction paper. Paint completely over the sheet and clover with the paint. While the paint is wet, sprinkle streams of gold and/or green glitter onto the page. When the project has dried, carefully pull away the clover, revealing two glittering masterpieces. See the bulletin board on page 56 for a magically delightful way to display both parts of these St. Patrick's Day projects.

Connie Bryant—Preschool
Emerald Isle, Mother's Morning Out
Emerald Isle, NC

A Springtime Tulip Bouquet

Spring is the perfect time for student-made tulip bouquets! For each child, trim six cuplike sections from a Styrofoam® egg carton to resemble tulips. Poke two holes in the bottom of each cup, insert a pipe cleaner through the holes, and then twist the pipe cleaner to create an imitation tulip. For each of several tulip colors, mix three teaspoons of water and one-half teaspoon of liquid dishwashing detergent into a cup of tempera paint. As a final preparatory step, create a clothesline-type drying area, label a section of the line for each student's flowers, and protect the floor beneath it with newspaper.

To make a bouquet of tulips, have a child hold each of his six flowers, in turn, by the pipe cleaner stem and then dunk the bloom into his choice of paint. Assist him in curving the end of the pipe cleaner to form a hook and hanging it on the drying line. When the paint is dry, cradle the flowers in a green construction paper cone for transporting home.

Lisa M. Quintal—Four- and Five-Year-Olds, McLean Child Care Center, Belmont, MA

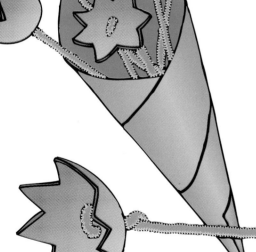

"Spectacularsaurs"

To make one spectacular dinosaur puppet, fold a paper plate in half and then glue the halves together. Repeatedly cut triangular shapes from around the rim area. Next embellish the dinosaur with markers, bingo markers, paint, stickers, and other craft supplies. Finally, glue halves of craft sticks to the straight edge of the plate for legs. Personalize the back of each project with a dinosaur name based on the artist's name. Look, guys! It's the gentle, plant-eating giant, Jacobosaurus!

Janie Rabb—Four- and Five-Year-Olds
Alphabet Alley Learning Center
Llano, TX

 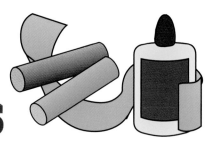

Crafts For Little Hands

Flower Basket

A-tisket, a-tasket, turn a cereal box into a flower basket! To make a basket, trim the panels of a cereal box to create handles as shown. Paint the box twice with tempera paint. When the paint is dry, glue on construction paper flower shapes. Fill the basket with plastic grass and Easter goodies. These sturdy boxes hold lots of treats, so fill them well!

Suzanne Mayo—Pre-Kindergarten
Our Lady of Peace
Fords, NJ

Make Way for Ducklings!

This springtime project is a textural treat for little fingers to make. To create the scene, first fingerpaint blue paint onto a piece of fingerpainting paper. When the paint is dry, cut out a pond shape; then glue it onto a large piece of construction paper. Next cut cloud shapes out of white felt to glue above the pond. To make each fuzzy duck, gently pull one end of a yellow cotton ball; then twist that part of the cotton ball to represent the duck's tail. Glue the cotton ball onto the scene; then add a felt beak and a wiggle eye to the cotton ball to complete the duck. After each duck has been added, use markers to add legs to the ducks and other details to the scene.

adapted from an idea by Angelia Dagnan—Preschool
Royale Childcare and Learning Center
Knoxville, TN

Circles and Centipedes

Invite youngsters to wiggle right over to an art center to print these circular creepy crawlers. To prepare, pour each different color of paint into a separate shallow container. Provide a number of different circular items for students to print with, such as corks, film containers, plastic spools, and bottle tops. Provide each child with a length of white construction paper. Direct him to use the objects to print a caterpillar onto his paper. Then have him use a fork to print grass. When the paint is dry, have him add wiggle eyes and marker details. These art prints also spark counting conversations. "How many circles long is your caterpillar? How many circles are red?" Cool!

Janet Polizois—Preschool
Play 'n Learn Childcare
Flanders, NJ

A Handful of Lilies

Since the lily is a favorite flower this time of year, have your little ones make a handful to give to a special staff member or class helper. To make one lily, trace a child's hand onto white construction paper; then cut it out. Also cut out a stem and leaves from green construction paper. Wrap the hand cutout into a cone shape; then staple the leaves, stem, and flower together as shown. Bend down the fingers to resemble petals. Insert yellow pipe cleaners into the flower. Finally, twist green chenille around the stem of the flower. Wrap a piece of tissue paper around several of the flowers or insert them in a vase. Happy Easter!

Jeri Gardner—Four-Year-Olds
Reid Memorial Preschool
Augusta, GA

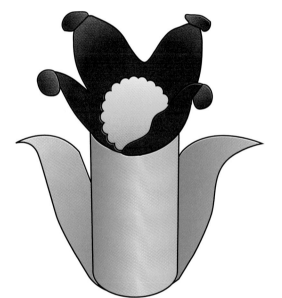

Tulip Time

Have youngsters make a row of tulips to brighten windowsills and shelves this spring! To make one tulip, use tempera paint to paint a cardboard roll green. For each tulip color, mix three teaspoons of water and one-half teaspoon of liquid dishwashing detergent into a cup of tempera paint. Cut one section of a Styrofoam® egg carton to resemble a tulip; then paint it. When the paint is dry, glue paper leaves onto the side of the cardboard roll, glue the tulip onto the top of the roll, and glue a colored cotton ball onto the center of the tulip. Ta-da! Tulips!

Cathy McDonald—Preschool
Thompson Elementary School
Jacksonville, NC

Spring Flowers Galore!

These flowers are so simple to make, your little ones will want to make a whole garden full. What makes this project even prettier? Making the flowers can help little ones understand patterns! Stock an art center with craft sticks, green construction paper, scissors, glue, markers, and white paper condiment cups from fast-food restaurants. Also put flowerpots filled with green Styrofoam® in the center for "planting" the finished flowers. To make a flower, flatten a cup. Color the cup's center and then its sections, alternating colors if desired; then color a craft stick green. Glue the flower and green paper leaf cutouts to the stick. Red petal, yellow petal, red petal, yellow petal...pretty patterned petals!

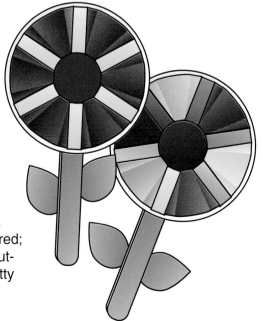

Donna Moseley—Pre-Kindergarten
Happy Kids Learning Center, Inc.
Hull, GA

Floral Greetings

Pressed for a Mother's Day card idea? Here's an idea that uses flowers and your children's special artwork. First, have your class help you press wildflowers or pansies. Put the flowers between layers of paper; then stack heavy books on top of the paper for several days. For each child, cut a 9" x 12" piece of Con-Tact® covering. To make a card, tape the cut paper to a table so that the sticky side is facing up. Have a child arrange some flowers on the paper; then press a piece of light-colored construction paper onto it. Fold the paper in half so that the pressed flowers are on the outside of the card. Have the child dictate a message for you to write inside the card, and then have her add her own artwork.

Laura Haden—Toddlers to Four-Year-Olds
Ft. Meade, MD

Lovely Frames

These beautiful frames are sure to touch every mother's heart. Following Valentine's Day, ask families to send in empty heart-shaped candy boxes. (You'll only use the lids to make these frames, so save the bottoms of the boxes for future projects.) Spray-paint both sides of the boxes' lids white. To make a frame, a child uses Mod Podge® to paint tissue paper pieces onto the lid. When the lid is dry, glue a photo of the child to the center of it. Complete the frame by hot-gluing lace around the rim of the lid. Also hot-glue a string of beads around the photo and a separate string at the top of the lid for a hanger.

Lori F. Hartley—Pre-Kindergarten
George Hildebrand Family Resource Program
Morganton, NC

Mother's Day Placemat

Give Mom a place of honor with this placemat made just for her. To decorate a placemat, paint a child's fingers green (excluding his thumb). Have the child press the print onto the center of a large oval doily. Next have the child repeatedly dip a finger in a color of paint and then onto the doily above the green stems to create flowers. Have him add a drop of paint to the center of each flower. When the paint is dry, have him glue on a paper flowerpot shape. Write a message and then have the child write his name. Laminate the doily or cover both sides with clear Con-Tact® covering.

Susie Fox—Two- and Three-Year-Olds
Jensen Beach Community Church Preschool
Jensen Beach, FL

Crafts For Little Hands

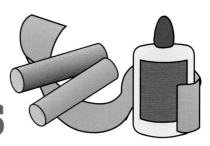

Garden Stones

These stepping-stones make precious gifts any time of the year! To prepare, collect a class supply of empty frozen-entree plates (without dividers). Also gather pretty stones, tiles, marbles, shells, and other items to include in these garden stones. Next, mix an amount of quick-setting concrete (such as Quikrete®) in a large mixing bucket away from the children. Follow the package directions to prepare enough thick pastelike mixture to fill an entree plate for each child. Put an amount of the concrete in a separate plate for each child. Direct each child to put a hand in his dish to make an impression; then invite him to add his choice of items to decorate his stone. When the concrete has hardened, remove each stone from its plastic dish. Finally, decoratively wrap each stone and attach the poem shown.

Donna Pollhammer—Three-Year-Olds
YMCA Chipmunk Preschool
Westminster, MD

My hands were once so tiny.
I needed so much care.
Thank you so much, Daddy,
For always being there!

My love for you grows and grows and grows!
Kirsten

Pretty Posies in Pots

If you can say, "Pretty painted posies in pretty painted pots" several times quickly, then this is the project for you! Start by asking each child to paint a colorful piece of construction paper using the painting tool of his choice, such as a sponge, a marble, or a brush. When the paint is dry, cut each child's page into a large flower shape. Next, have each child use tempera paint to paint his own terra-cotta pot. Take a picture of each child standing in front of a brightly colored piece of bulletin board paper. After having the photos developed, cut each child's picture into a circle; then glue the circle to the center of his flower. Laminate the flowers. Mount each flower onto an unsharpened green pencil. Insert a piece of green Styrofoam® topped with plastic grass into each child's pot. Insert the child's pencil flower into the pot. Finally, add the message shown by sliding it into a plastic card holder that has been inserted into the pot.

Martha Briggs—Four-Year-Olds
Rosemont Tuesday/Thursday School
Fort Worth, TX

Slithering Snakes!

These colorful reptiles make great craft projects as you slide into summer! To make one, use bingo markers to paint different-colored circles on both sides of a paper plate. Starting along the outside rim of the plate, cut spirals, leaving an oval shape at the center of the plate for the snake's head. Glue wiggle eyes onto the snake. Punch a hole at either tip of the snake; then tie on a length of string for hanging from the ceiling. Sakes alive! Are those snakes alive?

Christa J. Koch—Pre-K
Wesley Circle of Friends
Bethlehem, PA

Open Wide!

Folks are sure to say "Aaah" when they see these awesome alligators! To make one alligator, tear green paper to make the alligator's long body. Next, tear another long piece for the tail and then glue it to the body. Continue tearing pieces and gluing them together until the alligator has jaws and legs. Add torn white and black paper eyes. And, of course, don't forget to give the alligator lots of sharp, white teeth! Display the alligators on a swamp scene made with blue plastic wrap and torn-paper trees and plants. Onlookers will be awed by the different sizes and shapes of alligators! Awesome!

Julie Shields—Pre-K
Brookeland School
Brookeland, TX

Turtle Love

Youngsters are sure to love making as many of these terrific turtles as their hearts desire! To make one, simply make a fist and then dip your knuckles and thumb into a shallow pan of green or brown paint. Press your knuckles and thumb onto paper. When the paint is dry, use markers or more paint to add facial features, legs, and details to the turtle's shell. Youngsters can make all types of turtles with this easy project that's tops!

Al Trautman—ECEEN (K3–K5)
Milwaukee, WI

Setting the Stage

Setting The Stage:

Reading Area

Bedtime Stories for Baby Dolls

Invite your little ones to pitter-patter to your reading area for bedtime stories. Place several dolls, small rocking chairs, doll beds, and baby blankets in the area. Next add plenty of board books that your students can "read," such as nursery rhyme books. Encourage your youngsters to visit the area to read bedtime stories to the dolls.

Laura Bentley
Captain John Palliser Elementary
Calgary, Alberta, Canada

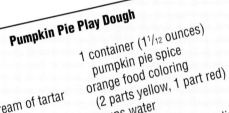

Pumpkin Pie Play Dough

5½ cups flour
2 cups salt
8 teaspoons cream of tartar
¾ cup oil

1 container (1¹/₁₂ ounces) pumpkin pie spice
orange food coloring
(2 parts yellow, 1 part red)
4 cups water

Mix all of the ingredients together. Cook and stir over medium heat until lumps disappear. Knead the dough on a floured surface until it is smooth. Store in an airtight container.

Jeanette Jonas—Pre-K
Rainbow Child Care Center
Bakersfield, CA

Play-Dough Center
Pumpkin Pie Play Dough

This yummy-smelling dough is sure to add spice to your play-dough area! Place a batch of this scented dough and some white play dough in your center. Add some fall cookie cutters, small pie tins, and rolling pins to the area. Invite your little ones to make fall cookies. Or encourage them to make play-dough pumpkin pies, using the white dough for crust and the scented dough for filling. Encourage your little bakers to make as many pastries as they want, but remind them that these goodies only smell good. No tasting please!

Water Table

Spooky Water Shakers

Set these spooky shakers in your water table and it will be floating with fun. Remove the labels from several small, clear plastic water bottles with tops. Place some scary things—such as small rubber snakes, plastic bats, or plastic spiders—in the bottles. (You may want to invite your youngsters to assist you so that they will feel comfortable playing with the shakers.) Next add some green, purple, or black decorative grass and a little glitter to the bottles before filling them with water. Hot-glue the tops to the bottles. Finally, leave these spooky shakers bobbing in your water table for your youngsters to shake, spin, and swirl.

Dayle Timmons
Alimacani Elementary School
Jacksonville, FL

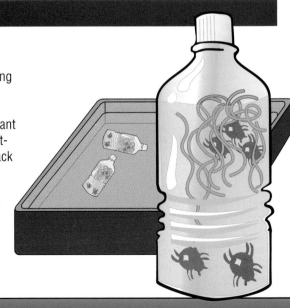

Interest Areas And Centers

Dramatic-Play Area

Call 9–1–1

Help your students learn when and how to call 9–1–1 with this idea and song. In advance, have parents donate used rotary or push-button telephones for your dramatic-play area. (Remove all cords for safety.) Discuss with your class the different emergency situations that might require a 9–1–1 call. Make a pretend emergency call, demonstrating how to use the phone and what to say during the call. Teach your youngsters the song at right; then encourage visitors to the area to sing the song and practice calling 9–1–1.

What Do You Call?

(sung to the tune of "The Mulberry Bush")

What do you call if you need help,
You need help, you need help?
What do you call if you need help?
Call 9–1–1!

Tonie Northcutt—Pre-K
Ancient City Baptist Church
St. Augustine, FL

Games Area

Seasonal Name Game

Your little ones will quickly learn to recognize their names and their classmates' names when they play this fun matching game. To make the game, cut out two seasonal shapes for each child. Have each child personalize his shapes. Place one set of cutouts in a large seasonal container; then glue the other set onto a piece of bulletin-board paper. Set the paper and the container in your games area. Challenge your students to match the shapes in the container with the shapes on the paper. What a fun game for all seasons!

Katie Padilla—Special Education Pre-K
Mittye P. Locke Elementary School, New Port Richey, FL

Sensory Table

Bean Search

This super sensory idea is sure to thrill your older preschoolers! Fill your sensory table with large dried lima beans. Program a number of beans with letters, shapes, numbers, or simple pictures relating to current themes. Mix these bonus beans in with the others; then place a few plastic magnifying glasses in the supervised area. After informing your little ones of the hidden surprises, invite them to use the magnifying glasses to find the special beans. Now let the bean search begin!

Cynthia Osbourne—Three- and Four-Year-Olds
Hickory U.P. Church Preschool
Hickory, PA

Literacy Center

Write 'n' Wipe

Your little ones will make memories as they use this photo album idea to practice their writing skills. Fill the pages of an album that has plastic page protectors with letter-shaped and geometric cutouts. Also fill the pages with cards labeled with students' names. Place the album in your literacy center along with dry erase markers and tissues. (Slim dry erase markers are less pungent.) Encourage your little ones to write, wipe, and then write again!

Jenny Unruh—Preschool, Special Education
Georgia Matthews Elementary
Garden City, KS

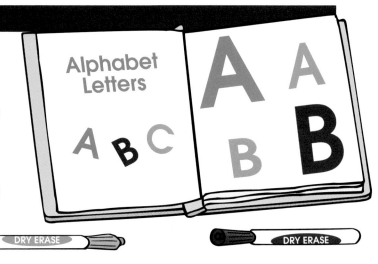

Blocks Center

Floor "Mat-tropolis"

Keep things moving at your blocks center by adding this easy-to-make floor mat that represents Your Town, USA! Using permanent markers, draw roads, buildings, and natural landmarks on a vinyl, felt-backed tablecloth (available at discount stores). Put the mat on the floor of your blocks center. Then encourage children visiting the center to use toy vehicles and blocks to get the city bustling with activity.

Maureen F. Guerin—Toddlers and Preschool
Hilltop Learning Center
Tewksbury, MA

Sand Table

Digging Up Bones

Youngsters will uncover their archeological skills when digging up these bones. During a study of dinosaurs, hide bone-shaped dog treats in your indoor and outdoor sand centers. Provide youngsters with buckets, shovels, and even paintbrushes to aid them in their digging.

Antares Narizzano—Pre-K
Rainbow Station Child Development Center
Richmond, VA

Dramatic-Play Center

Grocery Shopping Lists

Sooner or later you'll want to set up a grocery store in your dramatic-play area. When you do, be sure to provide these rebus-style shopping lists. They'll extend the dramatic play in your center, while promoting language and literacy skills at the same time. To prepare each list, cut out magazine or grocery ad pictures of items that you have in your store. Glue several pictures onto construction paper, label the list, and then laminate it. What's on your list? I'm looking for bananas, cereal, and milk!

Karen Still—Four-Year-Olds
Chevy Chase United Methodist Church Preschool
Chevy Chase, MD

Housekeeping Area

Take Time to Count the Roses

This dress-up prop might look like a hat to most people, but you're sure to see that it's a creative tool for reinforcing counting and classification skills as well as color words. To make the hat, attach the hook sides of a number of self-adhesive Velcro® stickers around the rim of the hat. Attach the loop side of a Velcro sticker to each of a number of artificial flowers that vary in color and type. Encourage a child to select flowers to put on the hat. Then ask lots of questions. How many flowers? Are they all the same? How many of each type? Now *that's* a thinking cap!

adapted from an idea by Audrey Englehardt—Early Childhood Education
Meadowbrook Elementary School
Moro, IL

Gross-Motor Area

Flower Toss

This beanbag tossing game reinforces colors just in time for spring! Collect a number of colorful round plastic baskets. Secure the bottom of each basket to the center of a matching paper flower shape. Add paper stems and leaves if desired. Arrange the flower baskets on the floor of an open area. Then give a child several beanbags and encourage him to pick the flowers in which he would like to toss the bags. It's a gross-motor garden!

Audrey Englehardt—Early Childhood Education

Setting The Stage:

Puzzle Center

Fishing for Puzzles

Here's a clever way to renew interest in your class puzzles. Invite youngsters to go fishing for the pieces! To prepare, hot-glue a flat magnetic item (such as a washer) to the back of each puzzle piece. Prepare a fishing pole with a magnet at one end of the pole's string. Place the pieces of each puzzle in a separate shoebox or other container. When visiting the center, a child chooses a box of puzzle pieces, fishes for the pieces, and assembles the puzzle as he makes his catches. For variety, put the box of puzzle pieces behind a divider. Have the child lower his fishing rod so that a child seated behind the divider can attach puzzle pieces to it.

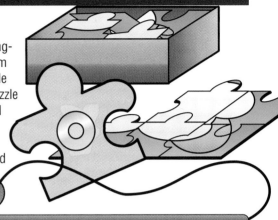

Kimberly Torretti—Preschool and Gr. K
Greystone House Montessori, Magnolia, TX

Water Table

Wash-o-matic

Children will line up for loads of fun at this water table laundry center! To prepare, stock the area with empty laundry product boxes and bottles, measuring scoops, a drying rack, clothespins, and doll clothes. If desired, add a small amount of mild dishwashing soap to the water to make it bubbly but still gentle on children's hands.

As a child participates in doing the laundry, he'll have the chance to gain loads of skills. For example, as he wrings out water, clips clothespins, and folds, he'll improve his muscle strength and coordination. Sequencing skills will be reinforced as he follows the steps for washing, adding soap, drying, and folding. And he'll also get hands on experience with the opposites wet/dry, heavy/light, dark/light, and big/little. Time to do laundry!

Helen Perth—Preschool, Special Education, Oswego County BOCES, Mexico, NY

Dramatic-Play Center

Space Shuttle

Invite your students to blast off into the final frontier of imagination with this space shuttle! Obtain a white display board from an office supply store. Spray-paint the board black or cover it with black paper. From poster board, design a space shuttle. Cut a circular window out of the shuttle; then attach the shuttle to the board. Next, cut a circle out of the board behind the shuttle's window; then tape clear plastic or cellophane to the back of it. When a child journeys into space in the shuttle, ask him to look back at Earth through the window and tell you what he sees. This also makes a great photo opportunity!

Bertha Cochran—Four-Year-Olds and Pre-K
St. Matthew's Preschool, Bloomington, IL

Math Center

Bubble Count

Something's fishy about this math center idea. It's how much fun youngsters have practicing counting and numeral recognition! To prepare the game, cut ten fish shapes (patterns on page 226) from colorful poster board; then write a different numeral from 1 to 10 on each fish. Arrange the fish on a piece of poster board; then trace around them. Use glitter glue to make a different number of bubbles from one to ten above each fish outline. Remove the fish. To use the game, a child counts the number of bubbles above a fish outline. Then he puts the fish with the corresponding numeral on the board beneath the bubbles.

Trish Draper—Pre-K and Gr. K
Millarville Community School
Millarville, Alberta, Canada

Literacy Center

M Is for Magnetic

To make a center that youngsters are sure to be attracted to, obtain a piece of sheet metal from a home supply store. Nail the piece to a wall. Then cover the sheet with bulletin board paper and add border if desired. Arrange magnetic letters and numerals on the board. Can you spell *F-U-N?*

Michelle West—Preschool
Denton City County Day School, Denton, TX

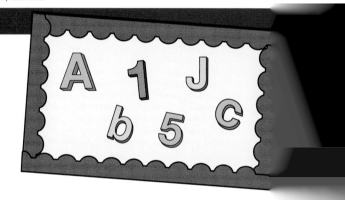

Discovery Center

It's a Jungle Over There!

This amazing idea is worth preserving! To create a rain forest environment in a corner of your room, attach lengths of green bulletin board paper to the walls; then create tree trunks out of brown bulletin board paper. From the ceiling, drape green tissue paper, netting, and green streamers. Arrange artificial greenery along the walls and trees. Fill the environment with toy rain forest animals, such as stuffed toy birds, rubber bugs and snakes, and student-made butterflies. Finally, play an audiotape of rain forest sounds.

To extend the learning while a child visits the forest, ask to him to find and count the animals in the area. Provide him with a recording sheet if desired. Or provide rain forest animal stamps, an ink pad, blank paper, and crayons. To create a reading area, add photo-illustrated books about the rain forest. Wild!

Susan Burbridge—Four-Year-Olds
Colonial Hills United Methodist School, San Antonio, TX

Patterns
Use with "Bubble Count" on page 225.

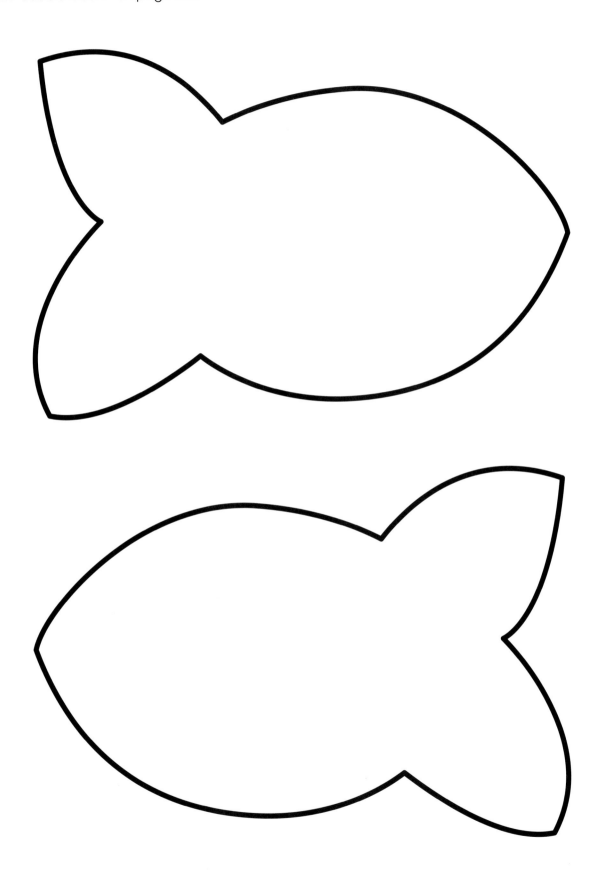

BUSY HANDS

BUSY HANDS

Creative Learning Experiences For Little Hands

KITCHEN CREATIVITY

Use kitchen utensils to help you cook up this batch
of fresh experiences for your little ones!

ideas contributed by Lisa Leonardi, Norfolk, MA

DISHWASHING DESIGNS

To prepare for this unique painting activity, cover a table with a solid-colored shower curtain liner or plastic tablecloth. Obtain several dishwashing utensils that are made to hold dishwashing liquid in the handle. Fill each handle three-fourths with liquid tempera paint and one-fourth with water. Encourage youngsters to squeeze the handles while moving the utensils over the liner or tablecloth. When it's time to clean up, wipe off the liner or tablecloth with a damp sponge and paper towels.

SPRAY 'N' SIFT

Invite youngsters to try this unusual way to paint using a flour sifter. Use a spray bottle filled with water to moisten a sheet of construction paper. Next use a flour sifter to apply a layer of powdered tempera paint onto the wet paper. Again moisten the paper. Watch the colors merge together into a bright masterpiece.

If desired, put more than one color of paint in the sifter at once. Or follow the first layer of paint with a different color.

SQUIRT AND SPLATTER

Use turkey basters to squeeze some fun into ordinary painting projects. In a center provide several pie tins of different colors of thin paint, a turkey baster for each different color of paint, a tub, and art paper. To use the items, a child places a sheet of paper in the tub; then he uses the turkey basters to squirt paint onto the paper. If desired, he takes his paper out of the tub, then moves it so that the paint drips in different directions. He's sure to enjoy watching the colors blend to create a one-of-a-kind painting!

I've "Bean" Busy!

That's what your little ones will say after trying this activity that develops visual tracking, coordination, *and* determination! Place a tub of different sizes of beans in a center along with a scoop. Poke several holes into an aluminum pie pan so that there are some holes only large enough for the smaller beans to go through and some large enough for the larger beans to go through. Challenge a child to put a scoop of beans in the pan and then try to sift the beans through the holes by shaking the pan. It won't take long before she'll realize that it takes careful shifting to get the larger beans through the larger holes.

Surprises by the Slice

Youngsters will improve their cutting skills when you provide them with butter knives and this fancy dough. Make a batch of your favorite white play dough. Then knead a handful of plastic confetti pieces into the dough. Roll the dough into a log; then put it in your center along with several butter knives. Encourage a child to slice the dough log to find the surprises inside!

What a Spread!

Invite youngsters over to a pretend cooking center to practice their spreading skills. Cut a number of colorful poster board "crackers" in various shapes and sizes. If desired, store the shapes in cracker boxes. Tint spreadable paste with tempera paint. Invite a child at the center to use a butter knife to spread the paste onto a cracker and then top it with another cracker. Aren't these delightful art hors d'oeuvres?

From Sink to Flower

Paint fanciful flowers by using a sponge dish mop, pot scrubber, or scalloped drain stopper! Just dip the items in a pie pan of paint, and then press them onto paper. When the paint is dry, use markers to add stems and leaves to these lovely flowers.

Spread and Squoosh

How do you turn white play dough into colorful dough? Spread on tempera paint; then squoosh it in! Invite a child to put a small ball of homemade white play dough onto a sheet of waxed paper. Next have him add a squirt of each of two different primary colors of washable paint onto the ball. After putting another piece of waxed paper on the dough, have the child use a rolling pin to blend the colors into the dough. After using this method several times, have him use his fingers to squoosh the colors together into the dough to create a new color.

BUSY HANDS

Creative Learning Experiences For Little Hands

STRINGS AND THINGS

ideas contributed by Lisa Leonardi, Jumpstart for Juniors, Norfolk, MA

LOVE TO LACE!

Sheets of plastic canvas make super sturdy lacing cards. Cut thin plastic lacing (such as S'getti Strings® lacing) into long lengths; then knot one end of each length. Invite a youngster to weave the plastic lacing in and out of the holes in the plastic canvas to make a design of his choice. Or use a permanent marker to draw (or trace) a simple shape onto a sheet of plastic canvas; then encourage a child to lace along the outline.

FUNNY FACES

Put smiles on your students' faces with this fun felt activity. Cut various colors of felt into large circles and ovals. Then cut colorful yarn or pipe cleaners into various lengths. Invite a child to choose a felt "face" and then shape features for it from the yarn or pipe cleaner pieces.

As a seasonal variation, cut orange felt pumpkin shapes and provide black yarn or pipe cleaner lengths. What jolly jack-o'-lanterns!

SPAGHETTI STATION

Serve up some fun with this water-table activity. To prepare, cut foot-long lengths of string, yarn, curling ribbon, and plastic lacing. Place them in your water table, along with pasta forks and colanders. Then invite little ones to stir, scoop, sift, and further explore the wet strings and things.

WEAVE IT

Make a few of these weaving trays to get lots of little hands busy with a weaving workout. To make one, use a pencil to poke an equal number of evenly spaced holes along two opposite sides of a Styrofoam® tray. Knot one end of a 36-inch length of yarn to a corner hole on the tray. Thread the yarn through the holes, making rows as shown; then knot the loose end to the last hole. Provide several lengths of yarn, ribbon, string, or twine in different colors. Invite a child to weave the strings and things over and under the rows on the tray.

When she's finished, she can save her work or remove the strings to prepare the tray for the next child who is wigglin' to weave.

SEASONAL STREAMERS

Get little ones involved in decorating your classroom for any season with this activity. Cut crepe paper streamers in colors coordinated to the current season. Invite little ones to use stamp pads and seasonal rubber stamps to stamp designs on the streamers. Or have children use seasonal paper punches to punch out designs from construction paper. Then have them glue the cutouts to the streamers. Dangle the finished streamers from your classroom ceiling or drape them across a bulletin board.

GET THINGS ROLLING

Little ones will have a ball with this variation on string painting. Wrap a long length of yarn around a large Styrofoam® ball, tucking in the loose ends of the yarn to hold it in place. Insert a craft stick or a pencil through the center of the ball. Provide shallow containers of tempera paint in different colors, as well as large sheets of construction paper. To paint, a child holds the string-covered ball by the handles, rolls it through the paint, and then rolls it onto a sheet of paper. Encourage him to repeat the process with other colors of paint as he desires. For added fun, have him sprinkle some glitter over the wet paint design.

JEWELRY WITH A TWIST

This pipe cleaner jewelry will be the fashion rage in your classroom! To make a necklace, twist together two pipe cleaners to make one long pipe cleaner. Then cut a length of yarn slightly longer than the extended pipe cleaner. Tape one end of the yarn to one end of the pipe cleaner; then wrap the yarn around and around the pipe cleaner and tape the opposite end. Twist the two pipe cleaner ends together and—ta da!—a nifty necklace! Try different lengths of pipe cleaners and yarn to create bracelets or headbands.

STICK 'EM ON

Here's a yarn collage that doesn't involve messy (and frustrating) glue. For each little artist, tape a piece of clear Con-Tact® paper sticky side up on a tabletop. Provide scissors and a variety of colorful string, yarn, ribbon, and rickrack. Invite a child to cut lengths of her desired materials and arrange them on the sticky paper. To display these masterpieces, just remove the tape and stick the Con-Tact paper to your classroom windows. Or seal the design with another piece of clear Con-Tact paper and send the projects home to admiring moms and dads.

BUSY HANDS

Creative Learning Experiences For Little Hands

CHILL OUT!

Keep little hands busy with these really cool and creative activities!

ideas contributed by Kathy H. Lee—Early Childhood Facilitator, Alpharetta, GA

SNOW CAPS

There's "snow" way your little ones will miss the chance to make snowball look-alikes at this sensory center. Combine enough grated Ivory® soap, torn white toilet paper, and cold water in a sensory tub to make a gooey mixture that can be shaped into messy mounds. Youngsters are sure to have a ball!

THE DEEP FREEZE

Ask your children to help you place small plastic fish or arctic animal toys into a number of resealable plastic bags. Next have the students help you fill the bags with blue water. Seal the bags; then put them in the freezer overnight. Ask the children to predict what will happen. The next day, ask them to describe how the bags look different. What happened to the toys? Place the bags in a science center for observation throughout the day.

POPSICLE® PAINTBRUSHES

To prepare for this cool creative experience, fill shaker containers (such as salt shakers or spice containers) with powdered tempera paint. Next fill ice cube trays with water. Cover the trays with aluminum foil; then insert a Popsicle® stick into each section of each tray. When the water is frozen, remove the cubes from the tray. Encourage a child to shake some paint onto white construction paper and then to use the Popsicle paintbrushes to turn the powder into a painting.

FUN CUBED

The fun just multiplies with this sensory activity. Fill regular or shaped ice cube trays with colored water; then put them in the freezer. Put the ice into a sensory tub along with measuring cups, bowls, spoons, tongs, and other items that the children can use to explore the melting cubes and cold water.

SHAKE IT UP

This activity mixes science with movement and results in tasty milkshake snacks! Provide each child with a lidded cup that has been half-filled with vanilla ice cream. Then help each child add some milk and a small amount of his choice of syrups or flavorings to his ice cream. Play some fun dance music as the children shake up their treats. Swing to the beat to make a sweet treat!

THE BIG CHILL

To give students a big thrill, put a box of cornstarch in a freezer for several hours. Dump an amount of the starch into a sensory tub; then invite students to explore the powder for a length of time. Next give the youngsters some warm water to mix into the cold starch. If your excited little ones can keep their cool, ask them to describe the experience.

SNOW DOUGH

All that glitters is not cold—but this snow dough sure is! Use your favorite recipe to make a batch of white play dough, adding iridescent glitter to the ingredients. Keep the dough chilled in the refrigerator until youngsters are ready to use it to make sparkly snow creations.

DO TELL, WHAT'S THIS GEL?

To get ready for this unique fingerpainting experience, chill several different colors of hair gel in the refrigerator. To use, give a child a length of waxed paper. Then squirt the hair gel color of her choice onto the paper. Little fingers exercise as they slip and slide through this chilly gel!

BUSY HANDS

Creative Learning Experiences For Little Hands

COLOR CONNECTIONS

RAIN MAKES RAINBOWS

Have a child arrange various colors of shredded tissue paper onto a white paper plate. Then invite the child to use a spray bottle filled with water to wet the paper. The colors from the tissue paper will transfer onto the plate, leaving behind a beautiful print when the papers are removed.

ROLLING RAINBOWS

To make a rolling rainbow for your little ones' enjoyment, fill a large clear plastic soft drink bottle with water and colorful plastic mosaic tiles (found in craft stores with the supplies for mosaic projects). Seal the cap tightly, adding a bit of hot glue for protection against leaks. Give it a roll and watch the colors whirl!

SIFT AND SORT

Add colorful beads to your sensory table sand. Encourage children to use slotted spoons and sifters to find the beads. Then challenge them to sort the beads by color. For even more fun, help them arrange the beads in rows to resemble a rainbow.

LET'S COLLABORATE!

In this activity, three colors *and* two artists are better than one! Gather red, yellow, and blue tempera paint; then put a small amount of each on separate trays. Add small rollers to the paint and provide a big piece of paper or tagboard for each pair of painters. Invite two children to paint, and it won't be long before rainbows appear!

MULTICOLORED DOUGH

As children make this rainbow dough, they'll also develop a whole spectrum of science process skills. Provide homemade white play dough and several colors of powdered tempera paint in salt shakers or spice containers. Invite children to sprinkle and shake the powdered paint onto balls of the white dough. Then have them squish the color in!

LAYER UPON LAYER

A little bit of clear Con-Tact® paper and a supply of different colors of cellophane strips are all your little ones will need to create these colorful collages. Help each child place a piece of the paper sticky side up. Then have her arrange her choice of the cellophane strips on the paper. Encourage the child to create some new colors by overlapping the strips. Be sure to adhere the collages to your windows for a room filled with rainbows of color.

RAZZLE-DAZZLE RAINBOW WEAVING

Put rolls of various colors of crepe paper streamers in a center along with plastic laundry baskets. Encourage children to weave the streamers through the baskets to create rainbows and to practice their fine-motor skills at the same time.

SERVE UP SOME COLOR

Develop some colorful creative-thinking and social skills in your little ones with this idea. Fill large mixing bowls with strips of colored cellophane. Put the bowls in your housekeeping kitchen along with kitchen tongs and wooden spoons. Would you like a rainbow, ma'am?

235

BUSY HANDS

Creative Learning Experiences For Little Hands

PITTER-PATTER, MUCK-MUCK

These creative ideas were inspired by the April showers and May mud.

by Michele M. Stoffel Menzel

MONET MUDSCAPES

Showcase youngsters' mud talent with this pudding-print twist! Fill three resealable plastic bags, each with a different flavor of prepared instant pudding (butterscotch, chocolate, and vanilla). Snip a small hole in the bottom corner of each bag. Encourage a child to squeeze the pudding through the hole in a bag onto a plastic plate. Then have him repeat the process, each time using a different pudding color. Encourage him to create a one-of-a-kind print by finger-swirling designs and then gently patting a piece of paper onto the plate. Lift the paper and discover the mudscape masterpiece!

THIS FORECAST CALLS FOR RAIN

Gear up for wet weather at this center! Create rain makers by punching or cutting holes in the bottom of plastic containers. Make tiny holes in one container, then gradually make bigger holes in each of the remaining containers. Invite little ones to visit the water table and explore by filling a container with water, holding it above the table, and listening to the rain sprinkle, drizzle, shower, and downpour. This rainstorm improves little ones' scooping and pouring skills while also tuning them into their sense of hearing!

PUDDLE STOMPIN'

Little ones create these rainy-day boot paintings by using their hands to do the stomping. Tape a length of white bulletin board paper to the floor of an uncarpeted area. Provide pairs of children's rubber boots or galoshes and shallow containers of brown tempera paint. Invite a child to place her hands inside a pair of boots, dip the boots in the paint, and then stomp her way across the paper.

ITSY-BITSY DOWNSPOUTS

Transform two pieces of PVC pipe—a one-foot length and a corner piece—into a downspout so that youngsters can explore how rainwater flows. Have children place the pipe inside a large rectangular plastic container, so that the corner piece is at the bottom of the container. Encourage children to watch what happens when they scoop water and pour it into the top of the pipe. Keep the fun flowing by adding plastic spiders. "Down came the rain and washed the spider out!"

MUD MUCKERS

Here's a clean way to play in the mud and build dexterity in little fingers. Fill a large, resealable plastic bag with dirt, water, and a plastic worm. Reinforce the seal with tape. Then invite little ones to muddle the mud using their fingers to create tunnels in the bag.

EDIBLE MUD MUCKERS

Are you looking for an edible muddy treat that also strengthens little fingers? Then try filling a bag for each child with whipped topping, one tablespoon of chocolate milk mix, and a Gummy Worm® candy. Encourage a child to use his fingers to squish and squeeze the mud mixture and then tunnel a path for the worm. When he finishes, consider providing him with a spoon. Mmm! Mud never tasted so good!

ROCKY ROAD MUD PIE

Head outside to create these one-of-a-kind mud pies. Have little ones moisten sand and press it into small pie tins to form piecrusts. Next empty potting soil into a small wading pool. Invite children to add water and stir until they make mud. Have them pour the mud filling into their crusts. Then have students garnish their pies with rocky road pebbles and shavings of grass blades. If desired, children can bake their pies in the sun until the mud has hardened.

"MARBLE-OUS" MUD MASSAGE

Improve flexibility and strengthen "little piggies" with this sensory experience. Cover the floor with a vinyl tablecloth. Prepare a batch of uncolored play dough and a batch to which brown tempera paint and dry coffee grounds (dirt) have been added. Give each child a small ball of each type of dough. Have him remove his shoes and socks; then encourage him to use his feet to knead the balls of dough together so that the colors begin to mix. For more fun, children can knead marbles into the dough, again using their feet. When finished, youngsters can place their dough into a zippered plastic bag to take home so they can share the marbleized effect with their families.

237

BUSY HANDS

Creative Learning Experiences For Little Hands

METALLIC MAGIC

Keep little hands busy with these shiny and reflective ideas.

by Michele M. Stoffel Menzel

FUN FOIL

Little ones will have a ball with this recycled foil idea. In advance, have children bring clean, recycled aluminum foil from home. To make a ball, begin by having a child form a piece of foil into a ball shape. Have children add more foil pieces, continuing this layering process until the ball has reached the desired size. Then invite children to roll, catch, or toss this shiny toy!

SLEEK DIGS

Brighten up your dramatic-play area with this sleek hideout. Place a refrigerator box on its side. With a utility knife, remove one of the long panels to create an opening. Invite children to assist you in taping lengths of foil to the inside walls and floor. Decorate the opening with strips of silver garland. Store some flashlights inside the box. Then encourage little ones to use the flashlights to explore these shiny new digs!

RIPPLIN' REFLECTIONS

Make some waves at your water table with all that glitters and gleams. Line your empty table with aluminum foil; then fill it with water. Add your favorite shiny or reflective materials including sequins, fake gemstones, or small pieces of shiny mylar paper. Then provide flashlights and handheld mirrors. Encourage children to use their hands to make waves in the water. Then invite them to use the flashlights to shine light into the water and onto the mirrors to reflect the light of the metallic objects. How's that for some ripplin' fun?

GLITZY GLOBES

Fill your room with dancing beams of light when youngsters make this glittering globe. Twist a paper clip into a hook shape and then insert one end into a large Styrofoam® ball. Have a group of children wrap sheets of foil around the ball until it is covered. If desired, have the children decorate the globe with foil star stickers. Tie a length of fishing line to the paper clip and then hang the ball from the ceiling at children's eye level. Darken the room and play some rhythmic music. Encourage children to take turns shining a flashlight on the ball to the beat of the music!

DO YOU SEE WHAT I SEE?

Set up this discovery center that invites little ones to explore light and color using compact discs. In advance, collect a supply of CDs such as the type that come in the mail promoting computer services. Place the discs on a tabletop in a well-lit area. As each child explores, encourage him to describe what he sees when he looks at the disk, such as his own image and the colors the disc reflects. Now that's music to his eyes!

ON THE FLIP SIDE

Set up this center for little ones to view reflections from the flip sides of compact discs. Place discs, simple pictures, and picture books on a table in a well-lit area. Have a child position the edge of a disc on a picture so that the shiny side faces toward the image. Invite her to look at the reflection as she captures each image. Wow! It's double vision!

CATCH SOME RAYS

After children have had plenty of time to explore CDs and how they reflect light, have them make these radiant suncatchers. To make his suncatcher, have a child use glitter paint or sequins and glue to decorate a compact disc. Then thread a length of metallic ribbon through the center of the disk, tie the ends, and hang the suncatcher from a sunny window for a dazzling display!

MIRROR, MIRROR...

Kids love seeing their own reflections, so create a looking glass that encourages them to make silly faces and practice drawing details. Place several colors of dry-erase markers near a full-length mirror. (Be sure the markers are used in a well-ventilated area.) As a child looks in the mirror, encourage her to draw the outline of her facial features on the mirror and then step aside to view her drawing. When finished, have her use a dry cloth or an eraser to wipe off the mirror. Now you see it, now you don't!

EXPLORATIONS

Explorations

Liquid Layers

Science concepts will flow quite naturally when youngsters try mixing two kinds of liquids—oil and water.

STEP 1

Launch your study of liquid layers by duplicating and sending home a parent note (page 254) with each child. Have a few extra bottles on hand for any students unable to bring them. Remove the labels from the bottles.

Dear Parent,
Please send one clean, empty 20-ounce clear plastic bottle with your child by
_____.
Don't forget the lid! Thanks!

STEP 2

Using a pitcher and a funnel, demonstrate to a small group of youngsters how to pour water into a bottle. Then have each child half-fill his bottle with water in the same manner, giving assistance when needed. Next help each child add several drops of food coloring to his water. Secure the lid tightly on each bottle; then have the children roll their bottles back and forth on the floor to blend the water and food coloring.

STEP 5

Have each youngster predict what will happen when his bottle is shaken. Then invite him to vigorously shake his bottle to find out! While students are shaking their bottles, have them sing the song below. For additional verses, substitute the word *up* with *left*, *right*, or *down*.

(sung to the tune of "The Wheels on the Bus")
I'll take my bottle and shake it [up],
Shake it [up], shake it [up]!
I'll take my bottle and shake it [up].
Will the liquids mix?

STEP 6

Have your little ones place their bottles on a table and carefully observe the contents for a couple of minutes. As they observe, ask some questions:
Did the oil turn the same color as the water when you shook your bottle?
Did the oil mix with the water?
Is the water on the top or bottom?
Where are the tiny materials that you added?

Science You Can Do by *Suzanne Moore*

To learn about mixing oil and water, you will need:
— one parent note per child (page 254)
— one plastic 20-ounce bottle (with lid) per child
— several funnels
— a pitcher of water (need about 10 ounces of water per child)
— food coloring
— 1/4 cup vegetable or baby oil per child
— 1/4 measuring cup
— plastic confetti or sequins

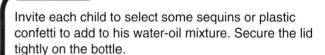

STEP 3

Remove the lid from each bottle. Assist each youngster in measuring 1/4 cup of oil in a measuring cup; then have him use the funnel to pour the oil into his bottle of water. Encourage each little scientist to describe what he observes when the oil is added to the water.

STEP 4

Invite each child to select some sequins or plastic confetti to add to his water-oil mixture. Secure the lid tightly on the bottle.

This Is Why

- Food coloring is made mostly of water, so it mixes with the water.
- Oil and water do not mix. They are *immiscible*.
- Although it appears that the water and oil blend together when shaken, they actually stay separate. The oil and water will always separate into layers, no matter how long or how hard the bottles are shaken.
- After the shaken bottles are left still for awhile, the oil moves to the top of the water because oil has a lower density than water.
- The tiny materials (sequins, confetti, etc.) will be suspended in the water or in the oil, depending on their density. Having a density about the same as water will suspend the items in the water. Having a density about the same as oil will suspend them in the oil.

What Now?

To reinforce the concept that oil and water don't mix, try this artistic science activity. Mix a small amount of vegetable oil with powdered tempera paint. For the best results, make several different colors in separate containers. Half-fill a rubber dishpan or cake pan with water. Spoon a few drops of the oil-based paints into the water and stir. Youngsters will observe that the paint floats on the water. Why? Because it is mixed with the oil! In turn, invite each student to place the bottom of a small paper plate on the water's surface. Let the plate float as your youngsters count to five. Remove the plate from the water and then set it aside to dry. Oil still doesn't mix with water, but it certainly creates a "marble-ous" paper plate!

243

Explorations

The Case of the Vanishing Ghosts

Scare up some science with this activity that makes ghostly water spots vanish into thin air!

STEP 1

Give each child in a small group a sponge and a piece of black construction paper. Using a spooky voice, announce that youngsters will use the items to make ghosts appear and disappear.

STEP 2

Continuing in a mysterious manner, demonstrate how to make a ghost appear and disappear. To do this, dip a sponge in the bucket; then squeeze out the excess water. Use the sponge to draw the outline of a ghost on the chalkboard; then fill in the shape to complete the wet ghost.

STEP 5

Encourage students to talk about their observations. Share the information in "Here's Why" to help students understand that fanning their ghosts helped them disappear.

Mine disappeared into thin air!

I think the chalkboard ate mine.

Here's Why

- *Evaporation* occurs when water disappears into the air.
- When water is exposed to air, it evaporates.
- The more air that water is exposed to, the quicker it will evaporate.
- Although the water on the chalkboard would have evaporated without the fanning motion, the moving air caused the water to evaporate more quickly.

Science You Can Do *by Suzanne Moore*

To learn about evaporation, you will need:
—bucket of water
—1 small sponge per child in a small group plus 1 extra
—clean chalkboard or 1 individual chalkboard per child
—1 sheet of black construction paper per child plus 1 extra

STEP 3

Next use the black construction paper to fan air onto the ghost to make it disappear. As you fan, recite the following chant.

> Mr. Ghost, you don't scare me!
> I know how to make you flee!
> With my fan I have no fear,
> 'Cause I can make you disappear!
> Ooooooooooh...oooooooooooh...
> *(Continue to say, "Ooh," as you fan away the ghost.)*

STEP 4

Invite each child to use his sponge and paper in the same manner to make a ghost appear and disappear. Remind youngsters to recite the chant as they fan their ghosts away.

What Now?

Prepare a science center where youngsters can try additional experiments with wet spots. To set up the center, put sponges and a bucket of water near the chalkboard (or provide individual chalkboards in the center). Suggest that students try these experiments.

• Make wet ghosts but do not fan them. What happens?
• Use clean paintbrushes to make wet ghosts. Do they evaporate more or less quickly than the ghosts made with the sponges?
• Make wet ghosts with warm water. Do they evaporate more or less quickly than ghosts made with cold water?

The water will float to the ceiling.

JB

The water might just sit there. But water ghosts disappear.

Shae

Develop youngsters' observation skills with this follow-up experiment. Attach a strip of tape to the side of a baby-food jar; then half-fill the jar with water. Place the jar near a window; then cut a large ghost from bulletin-board paper to display near the jar. Ask students to predict what will happen to the water if it is left sitting out. Record students' predictions on the ghost. Every few days, mark the water level on the tape; then record several students' observations on the ghost. Will this water vanish like the water on the chalkboard? There's more than a ghost of a chance that it will!

245

Explorations

Brrr! It's Frosty!

Jack Frost isn't telling all of his secrets, but he is willing to share one way to make frost so that your little ones can chill out with science.

JACK

STEP 1

Ask your little ones whether they have heard of Jack Frost or seen his icy work on cold days. Next explain that you have found out one of Jack's secrets for making frost. To begin the activity, give each child in a small group a can to fill with crushed ice. Ask the students to observe how the outsides of their cans feel.

STEP 2

Help each child measure one cup of water to pour over the crushed ice. Ask the children to watch the outsides of their cans for several minutes.

ONE CUP

STEP 5

Once a thin layer of frost forms on the outside of each child's can, ask youngsters what they think Jack's secret is. How was the frost made? Record their ideas.

I think the salt is his secret! My can has ice!

STEP 6

Use the information in "This Is Why" to explain how Jack Frost's secret ingredient (salt) made the water on the outsides of the cans turn to frost. Then sing this song to the tune of "Mr. Sun" to wrap up your chilly lesson.

Mister Frost, Frost, Mister Jack Frost,
Oh, we know your secret now.
Mister Frost, Frost, Mister Jack Frost,
Oh, we know your secret now.
Salt makes water very, very cold.
So cold it turns to ice—that is what we're told.
Mister Frost, Frost, Mister Jack Frost,
Oh, we know your secret now.

JACK

Science You Can Do by *Suzanne Moore*

To make frost, you will need:
— 1 empty 16-ounce can for each child in a small group (cover the cans' rims with tape for safety)
— crushed ice (enough to fill each child's can)
— 1 cup of water per child
— 1-cup measuring cup
— 3 tablespoons of salt per child
— tablespoon
— 1 plastic spoon per child

STEP 3

When water forms on the outsides of the cans, ask some questions: What did the water do to the crushed ice? How does the outside of the can feel now? What do you think makes the water on the outside of your can? Record each child's ideas.

The can shows it's cold by having water on its outside!

STEP 4

Tell your children that you have Jack Frost's secret ingredient for making frost. Then help each child add three tablespoons of salt to her can. Have her gently stir the salt into the ice water. Wait about five minutes.

TBSP

This Is Why

So what is Jack Frost's secret? When the salt is added to the ice water, it makes the water inside the can colder. When the water gets colder, the can gets colder. The water on the outside of the can freezes, covering the can with frost.

Pam Crane

What Now?

Here's another one of Jack's secrets for making frost. Slather some petroleum jelly on a glass pan. Invite several youngsters to use their fingers to make squiggly designs on the jelly. Place the pan in the freezer for two hours. When the pan is removed from the freezer, youngsters will find that a frosty coating has formed on their drawings.

Explorations

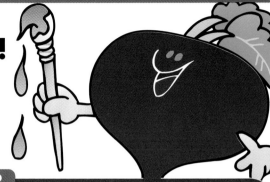

The Beet Goes On!

Youngsters will be tickled pink when they make this "un-beet-able" paint!

STEP 1

Chop the beets into half-inch cubes; then place them in a plastic bowl.

STEP 2

Invite each child in a small group to take a peek at the chopped beets. Have them brainstorm ways to use the beets to make pink paint. Record their responses on a beet-shaped chart.

Mush the beets. C.D.

Squeeze the beets. V.M.

Rub the beets on paper. A.G.

STEP 5

Direct each child to remove the lid from her container. Help her strain the beet juice into the second container. Discard the beets.

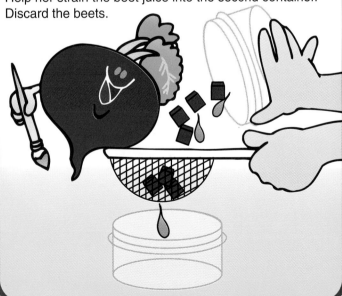

STEP 6

Help each student add one tablespoon of white paint to her beet juice. Then have her use a paintbrush to thoroughly mix the paint and juice. Next provide each child with painting paper and invite her to paint.

Science You Can Do by *Suzanne Moore*

To explore the natural dye found in beets, you will need:

— fresh beets (¼ cup chopped beets per child)
— sharp knife (for teacher use)
— large plastic bowl
— beet-shaped chart paper
— marker
— ¼ cup measuring cup
— 2 small plastic containers with lids per child
   in a small group
— tablespoon
— 1 tablespoon water per child
— strainer
— 1 tablespoon white paint per child
— 1 paintbrush per child in a small group
— white painting paper

STEP 3

Help each student measure one-fourth cup of chopped beets. Have her pour the beets into a plastic container and then add one tablespoon of water. Make sure the lid is secure.

STEP 4

Invite each child to vigorously shake her container (for about two minutes) as she repeatedly sings the song below.

(sung to the tune of "Did You Ever See a Lassie?")

Have you ever made some pink paint,
Some pink paint, some pink paint?
Have you ever made some pink paint
By shaking up beets?
I'll shake the beets this way!
I'll shake the beets that way!
Have you ever made some pink paint
By shaking up beets?

This Is Why

Some fruits and vegetables contain natural colorings, or *pigments*. Beets have a red pigment. Shaking the beet chunks with water made the water red. Mixing the red juice with white paint made the paint turn pink!

What Now?

Prepare a supervised paint center so that youngsters can experiment with another source of pigments—spices. To create a paint, help a child thoroughly mix one teaspoon of water with one teaspoon of either paprika or ground mustard. Provide him with a sheet of paper and invite him to use the spice mixture to paint a picture.

Explorations

Shake, Set, and Settle

Your little ones will really dig the science of soil!

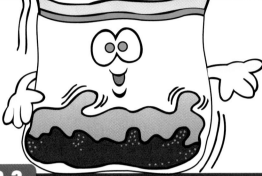

In advance, locate an area outside your classroom where you and your budding geologists can safely and easily dig up some dirt. If necessary, prepare the site by loosening the soil.

Give each child in a small group a craft stick for loosening the soil, a spoon for scooping the soil, and a plastic bag for collecting the soil. Encourage the children to get busy digging and putting spoonfuls of soil, small rocks, and leaf pieces in their bags. (If desired, give each child several aquarium rocks to add to his soil.)

Invite each child to stand and shake his bag while singing the following song to the tune of "The Hokey-Pokey."

You shake it to the left.
You shake it to the right.
You shake it up and down,
And you shake with all your might!
You shake toward the ceiling and
    you shake toward the floor.
Shake that dirt all about!

Attach each child's bag to a bulletin board that is at students' eye level by stapling it above the seal. Leave the bags undisturbed for several hours. Then invite each child to reexamine his bag (without touching it so that the contents stay settled).
Ask some questions:
Are all of the layers the same color?
Where are the rocks? Where are the leaves?
*Why do you think the water is in
    a different place from the dirt?*

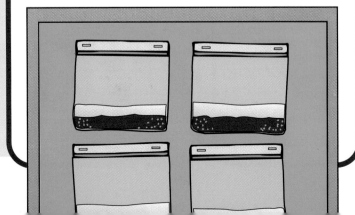

Science You Can Do by *Suzanne Moore*

To learn about soil and sedimentation, you will need:
—1 resealable plastic sandwich bag per child
—1 craft stick per child
—1 plastic spoon per child
—small rocks such as aquarium rocks (optional)
—1 paper towel per child
—magnifying glasses
—water
—small pouring container or cup
—masking tape
—stapler

STEP 3

After returning to your classroom, have each child pour his dirt onto a paper towel and then use a magnifying lens to take a closer look at it.
Ask some questions:
Is all of the dirt the same color?
Is the dirt wet or dry?
How does the dirt feel? Smell?
Do you see anything else
  (like bugs, rocks, or leaves) in the dirt?

STEP 4

Help each child return his dirt to his plastic bag. As you hold the bag open, have the child pour some water in the bag. Then seal the bag, securing the opening with tape.

Did You Know?

• There are different kinds of soils because there are many kinds of rocks. When the students look at their soil samples they might see different colors or types of soil, such as black soil, red soil, sandy soil, or soil that is like clay.

• Soil is a mixture of many things. For example, it might contain tiny bits of rock and pieces of plants. When a water and soil mixture settles, the larger pieces (such as the rocks) settle first. Then the different types of soil fall to the bottom. Some of the decayed materials may float. This is called *sedimentation*.

What Now?

• Have students make a dirt dessert by layering large cookie pieces (large rocks), small cookie crumbs (sand and clay), and chocolate pudding (mud) in a clear plastic bag as used in the activity. These sediment layers taste sweet!

• Try the activity described in Steps 1–6 using different types of soil, such as potting soil or sand. Will these kinds of soils also settle into sediment layers?

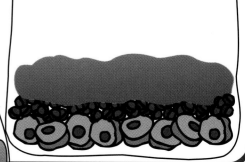

251

Explorations

Beautiful Briquettes!

Grow colored crystals with this simple activity using a summer staple—charcoal briquettes!

STEP 1

Give each child in a small group one or more charcoal briquettes on a separate paper towel. Then have the children use magnifying lenses to take a closer look at the briquettes. As they observe, ask some questions:

How does the charcoal feel?
Is the charcoal smooth or rough?
What happens to your fingers when you touch the charcoal?
Do you see anything else (like shiny specks) on the charcoal?

Have the children use moist towelettes to wash their smudged fingers after handling the briquettes.

STEP 2

Give each child a container filled with one-half cup of warm water. Next, give each child a small amount of salt to examine with a magnifying lens. Ask the children to predict what will happen when the salt and water are mixed together.

STEP 5

Have each child take her briquettes out of the water and then place them on her plate. Set the plate in a sunny area.

STEP 6

As a class, observe the briquettes each day. Record any changes the children observe. (In three to five days, crystals will begin forming on the briquettes.) After several days, have your little ones flip their briquettes over to discover even more crystals. If the air temperature is cool or humid, allow more time for the crystals to form.

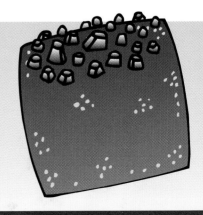

252

Science You Can Do *by Suzanne Moore*

To grow crystals, you will need:
— 1 or more charcoal briquettes per child
— 1 paper towel per child
— magnifying lenses
— moist towelettes
— 1 wide-mouth plastic container (large enough to hold one or more briquettes) per child in a small group
— measuring cups
— ¼ cup salt per child
— ½ cup warm water per child
— food coloring
— 1 craft stick per child
— a timer
— 1 paper plate per child
— crayons

STEP 3

Help each child add one-fourth cup of salt and several drops of food coloring to the water. Have her stir the water with a craft stick until the salt has dissolved. Allow time for discussion.

SALT

STEP 4

Direct each child to place her briquettes in the salt water. Set a timer for five minutes. While the children are waiting, have each child use crayons to decorate a personalized paper plate.

Jamie

This Is Why

So why did crystals form on the charcoal briquettes? Each piece of salt had a square shape. Each piece was a crystal. When the salt was added to the water the crystals lost their shape. They dissolved. When the charcoal was put in the water, it absorbed the salt in the water. When the charcoal was placed in a warm place to dry out, the water evaporated and the salt crystals were left behind on the charcoal. Crystals take longer to form when the air temperature is cool or humid because the water evaporates more slowly.

SALT

What Now?

To see the salt crystals in another way, try this artistic science activity. Invite several children to use their briquettes to make designs on paper. Finally, have the children use their magnifying lenses to observe the colored salt crystals on their drawings.

Dear Parent,
   Please send one clean, empty 20-ounce clear plastic bottle with your child by

_____ .

Don't forget the lid!
Thanks!

Dear Parent,
   Please send one clean, empty 20-ounce clear plastic bottle with your child by

_____ .

Don't forget the lid!
Thanks!

BUILDING BRIDGES

Building Bridges
Between Home And School

School: _____

Teacher: _____

Date: _____

Be Creative!

Creativity is thinking, expressing, or putting things together in a new way. Is your child creative? Chances are you say "yes!" Think about these characteristics you might see in your three- or four-year-old.

- Young children are naturally curious and adventurous.
- Young children are unself-conscious and open to expressing themselves in a variety of ways. They aren't concerned with being perfect.
- Preschoolers enjoy telling lengthy, imaginative stories.
- Older preschoolers may choose a favorite area of creativity, such as drawing and painting, listening and moving to music, or telling stories and making up songs.

Creative experiences establish feelings of self-confidence and satisfaction. They help children make decisions, solve problems, and improve language skills. So how can you take a new look at encouraging your child's uninhibited creative spirit?

- Display your child's artwork.
- Tape-record your child's music.
- Provide a variety of art supplies, such as clay, markers, all types of paper, paint, fingerpaint, scissors, and glue.
- Give your child enriching experiences at museums and musical concerts.
- Do something creative while your child is watching!
- Spark discussion about creativity by sharing the stories at the right. (Look for them at your library or bookstore.)

The Book Corner

Books About Being Creative

Matthew's Dream
After visiting an art museum, Matthew decides he wants to be a painter.
Written & Illustrated by Leo Lionni
Published by Alfred A. Knopf, Inc.

Frederick
Although it appears that Frederick is doing nothing while his fellow mice prepare for the winter, Frederick's creative work later saves the day.
Written & Illustrated by Leo Lionni
Published by Alfred A. Knopf, Inc.

The Art Lesson
Creative young Tommy loves to draw and receives encouragement from his family and friends. In kindergarten, however, he and his teachers must come to a compromise.
Written & Illustrated by Tomie dePaola
Published by Paper Star

Harold and the Purple Crayon
This simple story proves that with a little imagination and creativity, anything is possible.
Written & Illustrated by Crockett Johnson
Published by HarperCollins Children's Books

Hop Jump
All the other frogs hop, but Betsy finds a new way of moving—dancing.
Written & Illustrated by Ellen Stoll Walsh
Published by Harcourt Brace & Company

To the teacher: Duplicate a copy of pages 257 and 258. Complete the information at the top of page 257; then add class-related news to page 258. Trim away these instructions. Duplicate a copy for each child on the front and back sides of a colorful piece of paper.

Together Time

It's a Frame-Up

Encourage your child's creativity by displaying his/her artwork prominently and proudly in your home. Have your child choose or create a picture. Then creatively decorate a frame for it.

1. Obtain a frame with a border that is at least 1/2-inch wide.
2. Gather one or more types of items for decorating the frame, such as crayon wrappers, buttons, fake jewels, ribbon, dimensional paints, wood shapes, and more.
3. Help your child glue his/her choice of items onto the frame.
4. When the glue is dry, use the frame to proudly display your child's picture.

Kitchen Capers

Creative Creatures

Kitchens are creative places, too! Gather your choice of the food items listed; then invite your child to make a different creature each time you pull out the ingredients.

1. Give your child half of an English muffin or bagel.
2. Have your child spread either peanut butter or any type of cream cheese onto the bread.
3. Have your child choose from these ingredients to create his/her own mouthwatering monster: alfalfa sprouts, sliced vegetables and fruits, shredded cheese, dried fruits, pretzel sticks, and more.
4. Take a picture of your creative kid with the snack to preserve his/her creation long after it has been consumed.

Read All About It!
Our Class News

The ideas in this newsletter are contributed by Jan Brennan.

Building Bridges
Between Home And School

School: _____

Teacher: _____

Date: _____

Reading Aloud

What gift can you give your child that will

- foster feelings of love and security,
- increase his/her imagination and vocabulary,
- increase future success in reading and writing?

You can give the gift of time spent reading aloud. All you need is ten minutes a day and a good book! Keep these tips in mind for enjoyable reading times.

- Choose books with **words that are repetitive and fun to read.** Choose stories that are **not too long** in length and are **easy to understand** when listened to.

- Share picture books with **interesting illustrations** that you can stop to discuss together.

- **Read with expression!** Ask your child to join you in using a big voice, a scary voice, a sleepy voice, a quiet voice, and more to repeat phrases.

- **Be careful not to read too quickly.** A slower pace helps your child think about the story and form his/her own questions. It also lets his/her imagination develop possibilities as to what will happen next or how the story will end.

- Allow your child to **ask questions.** Develop curiosity by asking him/her questions as well.

- Set aside **a special time each day** for reading to let your child know that your time together is important.

- **Read it again!** Take advantage of your child's growing interest in reading by enjoying favorite books over and over again.

The Book Corner

The Read-Aloud Handbook (4th Edition)
The first part of this book explains the importance of reading aloud to children. The second gives reviews of more than 1,200 children's books that Mr. Trelease considers excellent read-alouds.
Written by Jim Trelease
Published by Penguin Books USA Inc.

Read-Aloud Rhymes for the Very Young
This child-friendly collection of poems for young children has over 200 short rhymes about picnics, puppies, special days, and more.
Selected by Jack Prelutsky; Illustrated by Marc Brown
Published by Alfred A. Knopf, Inc.

The 20th-Century Children's Book Treasury
This beautiful book contains 44 of the best children's stories for reading aloud. You'll find stories labeled for the young, the younger, and the youngest of your children.
Edited by Janet Schulman
Published by Alfred A. Knopf, Inc.

Recipe for Reading Aloud

Mix together:
1 enthusiastic and loving adult
1 curious and receptive child
1 good read-aloud book

Place in a comfortable chair and "set" for 10–15 minutes.
Yields: Feelings of warmth and security along with future reading success!

To the teacher: Duplicate pages 259 and 260. Complete the information at the top of page 259; then add class-related news to page 260. Trim away these instructions. Duplicate the pages for each child on the front and back sides of a colorful piece of paper.

Together Time

Listen to This!

Personalize your child's favorite stories by tape-recording the two of you reading them together. Begin by choosing a story with which your child is very familiar. A very predictable book or one that has a great deal of repetition makes a good choice. Practice reading the story together. Then begin recording by saying the title and author of the book. Read and describe the story together. If desired, add background noises or music to enhance your production. When your recording is complete, label the tape with the title, author, readers, and the date. You and your child will enjoy these tapes now and cherish them in years to come!

Kitchen Capers

Storytime Snack

For a super simple snack mix, have your child help you mix together equal amounts of Honey Nut Cheerios®, pretzel sticks, and raisins. Keep the container and your favorite books together so you can enjoy a book when you pause for a snack. Crunch, munch…read!

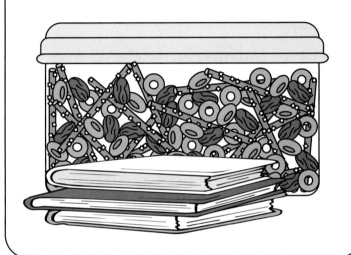

Read All About It!
Our Class News

The ideas in this newsletter are contributed by Jan Brennan.

Building Bridges
Between Home And School

School: _____

Teacher: _____

Date: _____

The "Write" Time to Start

Is your child writing at the age of three and four? You bet! You just have to know what you are looking for. Watch for your child to go through these stages of writing: 1) **drawing,** 2) **scribbling** lines and "reading" what they say, 3) **writing familiar letters** over and over again and reading what they say, 4) **sounding out words** when writing, and 5) writing with **correct spelling.**

Your child has been preparing for writing since he/she first grabbed a rattle in his/her tiny hand. The fine-motor skills necessary for successful writing develop over time. So does a child's understanding of writing. How can you set the stage for continued writing readiness?

• **Model writing.** When your child sees you writing daily for many different reasons, he/she will want to imitate you. He/she will also see how important and useful writing is. Write out such things as your grocery list, cards, and to-do lists in front of your child so he/she can learn by watching. Talk out loud as you write, telling your child what you are doing.

• **Provide supplies and opportunities for your child to exercise his/her hand muscles.** Designate a writing drawer or box somewhere in your house to fill with supplies such as

—paper of various sizes, textures, and colors
—writing tools including markers, crayons, and pencils
—play dough
—puzzles and building toys

• **Talk about your child's drawings and writing.** When presented with a drawing or a paper filled with scribbles, encourage your child by asking him/her questions about his/her work. Offer to write down his/her dictated story.

Still not sure if your child is writing? Keep encouraging him/her and when the time is "write," your child will let you know!

The Book Corner

Books About Writing

Harold and the Purple Crayon
With the power of a purple crayon in his hand, Harold draws himself some truly wonderful adventures.
Written & Illustrated by Crockett Johnson
Published by HarperCollins Juvenile Books

Purple, Green and Yellow
Brigid gets carried away as she draws and colors with her new markers, but comes up with a very satisfying solution to her problem.
Written by Robert Munsch
Published by Annick Press

Under the Table
A little girl enjoys drawing under the table. Fortunately, her parents understand when she draws on the underside of the table as well.
Written & Illustrated by Marisabina Russo
Published by Greenwillow Books

Cherries and Cherry Pits
Bidemmi draws four pictures and tells the story that each one depicts.
Written & Illustrated by Vera B. Williams
Published by Mulberry Books

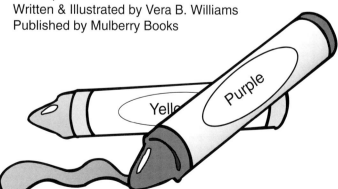

To the teacher: Duplicate pages 261 and 262. Complete the information at the top of page 261; then add class-related news to page 262. Trim away these instructions. Duplicate the pages for each child on the front and back sides of a colorful piece of paper.

My Big Book of Writing

Preserve some of your child's precious first writings to look at years from now when he/she has published his/her first book. To make a big book of writing, insert plenty of large sheets of drawing paper between two same-sized pieces of poster board. Punch holes through the left side of the book and bind it with adjustable metal rings or shower curtain rings. Invite your child to design the cover of the book; then write the title and author's name (your child's name) on it. Each time your child draws and "writes" a story on a page, write his/her dictated story on the bottom or back of the page. This book is sure to be a family favorite for years to come.

MBTCWS
ABBBRSS

My cat is so silly one day she climbed up the curtains

All "Write" Pudding

Here's a tasty way to help your child develop the fine-motor skills needed for writing. Make a batch of your child's favorite flavor of pudding; then spoon it onto a cookie sheet. Next gather together some writing tools such as spoons and straws. Encourage your child to use her fingers and the writing tools to write a story for you. Be sure your child tells you the story before she devours the evidence!

Read All About It!
Our Class News

Orange

Blue

The ideas in this newsletter are contributed by Jan Brennan.

Building Bridges
Between Home And School

School: _____

Teacher: _____

Date: _____

Rhythm

Your child's natural sense of rhythm began to develop before birth, as he or she listened to his/her mother's heartbeat. Rhythms are still a big part of your child's world—the ticking of clocks, the pitter-patter of rain, the steady panting of a dog. Encourage your child to respond to rhythms, not only for pure enjoyment, but also to
- strengthen listening skills
- promote self-expression
- improve body awareness, coordination, and balance

Use these simple activities to draw out your child's natural love of rhythm.

- Roam in and around your home with your child, listening carefully to the rhythms that often go unnoticed. Each time your child hears a different rhythm—like the bouncing of a basketball in the driveway next door, the purring of a cat, or the turning of the dryer—encourage him to talk about the rhythm. Is it fast? Slow? Soft? Loud?

- On another day, roam around the house listening for rhythms again. Each time the child points out another one, ask him/her to choose a way of moving (skipping, gliding, or marching, for example) that matches the rhythm.

- When the TV is on, ask your child to listen for rhythms and move to them. Talk about why some rhythms are relaxing to move to, while others leave you out of breath.

- Play several different musical recordings that vary in rhythm. Each time, ask your child to suggest a way for you to move together to each piece of music. Hold scarves as you move to music that has a more tranquil rhythm. After a few songs, ask your child why it seems right to move differently to different songs.

- Chant the nursery rhyme "Hickory, Dickory, Dock!" with your little one while you rock from side to side like the pendulum on a grandfather clock. Pretend to be chickens strutting and leading with your beaks as you move to the rhythm of "Hickety-Pickety, My Black Hen."

The Book Corner

Books With a Beat

Jamberry
This "berry" silly story about a boy and a bear invites you to join in the fun through its wonderful rhymes.
Written & Illustrated by Bruce Degen
Published by HarperTrophy

Chicka Chicka Boom Boom
The rhythm and rhyme in this clever alphabet book are as appealing as the vibrant illustrations.
Written by John Archambault and Bill Martin Jr.
Published by Simon & Schuster Books for Young Readers

The Train Ride
When you read this book, have your child put his/her bent arms at his/her side and keep the beat while pretending to be a traveling train.
Written by June Crebbin
(Check your library.)

Five Little Monkeys Jumping on the Bed
Five Little Monkeys Sitting in a Tree
Read, count, and keep the beat of these stories about five silly monkeys.
Written & Illustrated by Eileen Christelow
Published by Clarion Books

Bearobics: A Hip-Hop Counting Story
This whimsical countdown book is sure to lead to some rhythmic reading and fancy footwork.
Written by Vic Parker
Published by Puffin Books

To the teacher: Duplicate pages 263 and 264. Complete the information at the top of page 263; then add class-related news to page 264. Trim away these instructions. Duplicate the pages for each child on the front and back sides of a colorful piece of paper.

Together Time

Rhythm Sticks

Once your child has listened for rhythms in the world around him/her, it's going to be mighty tempting to create some from scratch. For these activities, you'll need a couple of pairs of homemade rhythm sticks. Use real sticks, wooden dowels from a home improvement store, chopsticks, or unsharpened pencils (especially the thick kind of beginner pencils). If desired, decorate the sticks with markers or paint, or by tying on ribbons, feathers, shoelaces, or beaded strings. Give your child a pair and keep a pair for yourself.

- Using your sticks, tap out three beats on the floor and have your child repeat them. Continue to tap out simple rhythms for your child to copy. Speed up and slow down.
- Lead your child as you tap your two sticks together while he/she copies your movements. Tap high, low, fast, and slow. Tap once. Tap twice. Tap them five times. That sounds nice!
- Have your child tap out beats for you to repeat.
- Play several very different musical recordings and tap out the rhythms together.

Kitchen Capers

Rhythm Shakers Snack

For a snack that has a rhythm all its own, pop a batch of popcorn with your child. Talk about the rhythm the kernels make as they pop. When the popcorn has cooled, mix it with Goldfish® crackers, pretzels, and sesame sticks. (Add or substitute ingredients as you wish.) Fill empty yogurt cups or other tubs with tight-fitting lids no more than halfway with this mixture. (If desired, partially fill each of several other lidded containers with a single type of ingredient to produce different sounds.) Replace the lids. Now play a recording of a lively song or two and use your shakers as musical accompaniment. When you're all done, remove the lids and enjoy your snack.

Read All About It!
Our Class News

The ideas in this newsletter are contributed by Jan Brennan.

Building Bridges
Between Home And School

School: _____

Teacher: _____

Date: _____

Dressing With Success

"I can do it myself!" Hearing these words from your preschooler means that he/she is growing more and more independent! However, if you have a three- or four-year-old who wants to dress himself but can't quite manipulate the buttons, zippers, and shoelaces, then dressing time can become a stressful time. Keep your child's abilities in mind; then consider the following tips for helping him dress independently with success.

Three-year-olds can usually:
• undress using simple fasteners
• button/unbutton large buttons
• unzip front zipper
• put on shoes (may be incorrect feet)
• fasten snaps

Four-year-olds can usually:
• undress and dress with little help
• button smaller buttons
• engage separating zipper with help
• lace shoes (but may not tie laces)

No need to get tied up! Use these helpful tips:
• When your child wants to dress him-/herself, select clothes that require minimal skills, such as elastic-waist pants, pullover shirts with wide openings, and shoes with Velcro® fasteners. As your child's confidence and skill level increase, match up one piece of clothing that is easy to put on with one that requires some skill.
• To assist your child, lay out the clothes correctly oriented to help distinguish front from back.
• If you are helping your child dress, work quickly. But if you are letting your child dress him-/herself, allow plenty of time.
• When you have time to play with your child, practice buttoning, zipping, and lacing skills by dressing dolls or playing dress-up. Why not let your child help *you* get dressed?

The Book Corner

Books About Clothing

Mrs. Toggle's Zipper
Kids are likely to have trouble with their zippers, but adults don't. Or do they? Children enjoy this funny story about a teacher, and are comforted by it as well.
Written by Robin Pulver
Published by Aladdin Paperbacks

Yes, Yes, Get Dressed!
To encourage your little one to get dressed, read this book. As your child flips the pages, animals will change clothes before his/her eyes!
Written & Illustrated by Jerry Smath
Published by Grosset & Dunlap

I Can Button
I Can Lace
I Can Snap
I Can Zip
Children can button, lace, snap, and zip over and over again with these interactive board books from the I Can Do It! Books series.
Written by Sara Miller and Rita Walsh-Balducci
Published by Reader's Digest Children's Books

Jesse Bear, What Will You Wear?
As Jesse Bear dresses, he adds extra items that make this rhyming story a sheer delight.
Written by Nancy White Carlstrom
Published by Aladdin Paperbacks

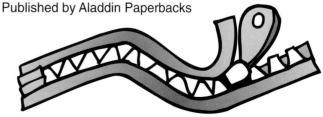

To the teacher: Duplicate pages 265 and 266. Complete the information at the top of page 265; then add class-related news to page 266. Trim away these instructions. Duplicate the pages for each child on the front and back sides of a colorful piece of paper.

Together Time

A "Zippy" Song

Here's a song to help you zip through dressing time. Soon the task will be a snap!

(sung to the tune of "Zip-a-dee-doo-dah")

Zip-a-dee-doo-dah, zip-a-dee-ay,
Watch me [zip my zipper] today.
Plenty of practice; then I'm on my way.
Zip-a-dee-doo-dah, zip-a-dee-ay.

Repeat the song, substituting one of these phrases for the underlined phrase.
…tie my shoelaces…
…snap my snaps…
…button my buttons…

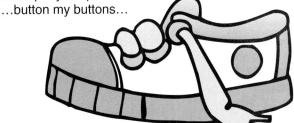

Kitchen Capers

Do "Knot" Play With Your Food!

All tied up keeping your child's shoelaces tied? This activity will give your little one the fine-motor practice needed to learn how to tie for him-/herself.

1. Prepare a small bowl of spaghetti or fettuccini.
2. Tell your child that he/she can *"knot-play"* with his/her food.
3. Demonstrate how to tie a knot with a piece of the cooled pasta.
4. After your child has practiced tying knots, invite him/her to eat them!

Read All About It!
Our Class News

The ideas in this newsletter are contributed by Jan Brennan.

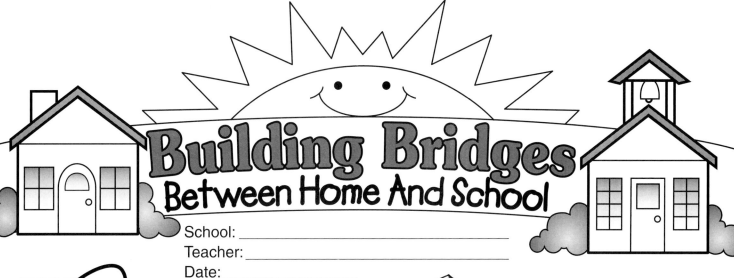

Building Bridges
Between Home And School

School: _____

Teacher: _____

Date: _____

Ready for ABCs!

Has your child shown

A (**a**wareness of letters)
B (interest in **b**eginning sound of letters)
C (**c**onnection between lettersand sounds) **readiness?**

Your child may show an **a**wareness of letters as you read to him or play games. He may ask you what certain letters and words are. He may sound out the **b**eginning sounds of words, such as names of cereals and stores, he sees in his surroundings. He may **c**onnect the sound to that letter as you point it out and say it clearly. These ABC readiness clues let you know that your child is ready to have fun with letters! Since children learn best through play, here are some fun suggestions for learning letter names and their sounds.

- Adapt the game I Spy to help your child identify beginning sounds. For example, you might say, "I spy something that starts with the sound /p/." Reinforce your child's guesses by saying the first letter sound of each item she guesses. You can say, "*Table* starts with the /t/ sound," or, "Yes, *piano* starts with the /p/ sound."

- Label things around the house with large letters you cut from construction paper or find in newspapers and magazines. Occasionally ask your child to choose a new item to be labeled. Sound out the beginning sound of the item together to decide what letter is needed. Then cut out that letter and let your child tape it onto the item.

- Select a special Letter of the Day and plan foods and activities that focus on that letter. For example, on *P* day eat pancakes, popcorn, and pizza. Go to the park, work on puzzles, or color with purple crayons. You might even try to read a story that emphasizes the letter, such as *The Poky Little Puppy*.

The Book Corner
ABC Books

The Letters Are Lost!
This hide-and-seek alphabet book will have your child searching for lost alphabet blocks and learning the letter sounds along the way!
Written & Illustrated by Lisa Campbell Ernst
Published by Puffin Books

Miss Spider's ABC
Miss Spider's bug friends are preparing a surprise party, one letter at a time.
Written & Illustrated by David Kirk
Published by Scholastic Inc.

On Market Street
A child goes shopping on Market Street and buys gifts, each one starting with a different letter of the alphabet.
Written by Arnold Lobel
Published by Mulberry Books

Dr. Seuss' ABC
Your child is sure to enjoy learning letters and sounds through this silly rhyming book!
Written by Dr. Seuss
Published by Random House, Inc.

Flora McDonnell's ABC
Bold, bright illustrations make this book a great way to introduce the alphabet to beginners.
Written & Illustrated by Flora McDonnell
Published by Candlewick Press

To the teacher: Duplicate pages 267 and 268. Complete the information at the top of page 267; then add class-related news to page 268. Trim away these instructions. Duplicate the pages for each child on the front and back sides of a colorful piece of paper.

Together Time

Letter Treasure

Searching for a fun way to reinforce letter sounds? Have a letter treasure hunt! Collect some items to hide that begin with the same letter. If possible, make one item an edible treat. For example, for the letter *B* you could hide a ball, a bottle, a bandage, a book, and banana chips. Write the letter that the items start with on a piece of paper. Show your child the letter, say its sound together, and then name the items for your child to find. After all of the items have been found, enjoy the edible treat. Adapt this idea for any letter you wish to treasure.

Kitchen Capers

Delicious Letters

Alphabet cookies, pretzels, crackers, pasta, cereal—all of these "letter-ific" snacks can be found at your grocery store. Buy some and put them on peanut butter crackers, on pudding, or in soup. What a fun way to learn how letters sound *and* taste!

For more letter fun, follow this recipe to make your own delicious letters.

1 tbsp. yeast
1/2 c. warm water
1 tsp. honey
1/2 tsp. salt
1 1/3 c. flour
1 egg
cooking spray
salt, poppy seeds, or sesame seeds

Preheat your oven to 425°. Grease a cookie sheet. Dissolve the yeast in the warm water. Stir in the honey and salt; then add the flour. Knead the dough. Form the dough into the letters of your choice. Brush them with a beaten egg. Sprinkle the letters with salt, poppy seeds, or sesame seeds. Bake the letters for about ten minutes.

Read All About It!
Our Class News

The ideas in this newsletter are contributed by Jan Brennan.

PEEK-A-BOO

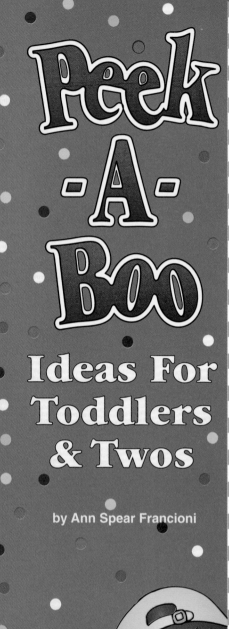

Peek -A- Boo

Ideas For Toddlers & Twos

by Ann Spear Francioni

A Day at the Beach

Did many of your little ones visit the beach this past summer? Replay that experience and build dramatic-play skills with this large-muscle activity. Lay out a few beach towels on a carpeted area. Then tape a blue crepe paper streamer on the floor about five feet away. Invite a group of youngsters to lounge on the beach towels, but tell them that the water (the blue streamer) is cold! Encourage them, one at a time, to tiptoe to the water and then scurry back to the beach towels. Encourage them to go faster and to not get wet. Add to the experience by spritzing little toes with a spray bottle of water whenever they get close to the water's edge.

I Can See

This song will familiarize children with one another's names. Use a different child's name in each verse.

(sung to the tune of "Head, Shoulders, Knees, and Toes")

I can see [Susie]'s here, [Susie]'s here.
I can see [Susie]'s here, [Susie]'s here.
Since she's here, I'll touch my ear.
I can see [Susie]'s here, [Susie]'s here.

I can see [Reina]'s there, [Reina]'s there.
I can see [Reina]'s there, [Reina]'s there.
Since she's there, I'll touch my hair.
I can see [Reina]'s there, [Reina]'s there.

I can see [Sam] is in, [Sam] is in.
I can see [Sam] is in, [Sam] is in.
Since he's in, I'll touch my chin.
I can see [Sam] is in, [Sam] is in.

King and Queen of the Slide

Here's a simple way to help toddlers learn one another's names, build self-esteem, and exercise large muscles—all during outdoor play! As each boy reaches the top of the slide, have him shout, "I'm King [child's name]!" As each girl reaches the top of the slide, have her shout, "I'm Queen [child's name]!" Then have the child slide down to a loud round of applause from you and the classmates. What a powerful feeling to shout out your name! Let's slide again!

I'm Queen Lucy!

Jumbo Ring Toss

Put some *big* rings into *little* hands for this active game that develops aim. Purchase a few 12-inch or 14-inch Styrofoam® rings from your local craft store. If desired, decorate the rings with scarves or yarn to make them more colorful. Provide a very large tub or box as a target. Ask children to toss the rings into the tub or box from increasingly greater distances. Ring a bell as each one lands in the target to signal success. Once little ones are proficient at tossing the rings into a tub or box, borrow a few rubber traffic cones from your tricycle track. Encourage toddlers to try to toss the rings on top of the cones. Ready…aim…toss!

Book Surprises

Want to get your toddlers into books? Try this tip to get them interested. Cut several circles from colorful construction paper, sizing them so they'll fit between the pages of a board book from your classroom collection. Tuck the circles between the pages in a few spots; then show the book to a small group of children. Encourage them to find the surprises hiding inside it. Tuck similar surprises (in different colors and shapes) into other books on your library shelf. Before you know it, little ones will be finding the *real* treasures hiding in books!

Runaway Balls

This silly activity will have your toddlers laughing, cooperating, *and* getting their exercise! Gather one or two fluffy bed pillows and some beach balls or large playground balls. Explain to a group of youngsters that the balls are tired and need to rest. Ask each child to put a ball on a pillow. (As one ball touches another on a pillow, one will roll off, making it difficult to put several balls on a pillow at one time.) Encourage youngsters to chase down the rolling balls and try again to "put them to bed." Good luck!

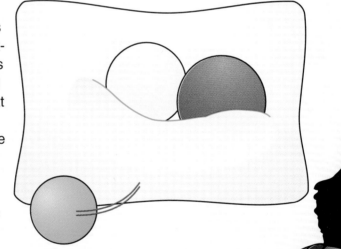

In Two Places at Once

Try this tip to help soothe a child who needs a minute away from the group. Record yourself singing a quiet song or reading a favorite story. Place the tape in a tape recorder in your quiet area. When a child needs a moment away from the group but you can't devote your attention to him at that time, have him sit in your quiet area and listen to the tape. This calming distraction will help give him the time he needs to collect himself.

Peek -A- Boo

Ideas For Toddlers & Twos

by
Ann Spear Francioni

Catch a Falling Feather

Since older toddlers enjoy the challenge of catching things, give them practice with this colorful activity. Drop a handful of colorful, nonshedding feathers from above the heads of several children. Encourage the children to bring their hands together to catch the slow-moving feathers. In the fall, provide red, yellow, and orange feathers and encourage the children to pretend the feathers are leaves. The colors are sure to excite them, and the whimsical movement of the falling feathers will entice them!

Leaf Catch

Your tiny tots are sure to catch on quickly to this leaf-dropping activity that develops gross-motor skills. To prepare, cut out several large hand shapes from laminated paper; then secure them to the floor. Provide a child with red, yellow, or orange beanbags. (Or tape paper leaf cutouts onto beanbags.) Ask the child to pretend that the beanbags are leaves and to drop them onto the hand cutouts so that they can be caught. As the child becomes more proficient with dropping the leaves, encourage him to stand a short distance from the cutouts and then toss the beanbags onto the hands.

Jack-o'-Lantern Mystery

This quick and simple jack-o'-lantern game will keep 'em thinking and grinning! From orange and black felt, cut out a pumpkin shape and jack-o'-lantern facial features. Put all the pieces on a flannelboard; then use them to play a What's Missing? game. Once the children are familiar with the game, vary it by asking a different child each time to take away a piece. Or make it more challenging by adding more felt pieces such as a stem, a leaf, or teeth for the grin.

Pack of Pumpkin "Stuff"

Tell your little ones that these bags are full of squishy pumpkin "stuff," and they'll be eager to give their fingers a no-mess, fine-motor workout! To prepare each pumpkin pack, put a spoonful each of yellow and red paint into a resealable plastic bag. Give a child a bag to squish until it is filled with orange paint instead of red and yellow. Next give him a black construction-paper workmat. Encourage him to put his bag on the mat and then use his fingers to draw designs in the paint.

Take a Closer Look at Leaves

Ask your little ones to help you collect fallen leaves; then invite the children to help you use the leaves to create leaf collages to stimulate observation skills all over your room. In turn, ask each child to help you press a number of the leaves onto the sticky side of a precut Con-Tact® paper square. (If you'd like to send the collages home later, save the paper backing from each square.) Then help the child press the square to his choice of one of your suggestions, such as on a low window, on a wall near a quiet area, on a mirror, or even on the floor. If desired, engage children in conversation as you notice them stopping to take a closer look at the leaves throughout your room all day long.

More Sticky Fun

Little hands won't have any trouble holding on to these shakers that stimulate the senses of hearing and touch. Partially fill oatmeal containers, cylindrical chip cans, or juice cans with rice or beans; then hot-glue on the lids. Tape a piece of Con-Tact® paper around each container *sticky side out.* Give each child in a circle a sticky shaker to rattle as you play music. Not only will your little ones enjoy hearing the sounds of the shakers, they'll love the feel of the sticky paper as well!

Are You Pulling My Bead?

No kidding! Children are sure to enjoy this game so much you'll almost be able to watch their minds figuring out how it works! To make one, punch four holes in a sturdy paper plate as shown. Thread an 18-inch length of yarn through each pair of holes; then tie a wooden bead to each end of each length. To use the toy, a child pulls on one bead to make the bead at the opposite end of the yarn move. *How* does that work?

Peek -A- Boo

Ideas For Toddlers & Twos

by Ann Spear Francioni

Family and Friends

At this time of year, children may see relatives and family friends who are not familiar. Make this baggie book to help them get acquainted before holiday visits begin. Invite parents to send in photos (to be returned later) of people their child may see over the holidays. Ask them to label the back of each photo with the name or names the child uses to identify the person or people pictured. Mount each photo on one side of a square of construction paper cut to fit inside a zippered sandwich bag. Label the paper with the person's name. Punch a hole in the corner of each baggie "page"; then use ribbon to bind this photo book together. During storytime, show the book to your group, encouraging children to name the people in the photos whom they recognize. Yes, that *is* your Grammy, Sarah!

Holiday Highlights

Parents will appreciate this keepsake, and it also makes a nice conversation piece for holiday visitors. Several days before your winter break, trace around each child's body on a length of bulletin board paper. Each day, have the child color in a little bit of his body outline as you talk with him about various body parts, his hair color, his eye color, and so on. Next to each outline, write in some vital statistics, such as the child's height, weight, current interests, favorite stories, or favorite activities. Send the finished projects home before the holidays. What a wonderful memory of 1999!

Elfin Excursion

Your youngsters are sure to be thrilled when you ask them to be Santa's helpers for this hide-and-seek game! To prepare, wrap several empty boxes in holiday paper and ribbon. Hide the boxes in easy-to-spot places in your play yard or play area. Then explain to your little ones that Santa has lost some gifts and needs their help to find them. Give clues as needed until all the gifts are rounded up. Play the game again on a subsequent day, increasing the difficulty of the hiding places as youngsters get better at finding the gifts.

Make a Snowstorm

Don't toss out that crumpled tissue paper that's left over in gift boxes after the holiday unwrapping! Put it to good use to make some faux snow that's soft and safe. Invite your little ones to scrunch the tissue up into small balls. When you have a tub full, let the snowballs shower down on some delighted toddlers! Encourage youngsters to toss these fake snowballs, pour them onto the floor and take a walk through the snowdrift, or try to make snow angels in them! When they're done with the snowy fun, just sweep it up!

Windblown Puzzles

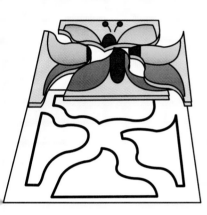

At this point in the year, your youngsters may be growing bored with your selection of puzzles. So try this twist to spark their interest. To prepare, assemble a puzzle on a sheet of paper (without any frame). Then spread the pieces apart a bit, to make it appear that the pieces have floated away from one another. Trace around each piece in its new position.

Give a child the tracing of the pieces and the puzzle pieces themselves (again, without any frame). Tell her that the winter wind has blown the pieces around and you need her help to reassemble the puzzle. Encourage her to match each piece to its outline. After she accomplishes this task, challenge her to move the pieces back together to assemble the puzzle.

Cool Spool Jewels

Toddlers just love to dress up in shiny jewelry! So ask parents to help you save some holiday trash that will make treasured "jewelry." Send a note to parents asking them to send in the inner spools from rolls of wrapping paper and ribbon. Cut the cardboard spools into shorter lengths. Then cover the spools with shiny foil or metallic wrapping paper. Your toddlers can use larger spools as bracelets, wear smaller ones as rings, and string some onto yarn to make necklaces. Cool!

Watch Out for Bigfoot!

If your toddlers like to try on adult-sized shoes (and what toddler doesn't?), they'll love this activity! To prepare, cover a piece of cardboard with colorful Con-Tact® paper. Then trace adult-sized footprints onto the paper and cut them out. Tape the cutouts to the bottom of a child's shoes and then invite him to walk around the room with the big feet on. It's a clown…it's an elephant…no, it's Toddler Bigfoot!

Peek -A- Boo

Ideas For Toddlers & Twos

by Ann Spear Francioni

Jingle, Jingle, Bounce!

Want to hear some music and see some movement? Just hand a toddler a ball with a bell inside! Purchase a couple of soft balls for infants that have bells inside or check the pet supply store for balls with bells. Then turn on the music and get ready to hear the jingling and see a whole lot of shakin' goin' on! Watch out—toddlers may discover that these balls bounce, too!

Find the Match

Use more balls for this activity that develops the sense of touch and works on toddlers' perceptual skills. Gather a few pairs of small balls with different, interesting textures—such as two golf balls, two tennis balls, two Ping-Pong® balls, and two Styrofoam® balls. Put one ball from each pair in a "feely" box or a cloth bag, making sure they are covered so children can't see them. Then invite a child to choose one of the remaining balls. Have him reach into the box or bag and try to find the ball's match using only his sense of touch.

Special Delivery

Encourage your youngsters to spread a little love this Valentine's Day with this easy activity. To prepare, cut hearts in several sizes from red, pink, and white shelf paper (the type that clings but doesn't stick permanently). For each child, peel the backing off a few hearts and stick them onto a sterilized foam tray. Take your little ones on a walk around your school and have them stick hearts on the walls, windows, and doors of other classrooms. The toddlers are here, spreading love and cheer!

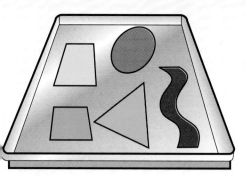

Magnet Mania

Bring out your scissors to prepare this magnet activity that will build your tiny tots' dexterity. Cut flexible magnetic sheets into short and long pieces, as well as simple shapes and curvy lines. Stick the pieces onto cookie sheets and invite your youngsters to experiment!

Flower Friends

Even if it's still cold where you live, you can bring some spring flowers into view with this matching game. Label a sheet of poster board "Flower Friends." Then cut out several matching pairs of flowers (patterns on page 282). For younger children, use the same flower shape and vary the color of each pair. For older toddlers, vary the flowers' shapes, as well. Glue one of each flower pair to the poster board. If desired, laminate the board and the remaining flower cutouts. Then invite your little ones to match each flower to its "friend" on the board.

Cool and Yummy for Your Tummy

This St. Patrick's Day activity tastes great! Put a small dollop of cold whipped topping into a zippered plastic bag for each child. Add a drop or two of green food coloring; then seal the bag. Invite each child to squish the contents of her bag together to make green fluff. After youngsters see the color mixing and feel the cold temperature of the bag, get another sense involved by inviting each child to taste her bag's contents. Have her open her bag and dip in a cookie or a finger to scoop up a bite of this sweet green treat!

The Tearin' of the Green

Everyone can participate in making this green-as-you've-ever-seen mural for St. Patrick's Day. Give each child a large sheet of green construction paper or green tissue paper. Encourage youngsters to tear the paper to their hearts' content—up, down, or sideways! When the tearing's done, paint some diluted glue onto a large piece of bulletin board paper. Have each child put her pieces on the mural. My goodness, that's *green!*

Peek-A-Boo

Ideas For Toddlers & Twos

by Ann Spear Francioni

Egg Carton Construction

Before Easter, ask parents to save all their empty egg cartons and send them to school after the holiday. Sanitize the Styrofoam® cartons by putting them in a dishwasher. Spray the cardboard cartons with a 10:1 water and bleach solution. Tape the cartons closed. Now you have wonderful, sturdy building blocks! Cut some cartons into smaller blocks to provide a variety of sizes. Invite youngsters to help you decorate the cartons with paint or stickers, if desired.

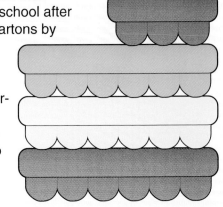

Garden Soup

Take advantage of a warm spring day to conduct this messy-but-fun outdoor experience! Have youngsters put on paint smocks. Head outdoors and have them gather around a few large bowls of water. Explain that you need help making some Garden Soup for the plants and bugs in your play yard. Have them toss in grass, leaves, dirt, twigs, or any other natural materials they find. Provide a few large mixing spoons and make sure everyone gets a turn to stir the earthy concoctions in the bowls! When it seems "just right," pour the Garden Soup onto a natural area or a class garden. Then wash up the bowls, the spoons…and the children!

Wind Races

On a really breezy day, take little ones outdoors again to feel the power of nature. Give each child a leaf or a feather. Have the children toss their objects up into the air and then watch how the wind carries them along. Which one travels the farthest? Do any escape the wind? Encourage little ones to chase down their wind-blown treasures before returning to the classroom.

Spreading Some Skills

Toddlers can practice their coordination skills as they prepare their own simple snacks. Give each child a rice cake, a cracker, or a slice of toast on a napkin. Then provide her with a plastic knife and invite her to choose from a variety of spreads, such as softened butter, cream cheese, or jelly. What a delicious way to learn!

Oh, how I love the springtime...

"Spring-y" Singing

After little ones have observed and talked about the changes that take place at this time of year, teach them this song about spring.

(sung to the tune of "Did You Ever See a Lassie?")

Oh, how I love the springtime, the springtime, the springtime!
Oh, how I love the springtime, and I'll tell you why:
I love [all the flowers]; they make me so happy!
Oh, how I love the springtime! Do you love it, too?

Repeat the verse several times, each time substituting one of the following phrases for the underlined words:

> sunny warm days
> the warm breezes
> animal babies
> springtime showers

Pie Plate Symphony

Rumbling spring thunderstorms may make some toddlers uneasy. Help them control their fears by making some rumbling thunder of their very own! Give each child an aluminum pie plate or other disposable baking pan. Then have each youngster roll a piece of aluminum foil into a tight ball. Have each child drop her foil ball into her pan and roll it around to create a thunderous noise. Play some lively music and listen to the symphony begin!

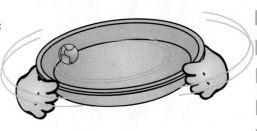

Snuggle Buddies

Baby animals abound in spring, and toddlers love to hold and cuddle warm, fuzzy critters. So give each child his own Snuggle Buddy to stroke, hug, and baby. For each child, cut a six-inch circle from fake fur. Add wiggle eyes or use a permanent marker to draw eyes. Invite youngsters to keep their Snuggle Buddies in their cubbies, and you'll be surprised at how often the children will check on their furry companions!

Peek -A- Boo

Ideas For Toddlers & Twos

by Ann Spear Francioni

Ant Detectives

Ants seem to be everywhere in summer, so spend a day focusing on these little critters. Before your toddlers arrive, collect a few ants from your play yard in a clear jar. Invite youngsters to observe them and talk about how they move and climb. Then encourage little ones to make pictures of your insect visitors. Have a child press a fingertip first onto an ink pad (black or red) and then onto paper three times to form the three parts of an ant's body. Have the child use a crayon to add six legs. Keep going and you'll have ants galore! Top off your ant exploration by playing a recording of the classic "The Ants Go Marching" as your youngsters hold their artwork and march around your room in an ant parade!

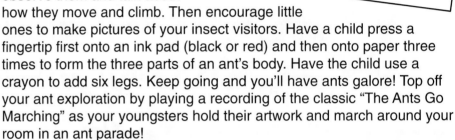

Crunchy 'n' Cool

When it's really hot outside, try this idea for a cool treat that's healthy, too! Give each child an ice-cream stick that is long and narrow. Set out a bowl of wheat germ and have each child roll her ice cream in it. Then head outdoors, find some shade, and invite youngsters to enjoy this cool treat with a crunchy coating.

A Summer Song

Help children think of all the fun things they can do in the summer heat. Then personalize this song for each child, inviting her to fill in her favorite summertime activity in the third line.

(sung to the tune of "You Are My Sunshine")

You know it's summer! Oh, yes, it's summer!
It gets so bright and hot outside.
But [Erin] loves it, 'cause (s)he [goes swimming].
Oh, in summer we have so much fun!

Summer Storytime

With all the fresh fruits available in summer, it's the perfect time to read Eric Carle's *The Very Hungry Caterpillar* (Putnam Publishing Group). Create a sock puppet to resemble the caterpillar in the story. After reading, have your puppet pretend to eat through some of the foods from your kitchen center. Then invite each child to make a hungry caterpillar puppet of her own. Provide each child with an old, clean sock and a variety of geometric shape stickers. Have her apply the stickers to make eyes, a mouth, and a scale pattern for her puppet. Then have youngsters "crawl" their puppets over to your snack table, where they'll find a snack of fresh fruit salad. Look—it's the very hungry toddlers!

Pop...Pop...Just Can't Stop!

Some toddlers may be frightened of the loud popping sounds made by fireworks. To prepare them to enjoy the excitement of the sounds, put them in charge of some popping of their own! Give each youngster a square foot of bubble wrap. Tell the class that you'll count to three, and then each child may stomp on his square, popping as many of the bubbles as he can. Then let the stomping and popping begin! Have everyone stop periodically and look to see how many bubbles he popped. Older toddlers may want to try popping some bubbles with their fingers, as well. Your toddlers will get so involved with the fun of popping the bubbles that they won't mind the noise a bit!

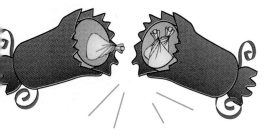

Firecracker Snackers

These treats will be a surefire hit for Independence Day! To make one, cut a toilet-tissue tube in half. Fit one piece halfway inside the other. Then slide a few treats, such as Hershey's® Kisses® candies, inside the tube. Wrap a piece of brightly colored tissue paper around the tube, and tie the ends with curling ribbon so that the package resembles an old-fashioned firecracker. During your Fourth of July celebration, invite each child to hold the tied ends of the tissue and then pull them in opposite directions. The treat inside pops out! It's an explosion of fun!

Picnic Leftovers

Since so many families have picnics at this time of year, ask them to send in leftover picnic supplies, such as plastic utensils, paper plates, and paper cups. Then recycle these picnic items for classroom use. Plastic spoons make great scoops for your sand table or for a bucket full of Ping-Pong® balls. Cut paper plates in half and have toddlers decorate them to make fans with craft stick handles. Use paper cups for help with pouring practice—in your water table, at snacktime, or with small manipulatives. And be sure to put some of the items in your dramatic-play area so little ones can have a picnic of their own!

GETTING YOUR DUCKLINGS IN A ROW

Getting Your Ducklings

You've Got Mail

This first-class way to create classroom mailboxes gets our stamp of approval. Obtain enough sturdy, compartmentalized boxes (such as those available at liquor stores) so that you have a separate compartment for each child, your assistant, and yourself. Tape the boxes together with duct tape; then cover the entire unit with decorative Con-Tact® covering. Label each compartment with a different child's name and a reduced photocopy or color copy of his photo.

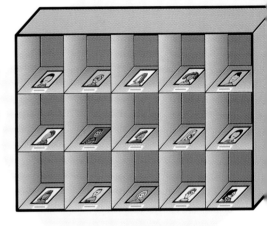

Put the mailboxes in a language center so that students can send each other messages and pictures. Or use the mailboxes as a handy way to communicate with parents. Have you checked your box lately? You've got mail!

Elizabeth A. Cooper—Pre-K
Meadowbrook Elementary School
Fort Worth, TX

Run for the Border

Run to get your next few months' worth of bulletin board border; then make use of this timesaving tip! As you prepare your next bulletin board, choose a neutral background; then layer and attach several borders for future planned displays. For example, mount a Christmas border, then cover it with a Halloween border, and finally top both of those with a fall border. When it's time to change the display, simply peel off the top layer of border. The next border is in place and ready to use!

Amy Barsanti—Four-Year-Olds
St. Andrew's Preschool, Nags Head, NC

284

Thematic Storage Boxes

Decorate your room and store your teaching materials at the same time. Here's how! Decorate boxes to reflect the thematic materials they will hold. For example, for a farm-related unit, cover a box and its lid with colorful paper. Then glue on farm animal die-cut shapes. Or, for a transportation unit, cover a box with yellow paper. Add black paper wheels, painted windows, and magazine cutout passengers. You'll be able to tell at a glance where your materials for each theme are located. Plus it's a great way to spark youngsters' curiosity for upcoming units!

Amy Aloi and Gwen
Blake—Four-Year-Olds
Berkshire Elementary
Forestville, MD

In A Row

Tips For Getting Organized

Transition Train

All aboard the transition train for a fun way to teach youngsters to line up! Use masking tape to create a railroad track on the floor in the area where students line up, making sure the track is long enough for each child to have her own space. During transition time, direct each child to stand in her own space on the track.

To make a transition time into a learning opportunity, add different-colored geometric shapes, letters, or numbers to the spaces in the track. Cover them with clear Con-Tact® covering for durability. Also consider creating matching picture cards. Then, during transitions, show each child a picture card and have her find and stand on the matching space. All aboard for transition fun!

Melissa Nelson
St. Nicholas School
Zanesville, OH

Easy Art Easel and Art Display

Got a clip? Use this tip! Use large plastic spring clips (such as those used to clip potato chip bags closed) to create instant easels and displays. Just nail each clip within student reach into a wooden surface, such as a thin piece of plywood, a wall, or the side of a wooden cabinet or shelf. Invite a student to slip a piece of art paper into the clip for an instant easel or hang his work from a clip for display.

Gayle J. Vergara—Preschool
Willowbend Preschool
Murrieta, CA

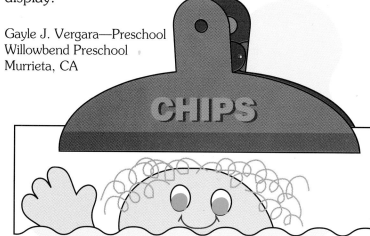

Next Stop!

This center-management idea is just the ticket for promoting decision-making skills! In turn, ask each child to name his center choice; then give him a train ticket to that center. Invite one student to be the engineer. Ask the other students to "get on board" (line up) behind him. Instruct the engineer to lead the student train around the room, stopping at each center. When the train arrives at a center, have him announce the stop and take the tickets of students who are disembarking to play at that station. Next stop, sand table! Toot, toot!

Margaret Mankiewicz—Special Needs/Preschool
Vineyard's Elementary School, Naples, FL

Getting Your Ducklings

Clip Hangers

Are you on the edge of your seat looking for more classroom display space? Link up with this clip hanging idea! Make a hanger for each child by linking a series of large colored paper clips together. Slide one end of each hanger under a different ceiling tile or hang it from a self-adhesive hook attached to the ceiling. To display a child's work, simply slide it into the last paper clip on the hanger. For heavier work, punch a hole in the project and bend the last paper clip so that it will hook through that hole. Then simply hang around!

Dayle Timmons
Alimacani Elementary School
Jacksonville, FL

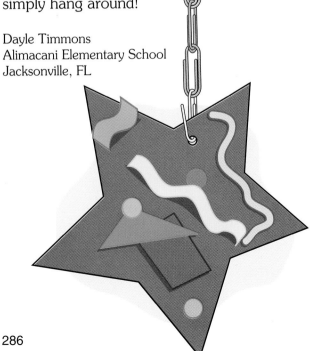

Recycled Paint Cups

Don't throw away those wonderfully sturdy, plastic frosting containers! They make great paint cups for your easel. To make one, use a craft knife to cut a paintbrush hole in the lid of the container. Then pour paint into the container, snap on the lid, insert the brush, and it's ready for action!

Teresa Edison—Four- and
    Five-Year-Olds
Luther Hospital Child
    Care Center
Eau Claire, WI

Playing Places

These tablecloth play stations help define children's play spaces, and they speed up cleanup too! To get started, arrange a few vinyl, flannel-backed tablecloths on the floor. Then place a different tub of toys or manipulatives on each tablecloth. Assign a different group of children to each tablecloth. Ask each group to play or work on its assigned tablecloth. When it's time to clean up, your little ones know where the little things go!

Joyce Cummings—Pre-K
First Baptist Day School
O'Fallon, MO

In A Row — Tips For Getting Organized

Easel Options

Need more easel space in your classroom? Try this easy easel option. Begin by attaching Con-Tact® covering to a low bulletin board or wall. For each art space that you'd like to have, hot-glue two spring-type clothespins to the background as shown. Provide art supplies in shoeboxes or plastic window boxes on the floor. Also keep a supply of art paper nearby. To work in this area, a child simply hangs a sheet of art paper from two clothespins, and the scene is set for creativity.

Patricia Parahus—Pre-K
Our Redeemer School
Levittown, NY

Smock Frock

Cut back on paint smock expenses with this thrifty idea. To make one, cut out a rectangle from an old vinyl shower curtain or tablecloth. (Adjust the size according to your children's needs.) Then, in the middle of the piece, cut a hole large enough for a child to slip his head through. Keep these smock frocks in your art area where they can easily (and independently!) be slipped on and off.

Peggy L. Emde—Preschool
Kids Under Construction, Inc.
Stillwater, OK

Supply Trays

Little hands can get just what they need when you use these handy supply trays. In advance, collect a supply of various types of divided microwave meal trays. When you'd like to have small supplies within the reach of your little ones, use the trays that suit your needs. They're small enough to move from place to place and can be gathered up again in no time at all. If you use these trays for glue, the leftover glue can be peeled right off once it has dried. Simply supplied!

Beth Hall
Parkway Elementary School
Virginia Beach, VA

Getting Your Ducklings

Remote Control

Empower children to display appropriate behavior with this tip. When it's necessary to ask your class to be quiet, suggest that they use their imaginary remote controls to turn down the volume of their voices. If a child is having difficulty, kindly offer him "fresh batteries" for his remote control.

Suzanne Costner—Preschool
Holy Trinity Preschool
Fayetteville, NC

Red Line, Green Line

Use colorful tape to create a visual guide that will help your class line up successfully every time! To indicate where your class should stand in line, adhere a strip of yellow tape (long enough for your entire class to stand on) to the floor. Designate the beginning of the lineup area by placing a strip of green tape on the floor so that it is perpendicular to the yellow strip; then similarly designate the end of the area with a red strip. When it's time to line up, ask one child to stand at the beginning of the line on the green strip, have another child stand at the end of the line on the red strip, and then direct the rest of the class to stand on the yellow line that's in between. We're ready to go!

Lisa Marks
Nelson County Elementary Schools
Lovingston, VA

No-Spill Glue

Do you have "no-spill" paint cups in your room? In addition to filling them with paint, fill some of them with glue. It's easy to squirt glue in the holes in the rims and the snap-on lids keep the glue from drying out. Best of all, children can use paintbrushes to apply glue to their projects so that there's less mess! Storage is easy, too. Just stack 'em up!

Ellyn Soypher—Preschool
Chizuk Amuno Preschool
Baltimore, MD

In A Row — Tips For Getting Organized

No More Border Clutter!

Feeling like you want to run from the border clutter created by the rolls of bulletin board borders in your closet or drawers? Here's a tip for you! If your school orders large amounts of crayons or markers that come in a divided box, save the box when the supplies are distributed. Then put your rolls of borders in the divided sections. The rolls stay neat, and they are easily accessible, too!

Claudia Johnson—Preschool, Special Education
New Kent Primary
New Kent, VA

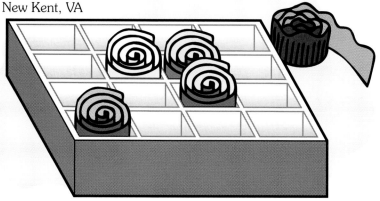

Take a Number, Please

Here's a management technique that promotes patience and teaches numeration at the same time. To help children wait their turns for your individual attention, label as many as five index cards each with a different numeral from one to five. Put the cards in order; then store them in a place that is easy for youngsters to access, such as the front pocket of your apron. When a child needs help, ask him to take a number! Who's next?

Karen Sheheane—Preschool
Killearn United Methodist Preschool
Tallahasee, FL

Dressed for the Weather

These easy-to-make weather folks will be a great addition to your daily circle-time weather discussions. Cut simple people shapes from cork (available in rolls from craft stores and home supply superstores). Also cut simple clothing shapes from a variety of fabrics to represent clothing for different seasons. Attach the cork shapes to a wall or display. During your group time, ask children to help you select clothing that is appropriate for the day's weather. Then use pushpins to attach the clothes to the cork people shapes.

Amy Aloi
Prince Georges County Head Start, Berkshire
   Elementary
Forestville, MD

Getting Your Ducklings

Play Dough Volunteers

Do you have parents who would love to help out but can't come to school during the day? Get them involved by asking them to make batches of play dough. At the beginning of the year, ask each interested parent to sign up for the month she is willing to make a batch of dough. Then distribute copies of the recipe. To give each parent a friendly reminder when it's her turn to make play dough, just give her a phone call or send home another copy of the recipe. This idea is sure to save you lots of time, and it will ensure that your children always have fresh dough for your play dough center.

Gerene Thom—Five-Year-Olds/Transitional Kindergarten
Denmark Early Childhood Center
Denmark, WI

Play Dough Volunteers		
Aug.	Gerene Thom	655-4331
Sept.	Susan Bowers	632-1174
Oct.	Mike Mann	605-7742

Naptime Boxes

Prepare these activity boxes for children who awaken from their naps early or who may not wish to sleep during your quiet rest time. If desired, cover several shoeboxes with colorful paper. Fill each box with items that can be played with independently and quietly, such as lacing cards, flannelboard pieces, or paper and crayons. A child may choose one of the boxes and take it back to his cot until rest time has ended.

Nancy Wolfgram—Four-Year-Olds, KinderCare Learning Center #1111
Lincoln, NE

Cooperative Learning

Teach your older preschoolers this effective way to participate in planned group work. Decide the number of small groups you would like to divide your class into. For each group, prepare a different-shaped group sign. Cut a number of smaller shapes to match the color and shape of each group sign. Then label these smaller shapes with the jobs needed for the group project. (If desired, use the patterns on page 292.)

When it is time for group work, place each of the group signs on a different table. Then randomly distribute the smaller shapes labeled with the jobs. Direct each child to use her shape to find the table at which she will be working. Demonstrate how each different job in the project should be done. Then have the groups get busy. Everyone has a job to do!

Suzanne Mayo—
   Four- and Five-Year-Olds.
   Pre-K
Our Lady of Peac
Fords, NJ

In A Row   Tips For Getting Organized

Learning and Lining Up

Reinforce basic knowledge with this smooth transition tip. At the beginning of the year, use clear Con-Tact® covering to adhere a paper star (for the line leader) and other colorful shapes to the floor so that they are in a line near your door. When it's time to line up, direct each child to find a specific shape or color to stand on. To vary the floor design through the year, create a pattern on the floor with the shapes or colors. Or adhere letters and numerals to the floor. What a smart way to get all your ducks in a row!

Amber Peters—Three-Year-Olds, First Baptist Church Weekday Preschool, Greensboro, NC

The Waiting Tree

Ever need a tool for helping your children wait patiently? Make a waiting tree, and you'll have just what you need at your fingertips! To prepare, locate a large potted plant or secure a branch in a pot. Cut out a supply of seasonal or thematic paper shapes. On each shape, write a different activity suggestion that requires only a few minutes to complete. For example, you could include a game of Simon Says, the words to a favorite song, several what-if questions, and a story starter. Attach a short yarn loop to each shape, and then hang it on the plant or branch. When you find yourself with short, unplanned time, just choose a shape off the waiting tree and follow the suggestion written on it. Time flies when you're having fun!

Cindy Lawson—
  Toddler/Preschool
Certified Family Daycare
Shell Lake, WI

Rebekah
Bright Day School
666-4431

Once upon a time there was a busy bee. He flew...

Free Nametags

Ask parents who attend seminars and conventions to save the plastic pin-on nametags that they receive. Collect enough for the largest class in your school. Then when a class is ready to go on a field trip, that teacher can program a class supply of sheets to slide into the nametags. Multiple classes can reuse the tags over and over again!

Joy Wallace—Preschool, Home Daycare
Centreville, MS

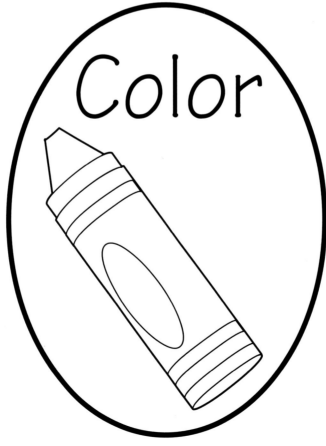

BULLETIN BOARDS AND DISPLAYS

Help your youngsters see the progression of their school day with this display. Cut a ladder shape from cardboard; then mount it on a wall along with a character. Screw a small eye hook into each rung. Next label a number of paint-bucket cutouts each with a different daily activity. Add a corresponding picture to each cutout. Also prepare buckets for special events such as field trips or parties. Laminate the buckets for durability; then punch a hole near the top of each one. Beginning at the bottom of the ladder, hang each bucket onto a rung according to the sequence of your day.

Cathy Mossbarger—Three-Year-Olds
St. Mark Lutheran Preschool
Lake Jackson, TX

To make one apple for this display, cut an apple shape from white construction paper. Glue on red construction paper that has been cut to fit the top and bottom of the apple shape. Add a paper leaf and stem; then mount the apple on a bulletin board. To make the apple's peel, glue a white strip of construction paper to a red strip of construction paper. Curl the strip; then staple one end to the apple. Add a number of these apples and students' work to a display, and you're sure to harvest a crop of compliments!

Jeanette Jonas—Pre-K, Rainbow Child Care Center, Bakersfield, CA

A BLOOMING GARDEN OF ABCs

Here's a display that blooms as your students' letter recognition grows throughout the year. Along a hallway or on a wide window, mount a paper picket fence and a title. As you study each letter, add a paper flower labeled with that letter to your garden. Invite students to bring in items that begin with the letter. Write the name of each item on a paper leaf to add to the flower's stem. What a way to plant seeds of learning!

Lisa Bigon—Four-Year-Olds, St. Mark Lutheran Preschool, Lake Jackson, TX

This colorful bulletin board is sure to draw a lot of attention. From bulletin board paper, create a large crayon box; then mount it to a bulletin board. Write each child's name in bold letters across a separate large white paper crayon cutout. Have each youngster color his cutout using his favorite crayon color. Mount the crayons around the box; then add a title. For an extra splash of color, surround the board with large inflatable crayons.

adapted from ideas by
Tonie Liddle—Pre-K, Central Baptist Christian
   Academy, Binghamton, NY
Nancy Goldberg—Three-Year-Olds, B'nai Israel
   Schilit Nursery School, Rockville, MD

If you'll be focusing on the color orange in October, use these ideas to make a bright fall display of students' projects. Cover your bulletin board with Halloween-themed fabric; then add an orange border and a title in orange letters. Use the display to show off any of the projects that students create during your orange studies, such as pumpkins and leaves.

Anita Edlund—Three-Year-Olds, Cokesbury Children's Center, Knoxville, TN

You're sure to get 101 compliments with this dalmatian display! Duplicate the dog pattern (page 304) onto white construction paper for each child. Have a child color and personalize the hat and then press black finger-prints onto the dog. Cut out the pattern. Write a student-given name on the dog tag. In a word balloon, write a fire safety rule dictated by the child. Finally, mount the dogs, the balloons, and a title onto a bulletin board.

AND DISPLAYS

If you study Native American tribes in November, you'll want to create this terrific totem pole display! Have each student paint a brown paper grocery bag to resemble a bird or an animal. Later, have him fill his bag with crumpled newspaper and then add construction paper features such as a beak and wings. Using staples or duct tape, stack and mount the bags onto a wall or a large bulletin board. After explaining that totem poles were used for storytelling, challenge youngsters to create tall tales their totem poles might share.

Barbara Meyers
Fort Worth Country Day
Fort Worth, TX

Our Corny Cornucopia

Out of the frying pan and into <u>my mouth.</u>

It takes two to play on the <u>seesaw.</u>

When the cat's away, <u>she's gone to the vet.</u>

A picture is worth <u>a dollar.</u>

What's good for the goose is <u>birdseed.</u>

You can lead a horse to water but <u>he might get wet.</u>

Too many cooks <u>make too much to eat.</u>

The early bird gets <u>no sleep.</u>

His bark is worse than a <u>loud siren.</u>

Place this corny cornucopia on display in a hallway to give passersby a hearty chuckle. Cut student fingerpainted paper into fruit and vegetable shapes. Add two wiggle eyes to each shape. In a word balloon, write each child's version of a well-known adage. For example, "The early bird gets [no sleep]." Mount a large paper cornucopia on a background; then add the fingerpainted shapes, the word balloons, and a catchy title.

Pat Thein—Preschool, St. Joseph School, Keyport, NJ

Each of the candles on this menorah will sparkle and glow as you go through the holidays. To create the mosaic-style menorah, have students glue paper pieces onto nine large bulletin board paper rectangles. Mount the pieces on a background. Next cut out nine more bulletin board paper rectangles to represent the candles. Mount the shammash (central candle) and "light" it with a tissue paper flame. Each day, have students help you add another candle and flame to celebrate.

Nancy Goldberg—Three-Year-Olds, B'nai Israel Schilit Nursery School, Rockville, MD

Looking for an "a-door-able" holiday display? Try this! Mount a large cookie jar cutout on your classroom door; then have each child decorate a gingerbread cookie cutout. Mount the projects as shown. How sweet it is!

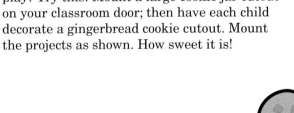

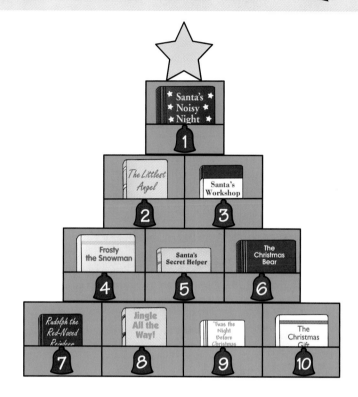

With this tree of books, you can use your daily storytime to count down to the holidays. To make the pockets, laminate ten 12-inch, green poster board squares. Fold up 3½ inches on one side of each square; then staple to make each pocket. Tape the backs of the pockets together to form a tree shape; then mount as shown. Label the pockets with programmed die-cuts. Finally, put a favorite holiday story in each pocket. Read a story a day, and Christmas vacation will be here before you know it!

Pat Smith—Pre-K, Bells Elementary, Bells, TX

Make sure parents take a look at their children's successes with this eye-catching display. For each child, cut out a construction paper mirror shape; then glue a circle of aluminum foil to the section where the glass would be. Laminate the mirrors; then attach a different child's photo to the center of each one. Display the children's mirrors along with their proud statements.

Nancy Goldberg—Three-Year-Olds, B'nai Israel Schilit Nursery School, Rockville, MD

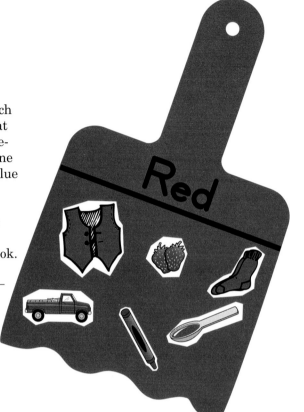

Color your world with these giant paintbrushes. Each time you study a color, cut a large paintbrush from that color of bulletin board paper and label it with the corresponding color word. Invite children to cut out magazine pictures of items that are that color; then have them glue the pictures onto the paintbrush. Display these giant paintbrushes on a wall along a hallway.

As a variation, cut paintbrushes out of construction paper. Then, after youngsters have glued on pictures, bind the brushes together on a ring to make a class book.

adapted from an idea by Sandra Faulkner and Traci Baker—
    Four-Year-Olds
Kernersville Moravian Preschool
Kernersville, NC

It's true! April showers really do bring flowers. And my, aren't these May blooms creative? To make an umbrella, a child glues portions of the weather section of the newspaper onto two pieces of construction paper. He then traces umbrella and handle patterns, cuts out the shapes, and then glues them together. Alongside the umbrellas, display flowers that students create from their choice of papers and a variety of craft supplies.

Lynn Anderson and Lauren Ingle, Friendship Connection, Maplewood, MN

AND DISPLAYS

This creepy-crawly attendance display provides learning opportunities for your circle time! Cut a picture of each child into a circle; then laminate the photos. Also laminate a class supply (plus one extra) of large green construction paper circles. Mount the circles on a wall near your group area to create the caterpillar, adding facial features to the first circle and the loop side of a Velcro® piece to each of the other circles. Attach the hook side of a Velcro piece to the back of each photo. When a child creeps into your room, she puts her photo on a circle. Count the faces present and not present each day!

Tina Mrozek—Two-Year-Olds, Children's World, Lisle, IL

SMILES BLOOM HERE!

Your children's faces on these pansies will bring smiles to all who see them. Have each child cut two pansy shapes from large pieces of construction paper. After gluing the shapes together, have the child paint the center of the flower. Finally, glue a photo of a child to a paper heart shape; then glue the shape onto the center of the flower. Display the flowers together for a display that just blooms with beauty!

Nancy O'Toole
Ready Set Grow
Grand Rapids, MN

BULLETIN BOARDS

Here's a shimmering display that gives parents a positive message about your school. Mount a paper treasure chest and tissue paper seaweed on a blue background. Add a sponge-painted octopus labeled with your school's director's name. Write your message on a paper starfish; then glue circular cereal pieces onto it. For each different class, label different colors of circles with the teacher's name and her students' names. Finally, ask children to help you glue faux jewels to the circles. A display to treasure!

Karen Gerton—Director
Robyn Lipstick—Parent/Toddlers
B'nai Israel Schilit Nursery School
Rockville, MD

Show everyone how much you value your class with this idea. Design a simple monetary bill from a paper rectangle as shown. Duplicate the bill onto green paper to make a class supply. Cut a picture of each child to fit on the center of the bill. Write each child's name on a bill and then glue on her picture. Arrange the bills on a background along with a real garbage bag (money sack), characters, and a title. This idea is worth a million!

Jill Beattie—Four- and Five-Year-Olds, The Apple Place Nursery School, Chambersburg, PA

AND DISPLAYS

We're BIG On Memories!

Make a big impression with this colossal collection of memories. Enlarge a dinosaur pattern onto bulletin board paper. Cut the dinosaur out; then attach it to the board. Cut photos from your year into geometric shapes and then mount the photos onto colorful paper. Also ask students to look at the pictures and dictate memories for you to write on additional colorful geometric shapes. Arrange the photos and the shapes on the dinosaur. Everyone will enjoy looking at this one-of-a-kind lizard!

This tree is sure to become a favorite gathering place for group time and storytime! To create the tree's trunk and branches, cut woodgrained Con-Tact® paper and then mount the pieces to the walls in a corner of your room. Depending on the season, hang large leaves, apples, or snowflakes from the ceiling directly in front of the tree. Hang the items with matching colors of yarn and vary the height at which they are displayed to create a truly inviting effect.

Angelia Dagnan—One- to Three-Year-Olds
Royale Childcare and Learning Center
Knoxville, TN

Dog Pattern
Use with the bulletin board idea
on page 296.

OUR READERS WRITE

Our Readers Write

Not Just for Notes!

Try these noteworthy ideas for using novelty-shaped notepads for more than writing notes!

- Write a child's name on a laminated notepad sheet; then pin it on his clothing for a quick nametag.
- Glue different notepad sheets in a pattern to a sentence strip. Laminate the strip and additional sheets to create a pattern-matching activity.
- Challenge students to match capital letters written on large sheets with lowercase letters written on smaller sheets.
- Give each child a personalized sheet for use on a graph.
- Program calendar dates onto seasonal notepad sheets.

Barbara Beeler and Linda Skidmore
Grapeland Elementary School
Grapeland, TX

Every Piece Counts

Use this idea to help your little ones feel a sense of belonging in your classroom. Purchase one or two puzzles so that you have as many pieces as you have children in your class. (Consider purchasing a puzzle with a few extra pieces or a duplicate puzzle to prepare for lost or forgotten pieces.) Before the beginning of school, mail each student a puzzle piece along with a note asking her to bring the piece on the first day. When the children arrive, invite them to work together to assemble the puzzle. What a wonderful way to begin the year!

Nancy Goldberg—Three-Year-Olds
B'nai Israel Nursery School
Rockville, MD

Where Is the Worm?

Your little ones will really be "up" on position words with this interactive class book! Program a number of construction paper pages with "Is the worm [position word] the apple?" Use a different position word each time. Glue an apple cutout to each page. (Glue the apple only partially if the word is *behind* and glue the apple in halves if the word is *inside*.) Bind the pages together between covers titled "Where Is the Worm?" Also cut out a paper worm. After you read each page, have a child hold the worm in the appropriate place on the page. Then encourage the class to answer, "Yes!" Or have the child challenge the class by putting the worm sometimes in the right place and sometimes in the wrong place. If desired, help each child make a small version of the book for take-home reading.

adapted from an idea by Tammy Lutz—Preschool, Head Start
George E. Greene Elementary
Bad Axe, MI

Is the worm behind the apple?

behind

Glue Shapes

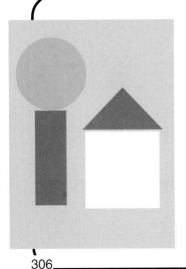

These manipulatives will have youngsters stuck on learning! To make the shapes, thickly squeeze colored glue onto laminated paper to create geometric shapes in a variety of colors. When the glue is dry, peel the shapes from the paper. Encourage children to use the shapes to create pictures on workmats of laminated construction paper. Or have them sort the shapes by color or type. If the shapes do not cling to the paper, wet the surface with a damp sponge.

Tonie Northcutt—Pre-K
Ancient City Baptist Church, Mother's Morning Out
St. Augustine, FL

Photo Fund

If you take a lot of photographs of your students throughout the year, this idea could help cover the expense of purchasing and developing film. Decorate a large container labeled "Photo Fund." During Open House, display the container and explain that parents are invited to donate rolls of film or money for developing film throughout the year. What a photo opportunity!

Shelly L. Kidd-Hamlett
Helena Elementary
Timberlake, NC

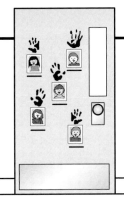

"A-door-able" Handprints

This idea doubles as a name-recognition center and decoration for a metal door (or other metal surface). Paint each child's hand with washable paint; then have her make a handprint on the door. Use a permanent marker to label each print with the child's name. Next laminate a photo of each child; then attach a strip of magnetic tape to the back of it. Put the photos on the door. Challenge students to match their classmates' pictures with the labeled handprints. When ready to remove the decoration, take off the handprints with soap and water and the permanent marker with nail polish remover.

Debbie Jerrett
Waterbridge Elementary
Orlando, FL

Johnny Appleseed Cupcakes

Celebrate Johnny Appleseed's birthday (September 26) by having the apples of your eye help you make this tasty treat. Prepare yellow cake batter according to the package directions; then stir in 1 1/2 cups of peeled, chopped apples and one-half cup of raisins. Pour the batter into muffin cups; then bake the cupcakes. (Baking time may be slightly longer than the package directions indicate.) After singing "Happy Birthday to You" to Mr. Appleseed, serve the cupcakes along with some refreshing apple cider. Delicious!

Cynthia Sayman, Harpursville, NY

Fake Cake Fun

One of the most exciting parts of a birthday is making a wish and blowing out the candles on a cake! To make sure you're ready for every child's special occasion, make this nifty pretend cake. Invert a plastic flower pot; then spread plaster of paris on all but the rim so that it resembles icing on a cake. Before the plaster hardens, add novelty birthday-candle holders to the top of the cake. When a child's birthday arrives, put the correct number of candles in the holders. After singing "Happy Birthday to You," have him make a wish and "blow" out the candles.

Pat Smith—Pre-K
Bells Elementary
Bells, TX

A Star Is Born

Have your class make this book to highlight the star qualities of your student of the week. Ask each classmate to dictate a sentence about the featured child for you to record on a piece of paper. Have each

child illustrate his page; then bind all the pages between titled covers. To make the front cover extra special, cut a star shape out of it; then tape the featured child's photo to the back so that her face shines through. Present the book to the star student and watch her face light up!

Suzanne Ward
Ancaster, Ontario, Canada

ABC Pictorial

A is for Amazing Alphabet book! To make a page to represent each letter of the alphabet, take a picture of children in activities or places that begin with each different letter. Or include children in each photo whose names begin with the corresponding letter. Mount each picture to a page; then add text, rhyming pairs of pages if desired.

Denise Cook—Four- and Five-Year-Olds
Children's Courtyard
Grapevine, TX

It's in the Cards

Recycle greeting cards you receive by turning them into postcards that you can send to your children on many occasions. Cut off the front of each card, trimming it to postcard size if necessary. When you need to send a thank-you, birthday, or get-well greeting, write your message on the back of the card. Add postcard postage, and then send it on its way. Mail from my teacher!

Bernadean Clothier, Neithercut TLC, Flint, MI

Creepy-Crawly Spiders

Youngsters will eagerly help these adorable arachnids climb in your classroom. To make one, cut out a spider-body shape from tagboard or heavy paper. Color one side to resemble a spider. Tape the centers of four chenille stems to the back of the spider cutout. Then bend each stem to form the spider's legs. Next tape two one-inch pieces of a drinking straw to the bottom back of the spider. Thread a 32-inch length of heavy string through the straws; then knot the ends. Suspend the spider within students' reach by hanging the string loop on a hook or doorknob. To make the spider climb, a child gently pulls the bottom of the string loop apart as shown. For added fun, sing "The Itsy-Bitsy Spider" with students while they make the spider climb.

Pam Wilson, Ebenezer School, Statesville, NC

"Jack-o'-Science"

Don't throw your pumpkin away after Halloween. Instead use it for an extended, easy science experiment. Place the pumpkin in a secluded outdoor spot such as a wooded area. (Consider marking the area by tying orange yarn around a nearby tree.) Invite each child to predict what will happen to the pumpkin over time. During the next few months, observe the pumpkin with your students, having them describe how it changes. What an easy way to introduce little ones to our ecosystem. Plus it's a fascinating way to strengthen observation skills!

Lisa Marks, Lovingston, VA

Magic Color Snacks

Here's a tasty color-mixing experiment! Have students observe as you prepare red, yellow, and blue gelatin each in a separate clear container. (Prepare enough packages so that each child will have his own quarter-cup snack. Do not refrigerate the gelatin.) Next ask the students to predict what will happen if you mix a drop of one color gelatin into a small amount of another color. Then mix the colors in separate clear cups to make small amounts of orange, green, and purple gelatin. To make her own snack, ask a child to choose two primary-colored gelatins. Pour a small amount (about 1/8 cup) of each gelatin into a personalized plastic cup for the child. After she has stirred her gelatin to create a new color, refrigerate it. These colorful snacks will disappear before you can say, "Abracadabra!"

Judy Sibol—Pre-K
Bear Creek Elementary
Baltimore, MD

Jack-o'-Lantern Baskets

Treat your students with these jack-o'-lantern candy holders. For each holder, collect two orange berry baskets (or spray-paint green baskets orange). To make one, use orange yarn to tie the tops of two baskets together along one side. Place one basket atop the other to close the holder. Next glue construction-paper features and a stem to the holder so it resembles a jack-o'-lantern. Fill the completed jack-o'-lantern holder with candy for a great Halloween treat.

Belinda Deas—Four- and Five-Year-Olds
Hubbard Elementary Pre-K, Forsyth, GA

Batty Bottles

Little ones will go batty over these Halloween water globes. To make one, fill a small, clear plastic bottle with water. Squeeze in one drop of liquid detergent and enough red and yellow food coloring to tint the water orange. Add a generous pinch of bat- and moon-shaped confetti (found at party-supply stores). Then hot-glue the cap onto the bottle. When the glue is dry, a youngster shakes the bottle to see the bats fly. Happy Halloween!

Barrie Facente—Three-Year-Olds
Pascack Valley Cooperative Nursery School
Park Ridge, NJ

Pretty Pumpkin Necklaces

Wearing these necklaces will put youngsters in the mood for Halloween fun! To make one, tint two different bottles of glue orange and green by adding several drops of tempera paint to each one. Line a tray with waxed paper. Squeeze the glue onto the waxed paper to form a thick, orange pumpkin shape with a green stem. Allow the glue to dry completely; then peel the pumpkin off the waxed paper. If desired, draw a jack-o'-lantern face on the pumpkin with permanent marker. Punch a hole near the stem and add a length of yarn to complete the necklace. Now "whoooo's" ready for Halloween?

Christa J. Koch—Pre-K
Circle of Friends School
Bethlehem, PA

Tree Gloves

Enhance students' number and season awareness with these terrific tree gloves. To make one, attach the loop side of a piece of Velcro® to each fingertip of a brown knit glove. Attach the hook side of a piece of Velcro® to the back of each of five decorative items—such as artificial fall leaves or snowflake sequins. Use this glove for fingerplays or to reinforce math skills all through the year!

Sheral Drake—Preschool
Mayflower School
Middleboro, MA

Couldn't-Be-Easier Cookies

Simplify baking for your tots with this tasty recipe that uses just four ingredients to make approximately four dozen cookies. Ready, set, bake!

1 box cake mix (any flavor)
1/2 cup oil
2 eggs
1 cup chocolate chips or small candy pieces

Mix the first three ingredients in a bowl. Stir in the chocolate chips or candy pieces. Drop spoonfuls of batter onto ungreased cookie sheets. Bake at 350° for approximately seven minutes. Cool the cookies; then serve them with cold milk.

Lisa Boyle Meyer—Two- and Three-Year-Olds
Garden City Park School
Garden City Park, NY

A Touching Experience

Encourage tactile exploration with this fingerpainting idea. Set out a variety of textured materials—such as bubble wrap, aluminum foil, cardboard, and ceramic tiles—on your art table. Tape the edges of each material to the table. Next add fingerpaint to each material and invite youngsters to take turns fingerpainting on each one. Afterward, discuss the experience with the children. Now that's a "sense-sational" experience!

Patricia Moeser—Preschool, U. W. Preschool Lab Site , Madison, WI

Easy Halloween Holders

Make these simple treat holders with youngsters and you're sure to see some jack-o'-lantern grins. To prepare, gather a class supply of clean, empty juice cans. Cut off and discard the top third of each can. Cover each can with orange construction paper; then personalize it. Have each child cut out jack-o'-lantern features from yellow and black paper and then glue them onto his can. Staple on a green construction paper handle to complete the holder. Trick or treat!

Fran Strauss—Pre-K
C. E. C.
Crown Point, IN

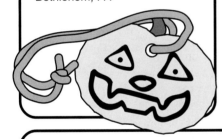

A Book of "Hand-some" Trees

Have students start this fall making these books and they'll have a project that's worthy of gift-giving by summer! To make a page of this book each season, have a child make a brown arm and hand print on a large sheet of paper to resemble a tree. Date the print; then encourage him to decorate it as described below to correspond to the season. Keep each child's pages through the year. Then when a child has completed the summer page of his book, bind the set of prints between covers.

Fall: Sponge-paint yellow, red, and orange leaves on the dry print.
Winter: Sprinkle clear or silver glitter on the wet print.
Spring: Glue bits of pink and green tissue paper on the dry print.
Summer: Use a green bingo marker to make leaves and then add red apple stickers to the dry print.

Wilma Droegemueller—Preschool
Zion Lutheran School
Mt. Pulaski, IL

Joey
Oct. 21,
1999

Our Readers Write

Holly Jolly T-Shirts

Want to add a special festive touch to school holiday events? Have your children sport reindeer shirts they made themselves! To decorate a child's white T-shirt, begin by painting a child's palm and fingers with tan fabric paint. Have him press his hand onto the shirt to leave a handprint. When the print is dry, use fabric paint to attach wiggle eyes and a red pom-pom nose to resemble a reindeer. Add a flurry of red and green fabric paint dots as the finishing touch. On Dasher and Dancer and Donner…!

Darlene Pruitt—Three-Year-Olds
Old Town Baptist Children's Center
Winston-Salem, NC

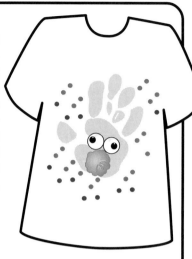

Puppets That Prance

These puppets prance and dance, bringing an extra spark of fun to your favorite reindeer songs and fingerplays. To make a puppet, trace the lid of a frozen orange juice can onto a brown grocery bag or construction paper and trace an antler pattern twice. Cut out the pieces, and then glue the antlers to the circle. On the opposite side of the circle, use craft glue to attach wiggle eyes and a pom-pom nose. Glue the back of the circle to the rimmed side of the lid. Tape a craft stick to the other side of the lid. Let the prancing and pawing begin!

adapted from an idea by Mary Corcoran—Preschool
Fort Wainwright Play Morning
Fort Wainwright, AK

Ring-a-lings

Looking for unusual tree ornaments your children can make? Transform deep colorful caps from fabric softener and detergent jugs into bright child-made bell ornaments. A few weeks in advance, spread the word to your students' families that detergent caps are needed for a craft project. Meanwhile, obtain small jingle bells (one per finished bell), plastic craft laces (or yarn), and several colors of fabric paint. When a classroom supply of caps are in, drill two holes in the top of each cap. To assemble an ornament, assist a child in threading the lace through the cap and the jingle bell and tying the lace for a hanger. To make his ornament truly unique, have the child decorate his bell with a few fabric paint embellishments.

Rosemary Kesse—Pre-K
Little People Playtime
Hampshire, IL

Feeling Good About Christmas?

Here's a perky little song to sing during December classroom transitions. Sing it to the tune of "If You're Happy and You Know It."

If you're glad it's Christmastime,
Just say, "Ho!" (Ho! Ho!)

If you're glad it's Christmastime,
Just say, "Ho!" (Ho! Ho!)

If you're glad it's Christmastime,
Then you'll sing this little rhyme!

If you're glad it's Christmastime,
Just say, "Ho!" (Ho! Ho!)

Suzanne Moore
Dallas, Texas

Guaranteed to Twinkle

Do you wish you could direct more attention to student work on bulletin boards? Gather some Christmas lights and some foil wrapping paper. Your wish is about to come true! Cut seven-inch circles from two or more colors of foil. Alternating the colors, place circles around the board for a border. If desired, staple extra circles and a character or two elsewhere on the board. Using pushpins and Christmas lights that conform to your school's safety guidelines (electric or battery-operated), wind the lights around the circles. (Take care not to prick the wiring insulation with the pins.) Have each child add something to this board. Turn on the lights and let the twinkling and the fascination begin!

Wendi Coker—Three-Year-Olds
Wonderland School
Bellflower, CA

A Present From a Child

This is the kind of gift that will be tucked lovingly away and kept from year to year. To begin, paint a child's hand red; then have him press his handprint onto the center of a large paper plate. Then have him make green thumbprints on or near the plate rim for holly. Have him finish the effect by using a brush to dab one to three dots of red paint near each green print grouping. Then attach the poem to the back of the plate. Have the child write his name beneath the poem and date the project. Little ones will beam with pride when they see the responses they get from the recipients of these gifts.

adapted from an idea by Desiree Magnani
   and Toni Ann Maisano
Babes in Toyland Preschool
Staten Island, NY

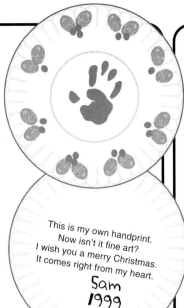

This is my own handprint.
Now isn't it fine art?
I wish you a merry Christmas.
It comes right from my heart.

Sam
1999

"Bow-dacious" Wreath

When you're telling your children about making these wreaths, leave out the part about how great it is for practicing their finger dexterity and counting skills—they'll have too much fun to notice anyway. To make a wreath, have a child cut an 8½-inch circle from his favorite color of construction paper. Then have him glue a card design of his choice to its center. Have him attach gift bows to the circle around the design. Provide assistance as necessary. Pulling the paper backing from the bow adhesive and counting to see how many bows are on the wreath can be a little tricky!

Molly Nagel—Preschool
Little Cherubs Christian Preschool
Cheshire, CT

Avoiding Sticky Situations

Here's an easy way to eliminate much of the mess associated with gluing projects. For each child, squirt a dab of glue into a film canister lid. Then provide students with Q-tips® cotton swabs for spreading the glue. No more sticky fingers!

Sharon Otto—Three-Year-Olds
St. Elizabeth Child Development Center
Lincoln, NE

Notable Thank-Yous

This year, when you receive gifts from students, send thank-you notes that are more meaningful to your little guys than thank-yous written to parents. Duplicate a coloring book or workbook design of your choice along with sentences 1, 3, and 4 of the message. For each gift that you receive, complete the second sentence and sign your name. Tuck the page into an envelope labeled with the student's name. Not only is this a special treat that the gift giver can color, but it's a timesaver for you too!

Nancy Goldberg—Three-Year-Olds
B'nai Israel Schilit
   Nursery School
Rockville, MD

Purple

Bianca,
Thank you for my Hanukkah treat.
It's a lovely yellow pin!
Here's a special Hanukkah decoration. Have fun coloring it on your vacation!
Mrs. Goldberg

Vivid in Vinyl

Convert vinyl placemats into snazzy photo ornaments. Before getting down to work, bargain-shop for vinyl placemats in holiday patterns or appropriate solids. Also obtain a picture of each child. To make an ornament, trace a holiday shape onto the placemat and cut it out. Punch a hole near the top of the shape; then insert a seven-inch length of ribbon and knot it for a hanger. Using craft glue, have a child attach a cropped photo to the center of the ornament and then glue sequins, glitter, or beads around it.

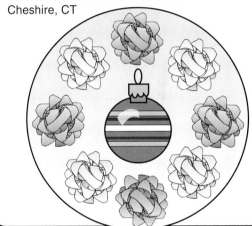

Becky Newberry—Three-Year-Olds
Briarcliff Christian Preschool
Fort Myers, FL

Increasing Shelf Life

Paperback books really take a beating in preschool classrooms. But you can double or triple their shelf life with a little forethought and elbow grease. Before placing a new paperback in your classroom library, cut it apart or remove the staples to separate the pages. Laminate each page; then resequence them. Using a binding machine and a plastic binding, reassemble the book.

Amy Reynolds, Diane Hamdun, and Brooke Jones—Four-Year-Olds
Merry Moppet Preschool
Belmont, CA

Our Readers Write

A Sweet Valentine's Treat

Looking for a gift your children can give for Valentine's Day? This sweet treat is just what you need. Have the children help you mix cinnamon and sugar together for a tasty toast topping. Then assist each child as she scoops some of the mixture into an empty baby food jar and fastens the lid in place. To make the jar look especially festive, have her place a seasonal cupcake liner upside down on the lid, fasten it in place with a rubber band, and tie ribbon around the jar. As a finishing touch, have the child sign a computer-generated label like the one shown and glue it to the jar.

Here's a little something sweet
To make your breakfast toast a treat.
Happy Valentine's Day!

Sarah

Maureen Wallace
San Bruno, CA

Where Is That Valentine?

Just in time for Valentine's Day, put a new twist on the traditional game Doggy, Doggy, Who Has the Bone? After reading about the misadventures of Clifford® at the post office in *Clifford's First Valentine's Day* by Norman Bridwell (Cartwheel Books), ask the children to sit in a circle. Choose one child to be Clifford and have him sit in the center of the circle and cover his eyes. Then give all but one of the other children a valentine to hide behind his back. Give the remaining child a small beanbag pup. Ask Clifford to uncover his eyes while the other children chant, "Clifford, Clifford, who has your valentine?" Each time Clifford calls a child's name, have that child reveal what he has hidden behind his back. When the pup is found, or a few names have been called, have the child holding the pup change places with Clifford to become the new Clifford for the next round.

Audrey Schanning
Waterford, WI

Hey, a Stamp With Me on It!

Wouldn't you love it if your children could address their own valentines? They can! Take a photo of each child (or use a wallet-size school photo of each child). Align the photos on a large sheet of paper and label each one with the child's name. Use a photocopier to reduce the page, so that the photos are about the size of large stamps. If you'd like to perforate the stamps, so they can be torn off the sheet like real stamps, use a sewing machine to stitch perforated lines through several pages at one time. It really works! Send a sheet of these awesome valentine stamps home with each child to make addressing valentines a breeze.

Gina Christensen—Preschool
Newton, KS

Hearts That Really Beat

With hearts posted everywhere, February is a great time to talk about our human hearts. To make a heart that "beats," use glue and tissue paper to cover one side of a paper heart cutout. Tape the neck of a balloon near the dip of an identical heart cutout. When the glue is dry, staple the tissue paper heart atop the other one, so that the balloon is wedged between the hearts. On the plain side of the heart, write "My heart beats." Ask each child to put his hand on his chest and try to feel his heartbeat. Then have children jump up and down a few times and feel for their heartbeats again. Talk about the work of the heart, pumping blood throughout the body. Using a sample of the heart project, show how to blow air into the balloon to make your paper heart "beat" something like your real heart does.

Danielle Reese—Pre-K
Check-Mate Learning Center
Freehold, NJ

Pearly Whites

Give your little ones a dental health lesson they'll remember long past February. Cut a half-circle smile from a sanitized Styrofoam® tray for each child. Then use a ballpoint pen to draw teeth on the cutout. Ask each child to paint his smile with yellow tempera paint. The following day, have the children help you mix baking soda, salt, and water to make homemade toothpaste. Then give each child an old toothbrush and his yellow smile cutout and have him go to work at the sink, brushing the yellow off of his cutout. Look how bright my smile is!

Karen Palmer—Four- and Five-Year-Olds
Stringfellow School, Coppell, TX

My heart beats

Mother's Day Necklace

Children will enjoy making these special necklaces for Mother's Day! To prepare for this activity, make a batch of dough by mixing together three cups of flour, a half cup of glue, one teaspoon of lemon juice, one cup of salt, and one cup of water in a large bowl. After a child rolls out an amount of dough, have him use cookie cutters to cut out the letters to spell *MOM*. Use a coffee stirrer to poke holes completely through the sides of each letter so that they can be strung onto a piece of plastic lace. Allow the letters to harden overnight. The next day, have each child paint his letters. When the paint is dry, have him string a length of plastic lace through the letters, adding beads where desired. Mothers are sure to treasure these unique necklaces!

Carol Corcoran—Pre-K
City of Bayonne, Department of
    Recreation Preschool
Bayonne, NJ

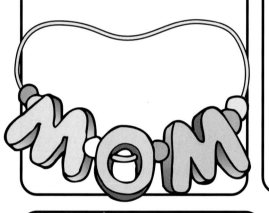

Blossoming Headbands

These sunflower headbands will make your dramatic-play area bright and cheery! They're also great for springtime performances. To make one, first cut a length of crepe paper streamer so that it is long enough to wrap around a child's face as shown. Next, glue a number of yellow tissue paper petal shapes onto the crepe paper. When it's time for a child to wear this sunny headband, tape the ends together under her chin. Look at those prancing springtime flowers!

Cindylee Villareale—Four- and Five-Year-Olds
Sister Helen Ann Wee Care Center
Pendleton, OR

Color-Coded Paintbrushes

Here's an inexpensive way to match paintbrushes with the colors of your paint to prevent the colors from getting mixed together! Spray-paint a number of wooden-handled paintbrushes to match the paint colors at your easel and art center. Your children will have no problem figuring out which paintbrush goes with each color. Paint away!

Kathleen Adair—Gr. K, Frey Elementary, Acworth, GA

Thank You, Mom!

Duplicate this poem onto sheets of construction paper; then have each child decorate a sheet to create a touching Mother's Day card that will be read over and over again!

Cheryl Schoell—Three-Year-Olds
Children's World Learning Center
Newtown, PA

Thank You, Mom

Thank you for reading me stories
And taking care of me.
Thank you for tying my shoes
And putting bandages on my knee.

Thank you for tucking me into bed
And kissing me good night.
Thank you so much for all your hugs
And holding my hand so tight.

Thank you for being my mommy
And that's not all I have to say.
Thank you so much for all you do
And have a Happy Mother's Day!

Painting on Wallpaper

Need a new and innovative approach to fingerpainting? Try fingerpainting on sheets of wallpaper! Just ask a local wallpaper store to donate discontinued sample books; then tear out the individual sheets. Each wallpaper sheet is just the right size for fingerpainting. In addition, students enjoy the various textures of the papers.

Eugenia Damron—Preschool,
    Special Needs
Ceredo Elementary
Ceredo, WV

Dandy Lions

Here's a dandy way to reuse yellow Easter grass and make a unique spring display! To make a dandy lion, paint a small paper plate yellow. While the paint is wet, press yellow Easter grass around the rim of the plate. When the paint is dry, use a permanent marker to draw a lion face in the middle of the plate. Glue construction paper leaves and a stem to the plate. Display these unforgettable dandy lions together and your classroom will be blooming with springtime flowers. No "lion"!

Jean Jaffe and Nancy Stevens—Preschool
Copeland Run Learning Center
Downingtown, PA

Our Readers Write

Buzzing Bees

After your youngsters have spent time watching the bumblebees outside, have them make their own little bees! To make a bee, cut two connected cups from a yellow Styrofoam® egg carton that has been sterilized. Use a permanent marker to draw a face on the side of one cup, adding wiggle eyes if desired. To create antennae, poke a hole in the top of this cup and then insert a four-inch length of pipe cleaner that has been bent in half. Next, draw stripes on the other cup.

Using a utility knife, make a small slit in the back of the cup. Insert a small black paper triangle into the slit to resemble a stinger. Finally, twist two oval tissue paper wings together and insert them into a hole in the top of the striped cup as shown. In no time at all, your classroom will be filled with buzzing bees! Bzzz!

Kathy Smith—Four-Year-Olds
Greenfield Child Development
Bossier City, LA

Father's Day Gift Bags

These shirt-and-tie bags make it easy to send home precious homemade gifts for Dad or other important male figures. Have each child use a variety of art supplies (markers, sequins, glitter glue, etc.) to decorate a construction paper tie cutout. Put the child's gift in a paper bag, fold down the top, and then staple on the decorated tie. What a perfect present for Papa!

Teri LaVelle, Zion Lutheran Preschool
Indiana, PA

Freshen Up!

Dads will be proud to hang these "scent-sational" gifts in their cars! To make an air freshener, trace two identical car shapes onto felt; then cut them out. Hot-glue the shapes together, inserting a length of folded yarn between them for hanging. Spray cologne on the felt. Place the freshener in a resealable plastic bag with a note attached. Your little ones won't be able to wait to take these gifts home to Dad. Beep, beep!

Judith Berdine—Preschool, World of Wonders Daycare
Canonsburg, PA

To the Moon!

If you're planning to do a space unit, this dramatic-play idea will create an atmosphere filled with excitement! In advance, spray-paint one or more rocks for each child silver. Hide the painted rocks around the room or outside. Explain to your students that on the Moon the children would weigh less and would float. Then gather your children for a pretend Moon landing. Challenge each child to "float" around and find at least one Moon rock. Once you've arrived back on Earth, invite each child to use a balance scale to compare the weight of his rock(s) to classroom items. Now that's a worthwhile trip to the Moon!

Bertha Cochran—Four-Year-Olds and Pre-K, St. Matthew's Preschool
Bloomington, IL

Bottled Art

Here's a unique painting technique—no brushes required. Simply squeeze! Clean several empty glue bottles. Refill each bottle with a different color of tempera paint and a squirt of dish soap. Then invite your youngsters to an art center to squeeze the paint onto their papers to create interesting designs and pictures. Your budding artists will squeeze many masterpieces out of this idea!

Janina Savala—Bilingual Pre-K and Gr. K
West Birdville School
Ft. Worth, TX